Engineering Stability

China Understandings Today

Series Editors: Mary Gallagher and Emily Wilcox

China Understandings Today is dedicated to the study of contemporary China and seeks to present the latest and most innovative scholarship in social sciences and the humanities to the academic community as well as the general public. The series is sponsored by the Lieberthal-Rogel Center for Chinese Studies at the University of Michigan.

Engineering Stability: Rebuilding the State in Twenty-First Century Chinese Universities
Yan Xiaojun

In Search of Admiration and Respect: Chinese Cultural Diplomacy in the United States, 1875–1974
Yanqiu Zheng

Seeking a Future for the Past: Space, Power, and Heritage in a Chinese City
Philipp Demgenski

China as Number One? The Emerging Values of a Rising Power
Yang Zhong and Ronald F. Inglehart

Paris and the Art of Transposition: Early Twentieth Century Sino-French Encounters
Angie Chau

The Currency of Truth: Newsmaking and the Late-Socialist Imaginaries of China's Digital Era
Emily H. C. Chua

Disruptions as Opportunities: Governing Chinese Society with Interactive Authoritarianism
Taiyi Sun

Rejuvenating Communism: Youth Organizations and Elite Renewal in Post-Mao China
Jérôme Doyon

Power of Freedom: Hu Shih's Political Writings
Chih-p'ing Chou and Carlos Yu-Kai Lin, Editors

Resisting Spirits: Drama Reform and Cultural Transformation in the People's Republic of China
Maggie Greene

A complete list of titles in the series can be found at www.press.umich.edu

ENGINEERING STABILITY

Rebuilding the State in Twenty-First Century Chinese Universities

Yan Xiaojun

University of Michigan Press
Ann Arbor

Published in the United States of America by the
University of Michigan Press
Printed and bound by CPI Group (UK) Ltd, Croydon, CR0 4YY

First published November 2024

A CIP catalog record for this book is available from the British Library.

Library of Congress Cataloging-in-Publication data has been applied for.

ISBN 978-0-472-07705-2 (hardcover : alk. paper)
ISBN 978-0-472-05705-4 (paper : alk. paper)
ISBN 978-0-472-90467-9 (open access ebook)

DOI: https://doi.org/10.3998/mpub.14364295

The University of Michigan Press's open access publishing program is made possible thanks to additional funding from the University of Michigan Office of the Provost and the generous support of contributing libraries.

To my family

Contents

Digital materials related to this title can be found on the Fulcrum platform via the following citable URL: https://doi.org/10.3998/mpub.14364295

Figures

Tables

Acknowledgments

To say that writing a book is a long journey is an obvious understatement. Without my even feeling the lapse of time, this book has already taken an entire decade to complete. This is the first major research project I decided to undertake after my graduation from doctoral studies at Harvard University. I wish to thank my doctoral adviser and also mentor for the past two decades, Elizabeth J. Perry, who has always been so generous and kind in offering help in this and other endeavors I chose to undertake over all these years.

I wish to express my gratitude to the late Professor Roderick MacFarquhar, who was on my dissertation committee and who was always willing to listen and to advise. I wish he had lived to read this book and say to me, "Aha, finally!" My thanks also go to Yoshiko M. Herrera, Susan Pharr, Grzegorz Ekiert, Alastair Iain Johnston, William C. Kirby, and the late Samuel P. Huntington, from whom I have learned so much.

My undergraduate student assistants and doctoral students gave me excellent assistance in undertaking this book project. They are Li Jia, Jiang Weikang, Zhou Kai, Li La, Yu Duo, and Xie Pengfei.

I am grateful that Mary Gallagher, Andrew G. Walder, Joel S. Migdal, Pei Minxin, Cai Yongshun, and Elizabeth J. Perry kindly read an earlier draft of the book manuscript and offered their comments and suggestions for improvement. I especially thank Mary Gallagher, editor of the current book series, for kindly providing advice on the publication of this project and for reading and endorsing the book manuscript. Of course, any remaining errors are purely mine.

Sara Cohen and Haley Winkle at University of Michigan Press are truly a delight to work with. I learned from their professionalism and collegiality, and the care they devoted to every detail in the publication process.

Last but not least, I wish to thank my family, who have supported me without reservation over all these years. Without the love, support, and understanding of my family, this and all of my works are simply not possible. I dedicate this book to them.

Introduction

> It is therefore manifest, that the Instruction of the people, depen-
> deth wholly, on the right teaching of Youth in the Universities.
> —Thomas Hobbes, *Leviathan*, 1996 [1651], 237

> Any understanding of "why men rebel" must be paralleled by an
> understanding of why they do not.
> —Alan Knight, "Weapons and Arches in the Mexican
> Revolutionary Landscape," 1994, 26

An Unusual Silence

From the Academic Legion during the Revolutions of 1848 to the lunch counter in Greensboro, North Carolina, and from Tahrir Square to Tiananmen Square, students across time and space have demonstrated their might as a dynamic social group that shapes historical trajectories. When student activism is on the rise, it threatens the hegemony of existing powers. When students become cynical about official ideologies and tired of the establishment elites, their lack of involvement in adult politics gives them "free rein . . . to adhere to absolute principles" (Lipset 1972, 4). University students are said to be the "repositories of the ideals of their nation" (Donahue 1971, 254) and college campuses "the central stage for the drama of democracy's ebb and flow" (Rhoads 1998, 2).[1]

The opening decades of the twenty-first century have seen a global resurgence of student activism that has challenged entrenched norms and called into question the wishful "end-of-history" illusion ingrained in the post–Cold War status quo. Between 2015 and 2020, at least thirty national student movements took place across more than twenty countries and regions (see figure 1). In 2020 alone, in the United States, students participated in the national March for Our Lives and Black Lives Matter movements, raising awareness of gun violence and racial injustice; in Hungary, students of the country's oldest university of arts blockaded its campus and took to the streets in defense of academic freedom; in Indonesia, university students became the backbone of a national joint force resisting the government's labor law reforms, which threatened to take away workers' rights and cause environmental damage; and in Iraq, student demonstrators from prominent institutions of higher learning in Baghdad stood arm in arm to demand the overhaul of a dysfunctional and perverted political structure.[2] In Asia, system-wide political battles fought by students take even more idealistic, confrontational, and revolutionary forms, attesting to youths' bravery, camaraderie, and pure willingness to sacrifice for a higher cause. In the words of Tony Vellela, writing three decades ago, "it never went away. It may have subsided, and it certainly changed, reflecting changing times and circumstances, but progressive student political activism never really stopped" (1988, 5).

"Young people come of age with three tools essential for renewal," said Marshall Ganz. "A critical eye of the world, a clear view of its needs and pain, and hopeful hearts that give a sense of the world's promise and possibilities" (Jason 2018). Yet against this backdrop, university students in mainland China—who have long been a sophisticated rebellious social group in history[3]—appear astonishingly quiescent. In sharp contrast to the vibrant global scene of student uprisings, university campuses in the most populous developing country today look like tranquil enclaves of conformity and compliance. This picture of calmness is both extraordinary and puzzling.

In 2019, when Hong Kong students were contesting the city's legislature and fighting the police behind street barricades, their mainland counterparts were busy training and rehearsing for the upcoming celebrations for the 70th National Day of the People's Republic of China (PRC). In 2021, at a celebration of the hundredth anniversary of the founding of the Chinese Communist Party (CCP), Feng Lin and Zhao Jianming, two university students representing China's educated youth, "expressed their commitment to the Party's cause," alongside two representative primary school pupils. The CCP's official English-language newspaper, *China Daily*, reported,

The four students jointly delivered an affectionate ode to the Party. "Today, we make a vow to the Party: Listen to the Party's call, be grateful to the Party and follow its lead," they said in unison. In order to realize the second centenary goal—to build China into a great modern socialist country by 2049, the centenary of the People's Republic of China, and achieve the great rejuvenation of the nation—young people are always prepared to fight for the socialist cause, they said. "Rest assured . . . we are ready to build a powerful China," they repeated four times at the end of the ode. (China Daily 2021)

Even more substantial than this centennial pledge of allegiance is the prevalent everyday political quiescence on Chinese university campuses—the "enemy territory" in the eyes of the communist state (Andreas 2009, 270). Indeed, there has been no major antiregime student movement since the tragedy that ended the 1989 Tiananmen Movement. When sporadic student demonstrations have occurred on a national scale—such as the one taking place after the United States bombed the Chinese embassy in Belgrade in 1999—the protesting students' target has been the Chinese state's mortal enemy: Western "imperialist" powers.

For the ultra-obedient Chinese students, conformity and quiescence signify not sluggishness and inactivity but national pride, dignity, and the willingness to "fly into a cyber-rage at the slightest provocation" (*Economist* 2016). Since the mid-2010s, the increasingly frequent online outbursts of the "little pinks" (*xiao fenhong*)—"young people fired with patriotic zeal . . . to guard China against even the remotest hint of critics" (Zhuang 2017)—have demonstrated that still waters run deep on the apparently submissive Chinese university campus.[4] The scene of a cooperative Chinese academy is so remarkable that Elizabeth J. Perry (2020) introduced the term "educated acquiescence" specifically to emphasize the contribution of this pattern of obedience to buttressing state power and to "[raise] questions with prevailing assumptions that associate the flourishing of higher education with liberal democracy" (1).

In early 2023, when a handful of students held blank paper to join the societal protest against the Chinese state's COVID-zero policy and its lockdown measures, this spasmodic contention was soon put down by the political control bureaucracy installed on university campuses without shaking the rule of the political regime. This book discussed how this control system is re-invented after 1989 and why it works so effectively to preserve political stability on university campuses in 2023. The White Paper

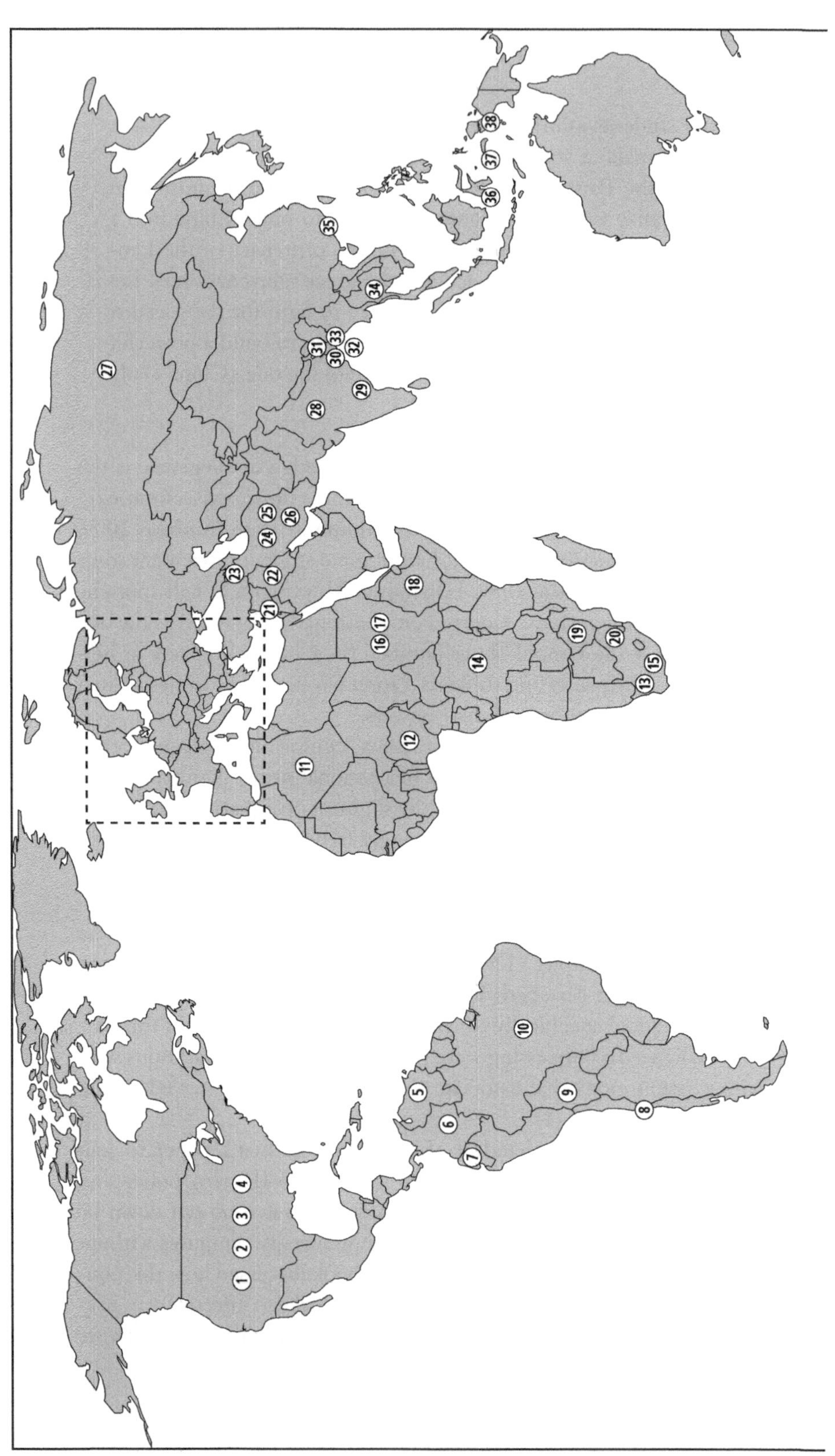

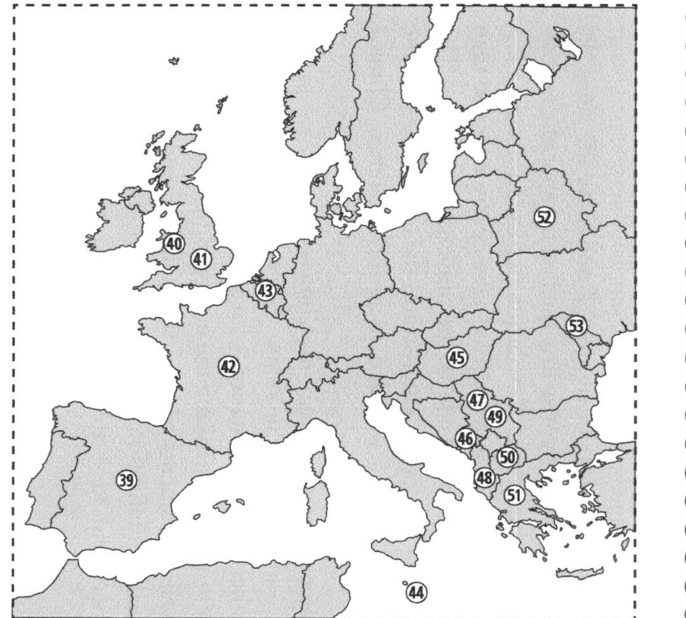

Figure 1. National student movements in the world, 2015–2020.

Figure 2. Student representatives deliver an ode to the Chinese Communist Party in Tiananmen Square (July 1, 2021). *Xinhua.*

Revolution was a crucial political occurrence; yet, this event supports—rather than challenges—the argument I present in this book.

First, prior to the White Paper Revolution, during the implementation of the "Zero COVID" pandemic control policy (2020–2022), the universities in China generally remained peaceful and compliant despite persistent campus lockdowns and the longest disruption of university life since the Cultural Revolution. The government swiftly quelled the sporadic expressions of discontent; the White Paper Revolution persisted for only a few days and on a much smaller scale, and incurred a less severe response than the anti–Zero COVID protests outside of the university campuses. The differences between these two cases demonstrates the effectiveness of the pervasive student-control system installed in post-Tiananmen Chinese universities.

Second, the student-control system in Chinese universities played a significant role in putting down the White Paper Revolution, just as it did in controlling other sporadic instances of student unrest in the post-Tiananmen era. The student-control regime equipped the Party-state not only with the political instruments to keep the student population from engaging in large-scale mobilization but the cognitive infrastructure for university management and for state bureaucrats to promptly respond to changes in the student's collective mentality during critical political moments (e.g., the White Paper Revolution, the Qiu Qingfeng Incident in 1999, and activities of the fundamentalist Marxist societies in the early 2000s).[5] In this book, I argue that the impact of the construction, optimization, and practice of this new control system over thirty years is reflected in the stark differences between the respective outcomes of the White Paper Revolution in 2022–2023 and the Tiananmen Movement in 1989.

Third, the White Paper Revolution (and other instances of Chinese student unrest since 1989) also indicated that the quiescence and general stability on university campuses should not be interpreted as a sign of the society's devoted agreement with the power and legitimacy of the Party-state; rather, the compliance and engineered stability in post-1989 Chinese universities is ostensive, fragile, and extrinsic. In contrast to the ideology-based, devoted, wholehearted embrace of the political regime during the early years of the PRC, the current compliance, carefully maintained through a sophisticated, quotidian, and bureaucratic state machinery of control, may be characterized more specifically as obligatory and directed outward.

Amid soaring student activism on the international scene, loyal college students and quiescent university campuses in China are puzzling. The military crackdown in the summer of 1989 abruptly ended the month-long national resistance movement led by students at China's elite universities, but dealt a serious blow to the legitimacy, capacity, and moral standing of the state. After all, as Hannah Arendt (1969) has famously argued, "violence appears where power is in jeopardy" (155). Soon afterward, the end of the Cold War and the demise of Soviet socialism left the communist regime of China disoriented and equipped with an ideology that needs immediate update. The Party-state's subsequent decision to undertake a full-scale transition to a market economy temporarily stabilized the regime and comforted the liberal-leaning intelligentsia and profit-seeking elites; nevertheless, with marketization, the state also lost its monopolistic control over the material resources and opportunities for upward mobility available to the country's younger generation, further weakening the already compromised set of tools used by state apparatchiks to induce compliance. The entry of global capitalism "led to a contagion of capitalism across the economy and ideological boundary of public ownership" (Gallagher 2005, 3) and brought in alternative narratives, visions, and ideologies for the future of China, which among other challenges posed new obstacles to the state's endeavors to keep the post-Tiananmen Chinese universities under its control.

A mere three decades after the event of 1989, how has the post-Tiananmen Chinese state managed to restore and maintain a state of general stability on the nation's 2,738 university campuses and steady control over the country's more than forty-one million college students?[6] Amid unfavorable global trends and geopolitical intrigue, how has the Chinese state prevented the country's university students from mounting another serious rebellion against the regime? In a broader sense, what does this reinvented model of control tell us about the updated form of state power at this time, when globalizing forces are overtaking local sovereignty, high-capacity surveillance apparatuses are replacing slow-moving traditional bureaucracies, and an entire generation of youth spoiled by access to a massive volume of information is taking the stage in place of the generations that grew up before the information revolution?

In scrutinizing the Chinese Communist Party's undertaking to reassert control and restore order on university campuses in the post-Tiananmen era, this book explores an overarching theme—namely, state reinvention—with rich materials gathered from in-depth field research in China. The pages that follow invite scholars of comparative politics, state theory, contentious politics, and political development to rethink and reimagine the ways in which a compromised state is rebuilt *within* and *from* itself after overcoming a traumatic moment of vulnerability. It further suggests that this rethinking proceeds along the lines of the widely felt but little-understood new phenomenon of state-led intra-regime institutional reinvention. On both fronts, China today is the most illuminating, and perhaps the only, case study.

The Compromised State

Political scientists have long studied the processes of building a state from scratch—"the founding moments"—and of constructing a new political order following the transition from an archaic mode of rule; however, much less attention has been given to how regimes that survive major political crises purposefully reinvent a postcrisis state pursuant to updated concepts, new circumstances, changed social demands, and a realigned elite consensus.[7] State rebuilding, in the sense of self-salvaging a compromised structure of power, is bound to be a laborious and wide-ranging project that must address urgent and intractable issues while operating in political fields that are often poorly defined. Yet if such an attempt is successful, order—the sine qua non of state power—would be reinvented on a carefully designed and effectively constructed infrastructural network commanded by a state operating on everyday terms, through which the discharging of power appears again natural, familiar, purposeful, and consequential to the citizens.

"Political order cannot be treated as a given" (Bates 2008, 5). In contrast with building a state from scratch or after the collapse of an ancien régime, a compromised state has the advantage of largely intact state machinery and the capability to maintain basic law and order; however, it suffers from a weakened ideological base of legitimacy, a lack of instruments to regulate citizens' behavior, and a compromised position in its competition for dominance with other centers of authority in the nation's public life. A compromised state is often observed in the aftermath of a national political crisis that features entrenched, confrontational, emotional, and ideologically charged animosity between the state and society. A compromised state's salvation hinges on its ability to rehabilitate its institutional capacity, legitimating footing, regulatory strength, and incentivization instruments for compliance, and doing so within an existing yet damaged state structure. Within these intertwined fields, state rebuilders strive to reconstruct its premises to effectively execute its plans at scale and reclaim the ability to produce, effectuate, project, and sustain a political order far and wide. As Timothy Mitchell (1991) wrote, "the boundary of the state never marks a real exterior" (90).

These fields in which the postcrisis state undertakes restorative work are interconnected processes and social spheres rather than separate structures with fixed spatialities. I use "process" in the sense of Joel S. Migdal, for whom it refers to "the ongoing struggles among shifting coalitions over the rules for daily behaviour" and it "determine[s] how societies and states create and maintain distinct ways of structuring day-to-day life" (Migdal 2011, 11). In its rebuilding project, the compromised state has to face an across-the-board obstacle: the alienation and disbelief, if not apathy or even disobedience, of the population. State rebuilding often takes place after a long and dreadful confrontation between rulers and the ruled that is characterized by violent insurrection, military crackdown, government collapse, or social disintegration. These events and situations have an impact for a long time in the collective consciousness of the national community as dreadful, traumatic, and disorienting memories. A state that orders the iron-fisted suppression of mobilized societal forces to swiftly terminate an otherwise lethal political crisis is consequently deprived of the possibility of "ruling as usual." The posttrauma hatred, resistance, and noncooperativeness provoked in the social sphere when a state seeks to restore its own authority may be subtle and even silent, but they are nonetheless pervasive and powerful. It is from these legacies that the vision of the state must be renewed, governing arrangements reformed, and the legitimating narrative of politics restored.

To effectively enact its reconstruction plan, the postcrisis state, more often than not, exercises a strategic alternation between, or hybridization of, visibility and invisibility during this convoluted process. Oscillating between visibility and invisibility gives a state high levels of operational flexibility and institutional resilience. To achieve this, the postcrisis state comes up with creative approaches—usually disguised as something else—to its restorative operations. Depending on the specific field in which the state operates and the precise goals it seeks, the state strategically deploys camouflaged institutional facades, procedural formalities, scientific disguises, discursive art, or functional concealment to smooth over its restorative undertakings when and where necessary. By hiding its true face behind various masks and veils, the postcrisis state circumvents the inconveniences and obstacles brought forth by massive social distrust, keeping itself out of public sight yet effectively commanding the undertakings that are imperative for the reinvention of a new institutionalized political order.

Why Universities?

But why does a book on state rebuilding nonetheless study the university? Ever since the Westphalian nation-state came to dominate the global political landscape, the university has evolved gradually from a medieval institution of masters and students into a cultural project that holds the "single and dominant image" and "fragmented practices" of the state together (Migdal 2011). In the modern age, prominent national universities also serve the nation-state as training grounds for the country's future political, economic, and cultural elites. Public life on university campuses thus not only has immediate political relevance, it carries important weight for the time ahead. As György Péteri argues, the university is a crucial "institutional field of human activity" and "a dynamic social field," where "conflicting loyalties" pertaining to the survival and future of the reigning political order are "cultivated and harmonised" (2005, 141, 163). To understand the process of state rebuilding, it is only natural to study the social space where this reinvented state power is effectuated to its fullest and the construction of the infrastructures for statism are the most encyclopedic.

For the modern state, national universities constitute an immensely precarious political site subject to a wide array of centrifugal forces pulling in different directions. As universities form the identities of young people in the temporal and social interval between childhood and adult life, a major centrifugal force is created by young students' strong desire to escape parental censure and state domination in their everyday experiences; this imagined separation from adult power becomes the natural road out of the wonderland of youth. The effect spills over to the political sphere and eventually forges an island of liberal ideals and the spirit of freedom in the university—a hotbed for defiance and resistance that is in constant confrontation with the state. When the time comes, the university can easily become "a ready infrastructure to serve the growing needs of a relatively independent public sphere" (Péteri 2005, 159).

The self-contradictory nature of the university as a social space creates political frustrations for any state builder who seeks to claim control over a national community. In universities, the state is obligated to provide students with maternal care and patriarchal control. University campuses are "spatial settings" in which order must be maintained, conformity nurtured, and control effectuated, but in which the life goals, career ambitions, personal welfare, and spiritual desires of young students must also be taken care of. In the process of attaining order, educational functionalities based on the teaching of knowledge may have to be balanced with a whole array of other sociopolitical purposes. Often, universities are given the dual and often self-contradictory missions of facilitating development and breeding loyalty. For development, the university is supposed to nurture the next generation of learned professionals and technocrats, armed with the necessary qualities for the free pursuit of knowledge, creativity, innovation, critical thinking, and individuality; but to nurture loyalty and compliance, the state needs to restrict each of these attributes. The inevitable result is what Susan Bregnbaek has noted—"the state promotes innovation while at the same time expecting conformity by limiting critical thinking and creativity" (2019, 8), and it can be taxing to strike a balance between these two goals.

Naturally, no ruler in China can afford to take university students lightly in its national political operations. The *Book of Han* (*Hanshu*) records perhaps China's very first student uprising, which took place in the Royal Academy (*taixue*) more than 2,000 years ago, in 2 BCE, when over 1,000 academy students gathered to protest against an unfair penalty imposed by the emperor on a senior scholar-official of the court. The emperor conceded, and the incident has since been known in the annals of history as "Wang Xian Raising a Banner" (*Wang Xian Ju Fan*)—a symbolically heroic act by educated young men with humble origins courageously confronting the mighty power of the imperial state. Throughout Chinese history—from the nationalist protests in the Song dynasty against alien conquerors from the north to the reformist petition drives of the late Qing dynasty to democratize the imperial court—elite university students in the empire's capital city have appeared frequently in the official records as upholders of moral principles, defenders of national dignity, pursuers of political justice, supporters of political reform, and loud critics of the corruption, despotism, nepotism, and misrule that plagued various imperial courts in their late years. When elite students as a social group are belittled by whoever occupies the throne of power of the day, the entire intelligentsia feels ridiculed.[8]

The collapse of China's imperial regime and the subsequent modernization of the country's governing superstructure did not weaken the political status of elite students as a crucial social group. Indeed, China's rich and colorful tradition of student rebellion resonates even more strongly in the modern political landscape. Throughout the twentieth century, as Jeffrey N. Wasserstrom and Liu Xinyong noted, "student-led mass movements [were] a recurring feature of Chinese city life" (1995, 362). Their status as presumptive elites, their ability to create theater for public display, their capacity for movement mobilization by deploying official symbols and discourse, and their propensity for creating organizations that resemble the state bureaucracy have all been channeled to challenge and undermine the political legitimacy of successive ruling regimes (Wasserstrom 1990, 1991). The intrusion of modern partisan politics into almost every aspect of campus life in the twentieth century further intensified student engagement in political movements of modern China (Huang 2010).

Four critical moments particularly signify the extraordinarily important role played by university students in China's contemporary political scene. In 1919, it was the university and high school students in metropolitan Chinese cities who propagated the news of the diplomatic humiliation the nation had suffered at the Paris Peace Conference, which finally outraged and mobilized an anxious and unsettled Chinese society into a nationwide awakening, precipitating the birth of a national communist party. In 1966, it was again the student population that came under the spell of the Great Helmsman, Mao Zedong, who recruited and deployed the nation's educated youth as the *troupes de bénévoles* to start a vehement attack on the Party-state bureaucracy that would eventually paralyze the corps of the old guards who had constituted the backbone of the communist revolution less than two decades earlier. In 1989, university students again took their place on the central stage of Chinese politics. By occupying the country's most symbolic space—Tiananmen Square—for two and a half months and demanding democracy, the students inherited a historical tradition of Chinese educated-youth protest and revealed to the world the renewed political momentum that had accumulated in the reformist era. In the words of C. Wright Mills (1960), throughout the twentieth century, Chinese students have remained the "possible, immediate, radical agency of change" (19).

Thus, in China, the university is a critical space in which the hegemonic rulers set to fight with actual or perceived enemies in the realm of ideas, organization, or allegiance.[9] "All these interactions," argued Tony Vellela, "both complicate the atmosphere on the campus, and make that campus a test area for future encounters" (1988, 5). Chinese universities have never been merely teaching institutions that cater to the population's educational needs; instead, they are spatial enclaves with various entrenched and inherent tensions that the state seeks to regulate, shape, and discipline as it looks to reclaim authority, conformity, and submissiveness. The study of Chinese universities in the post-Tiananmen era provides an unusually detailed glimpse into the operations undertaken by a compromised state to rebuild an institutionalized political order within and from itself and to reassert control over an increasingly pluralistic social realm.[10]

Reinventing a State from a State

The structure of state power, given the alternation between its visible and invisible operation, is most discernible when it is rebuilt. The political tragedy that ended the Tiananmen Movement of 1989 is both an indicator and a cause of the compromised state power. The epicenter in the national uprising—the university—has naturally become the most crucial social space over which the postcrisis state sought to reassert control. While the making of the modern state has been conventionally seen as the "cumulative product of [a] successive 'extraction-coercion cycle'" (Loveman 2005, 1652), the state's operation to remake itself on university campuses lacks precisely the necessary extractive and legal-coercive attributes and devices, proffering a unique angle from which the more hidden and nuanced structure of state power can be examined. By scrutinizing the post-Tiananmen Chinese state's efforts to reassert control over university campuses, this book advances arguments about state rebuilding on four fronts.

The Infrastructures for Statism. The state rebuilders' project to reassert control is upheld by the reconstructed institutional, significative, regulatory, and incentivization infrastructures. State rebuilders strive to revamp an institutional infrastructure that diffuses the state's organizational form, colonizes societal spaces, and places social networks back under state control; the goals are a significative infrastructure that projects the state's new legitimating message as widely as possible, a regulatory infrastructure that enables the state to regain its decisive edge in combating rival suppliers of authority in public life, and an incentivization infrastructure that properly rewards loyalty, punishes defiance, and deters the formation of oppositional forces. For this purpose, a refurbished surveillance framework is put in place so that compliance can be measured, monitored, created, and enforced. Within these intertwined infrastructures, state rebuilders can reconstruct the state's premises to reclaim the ability to produce, effectuate, project, and sustain political order.

The People and the Space. Postcrisis state rebuilders focus on reestablishing control over the nation's critical social groups and reclaiming dominance over its critical social spaces. Critical social groups—such as the technical intelligentsia in the Soviet Union and tenant farmers in the British Raj—live on the margins of the radiant network of state control, but hold subjectivities that may diverge greatly from the state's hegemonic cultural influence and political will. In the postcrisis context, critical social groups are ostensibly made up of citizens who share a similar identity, who suffered the most prior to the crisis, and who endured the largest share of collective loss during the crisis. Members of critical social groups inhabit and live their everyday experiences in critical social spaces, within which mobilization networks, political symbolism, or a shared identity may be nurtured and activities that are deemed harmful by the ruling political order may take place. Critical social spaces, such as the universities in post-Tiananmen China, are containers of specific practices, actions, networks, and identities that state rebuilders seek to monitor, regulate, and govern.

State Rebuilding in the Everyday. Critical social groups and critical social spaces meet in people's everyday lived experience. The silhouettes of the political everyday reflect the contours of state order. Lived experiences give life and form to the otherwise docile and formless spatiotemporal structure of political order; they offer a handle and pathway for the order-seeking state to exert its influence on the everydayness of the social sphere. The political everyday is the confluence point of institutional dynamism, societal networks, and state imperatives. The spatiotemporal structure of the political everyday is shaped by and reflects the interaction between grand statecraft and on-the-ground negotiation, the synergy between elite vision and mass imagination, and the convergence of high politics and subaltern networks. In Chinese universities in the post-Tiananmen era, the transmutation between time and space in the everyday brings political order into focus and is the natural site for the state to begin its project of building a new order. For state rebuilders seeking to reinvent a political order, the state simply must win the day.

Visible and Invisible State. "Social order is secured," as Jon Beasley-Murray (2010) argued, "through folding the constitute power of the multitude back on itself to produce the illusion of transcendence and sovereignty" (ix). This book illustrates that the post-Tiananmen state rebuilders seek to "demobilise" society and to engineer social stability through a normalized, quotidian, and pervasive web of control and operations that signify the state's baseline political narrative, regulate public life, and dispense incentives for conformism, thus securing the regime's claim to power. This process of reeffectuating and sustaining control has visible and invisible methods of operation. At times, the state is loud and vigorous in declaring its presence, injecting its ideas and performing its spectacles to targeted social groups and openly rallying loyalists. On other occasions, the state elects to remain out of sight, submerged in the everyday, taking care of the routines of life; it then operates silently, often disguised behind a normalized, bureaucratic, scientific, or mundane facade, strategically downplaying the political side of the undertaking in question. The combination of visible and invisible modes of operation forms the most important dimension of the state rebuilding project.

The State Reinvented

With the completion of the state-rebuilding project, the post-Tiananmen Chinese state presents a case of a compromised state being reinvented into an overbearing new type of state power that differs from both its predecessors and its peers—a kind of governing arrangement that gradually gains popularity as the guiding project for the future among rulers of the developing world. At the core of this reinvented state is an institutional edifice of control that is routinized, silent, quotidian, and seemingly casual, yet carefully designed and implemented.

The reinvented state is not essentially an institution for political agitation; its highest virtue and goal are the maintenance of political stability—that is, securing the survival of the regime.[11] To reach that goal, the reinvented state operates three projects in distinctive fields, building infrastructure for statism with significative, regulatory, and incentivization parameters. In the project of signification, the reinvented state advocates a realistic, depoliticized, materialistic, and nationalist narrative and discourse, advocating and projecting the state's baseline political rhetoric not through spectacular mass movements but by occupying the citizens' everyday timetables. The messages of the state are no longer transcendental values or utopian plans; by nature, they become secular, this-worldly, reachable, and issue-oriented. In the state's significative operations, the normative and value-rich vision for the future has been replaced by a down-to-earth hedonistic imaginary of latter-day prosperity, in which purpose and meaning are taken over by concrete goals and material gains, and the joint endeavor between the Party-state and the people for a brand new society is substituted with a sybaritic promise—with certain undeclared trade-offs—made by the former in exchange for willing conformism based on the rational calculation of the latter.

Regulatory operations secure the state's advantageous positioning in public and organizational life. The reinvented state must work on competitive terms. In the gradually diversifying fields of public life and the expanding associational space, the reinvented state competes with rivalry suppliers of authority with its increasingly aggressive regulatory project for a decisive edge in influence, control, domination, or shaping power over the communal experiences of the people under its rule. This must be accomplished amid a new social reality in which the dismantling of the Soviet-style economic regime has led the Party-state to lose its monopoly over the allocation of resources, opportunities for upward mobility, career prospects, or the administrative power to control people's movements, residence, or associational activities. As this book shows, the reinvented state strives to reclaim an advantageous position in its competition for control with a variety of new, alien or globalized forces through institutional design, interagency collaboration, and strategic manipulation and using a mixture of overt and disguised means.

The baseline guarantee of security for the reinvented state is its disciplinary power at the individual level, which is manifested through the state's incentivization project; however, this also relies on a highly extensive network of human and digital surveillance, preemptive operations, and punishments for political trespassing. The instruments and devices for incentivizing loyalty and monitoring compliance are maintained through a state-designed and state-managed machinery—the incentivization infrastructure—that is nevertheless kept outside of the scope of attention of ordinary people, submerged into the everyday lifeworld and disguised with a bureaucratic, administrative, nonpolitical, scientific, or even medical veneer. Especially when undertaking its punishing or deterring work, except for on rare occasions, the reinvented state remains out of sight. There are many fewer Maoist struggle sessions, parades, demonstrative spectacles, rallies, and the like; the reinvented state prefers to do its work in silence, masked and unheeded, or through state rituals that more often than not appear to be something else.

In Perspective

This book speaks to foundational literature in both political science and China studies, inviting its readers to rethink and reimagine crucial political processes that have for too long been taken for granted. First, the book speaks to the state-building literature by departing from its predominant focus on the process through which modern nation-states came into being, or the "founding moments," to scrutinize an overlooked yet equally important process through which a broken-down state reinvents itself from an existing but outdated and dysfunctional state structure. Going beyond the conventional discussion of static concepts such as "state strength" or "state weakness," this book examines the structure of state power through exploring the dynamic, nuanced, and everyday process of state rebuilding. This book is among the first to study the important but neglected phenomenon of state rebuilding—the reversal process of state decay.

Second, this book contributes to the literature on regime studies by explaining the process of intraregime reinvention. People can remotely feel the significant within-regime changes taking place in many non-Western countries, but there are few on-the-ground analyses of these historical occurrences. An emerging literature has started to unravel this political change both empirically and theoretically. To name just a few: Jeremy L. Wallace (2023) names this change a "neo-political turn," referring to the Chinese state's recent turn from a quantified governance model of its officialdom to one that relies more on ideological conformity, political standard, and subjective judgment. Elizabeth C. Economy (2022) explores the assertive turn of China's foreign policy and worldview at large in the past decade. Yuen Yuen Ang (2020) examines the relationship between corruption and the expansion of China's capitalist economy, scrutinizing the logic and effect of the country's anticorruption movement since 2012. This book traces the everyday origin of within-regime institutional reinvention to the postcrisis state rebuilding process of one of the largest developing countries of our time and looks into the features of the reinvented state—the institutional outcome of state rebuilding.

Third, whereas most scholarship on the making and functioning of the state has focused on elements of high politics, such as elite bargaining, coalition forming, and institution building, this book joins a growing body of literature exploring the everyday political processes that take place under the rule of the state. By scrutinizing how the post-Tiananmen Chinese state re-establishes control over the everyday experiences lived by university students, this book elucidates how the infrastructures of statism work to invent, effectuate, and sustain a political order in the political everyday. Echoing calls for a recognition of the importance of the political everyday lifeworld,[12] this book seeks to shift scholarly attention from a dominant focus on the high politics of state building to the down-to-earth, mundane, concrete, and lived experiences. It shows how latter-day state rebuilders are managing to consolidate state power by turning it into a form of everyday life.

This book also opens new ways of thinking for contemporary China studies. With most of the literature on Chinese universities, which are among China's most precarious social spaces, covering the periods either of the Cultural Revolution or of the Tiananmen Movement of 1989, this book updates knowledge of the sociopolitical ecology and state control of Chinese universities in the twenty-first century. More importantly, this book offers a fresh glimpse into China today and provides a theoretical framework for understanding the growing assertiveness, expanding control capacity, and changing political rhetoric of China. The book demystifies the fundamental political changes taking place at a time in which China is widely seen as a revisionist superpower gathering momentum on both domestic and international fronts. For readers who are deeply puzzled by China's ubiquitously obedient society or its overly zealous "little pinks" (again, a nickname for ultrapatriotic Chinese youth), this book offers new knowledge of the routinized, normalized, and socially embedded political structure—the reinvented state—that is bound to shape the contours of China in the years to come.

Plan of the Book

This book conducts a study of the post-Tiananmen remaking of the Chinese state—a perplexing institutional process through which a state has reinvented itself from and within itself after overcoming an internal political trauma. The introduction opens the book with sketches of the puzzling silence of Chinese universities in the post-Tiananmen era and an overview of the theme of the book: the reinvention of a compromised state. Chapter 1 provides a conceptual discussion of state remaking. With a critical review of the literature, this chapter provides a theoretical framework to understand the process of posttrauma state rebuilding, the infrastructures for statism, and how the state reinvention process leads to within-regime changes. State remaking is not a mere jump-starting of old engines; rather, it is a multivocal process of building a state from a state, in which rulers focus on regaining their capacity to mold, shape, and control the political everyday—the quotidian yet foundational activities and processes that buttress the order that the political elites seek to reinvent.

Chapter 2 explores the post-Tiananmen state's efforts to rebuild the institutional infrastructure of Chinese universities, which includes a concentric-circle structure with different layers of students in a framework of political trustworthiness and a "grid-structure" that organizes the campus community into hierarchically interlinked cells. This infrastructure diffuses the state's organizational form, colonizes social spaces, and places social networks back under state domination. This chapter sets the institutional stage for the state's operations by detailing the institutional infrastructure for student control in the post-Tiananmen era. A triple-pronged bureaucracy—comprising the Communist Party System, the Communist Youth League System, and the Student Work System—was reinvented to govern the critical social space of the university. Through a corps of cadres with dual identities as academic staff and Communist Party cadres, the state extends its reach into every corner of students' everyday lives. The concentric-circle structure, along with a "grid-like" institutional web, both forged by the state, are invented to organize and engage the students in repetitive experiences that mirror national political processes and render these processes habitual and natural.

Chapter 3 examines the post-Tiananmen Chinese state's reinvention of a significative infrastructure on university campuses to forge, project, and solidify a renewed discourse of legitimacy, an updated founding myth, and a new vision to justify the state's overhauled political lines. With this revamped footing of legitimacy, the state constructs its desired social reality through a variety of channels and arenas, combining passive training and active participation in ways that are woven into the fabric of the student community's everyday experiences. The signification project manifests the communist regime's efforts both to reform the state's baseline political rhetoric and to reconstruct the devices for projecting that narrative into the everyday experiences of the populace. This state-made "cultural milieu" not only ensures the all-round exposure of the student population to the state's legitimating discourses, it also eliminates the spatiotemporal share of alternative narratives. Eventually, it becomes so pervasive that students, despite their weariness with these activities, consider them familiar, natural, and instinctive, thus effectuating a firm cognitive foundation for the political order that the reinvented state seeks to reestablish.

Chapter 4 studies the post-Tiananmen Chinese state's operations in controlling the public life within university walls. The unique qualities of the university as a sociopolitical institution—its dense connectivity with society at large, its latency as an abeyance structure for youth progressing into the adult world, and its centrality to the production of the state's cultural capital—make it a critical site for the order-seeking state to control and command. However, the open nature of the public space of the university precludes the state from conquering it in monolithic terms; rather, in the lively public life and associational space of the university, the state must compete with rival suppliers of authority for dominance. This chapter explores the ways in which the post-Tiananmen Chinese state reestablishes control over the four major components of the university public space: the associational space, the virtual space, the field of the spiritual, and the institutional subculture. This vast operation to shape and control people's communal experiences again illustrates the emphasis of the state on structuring the political order to reinvent a political order.

Chapter 5 examines how a new incentivization infrastructure is being established by the post-Tiananmen state in place of the old system of generating incentives for compliance in Chinese universities. Positive incentives, comprising elite membership, preferential advantage, and earmarked opportunities, supply additional information about the state's favored behavior pattern, increase the opportunity costs of overt defiance, and enhance competition among elites when these rewards are dispensed in a hierarchical manner. Meanwhile, the system of punishment has both reforming and deterrence functions, correcting the wrongdoer and warning other members of the social group not to follow suit. Public punishment serves an expressive function by setting a clear boundary that lay members of society are not supposed to cross. The state's incentivization infrastructure is not complete without a mechanism that provides accurate and permanent real-time surveillance of the critical social spaces. Such a surveillance mechanism, often disguised in an administrative or scientific form, facilitates the monitoring and measuring of loyalty, defiance, and indifference.

Be it the death of a popular political figure, the anniversary of a rebellion discredited by the ruling elites, or a major international event in which China might be considered to have "lost face" in one way or another, politically sensitive occasions are the reinvented state's most vulnerable and exposed moments. Chapter 6 studies the post-Tiananmen Chinese state's invention of an entire responsive apparatus on campus for the "Critical and Sensitive Period," referring to a designated period when political or social tension is expected to be at a high level and the Party-state anticipates a higher likelihood of student unrest or collective action. Critical and Sensitive Periods on Chinese university campuses are politically precarious and demanding moments for the state. To guard order, the state takes extraordinary measures to pacify simmering tensions by monitoring critical social spaces, exerting tightened control over critical social groups, and preventing the mobilizing energies of the campus from materializing in the most critical moments of national and international politics.

Chapter 7 concludes the book by placing the story in perspective. It summarizes the main arguments, discusses the concept of state remaking, defines the primary state projects of signification, regulation, and incentivization for state rebuilding, reviews the need to anchor the state revival projects in the political everyday, details the four types of infrastructure—institutional, significative, regulatory, and incentivizing—that state rebuilders need to overhaul, and looks into the campaign of state rebuilding in post-Tiananmen Chinese universities and its implications for our understanding of politics in general.

ONE

The Compromised State
and Its Reinvention

Great power announces itself by its power over order. It discovers order, creates order, maintains it, or destroys it. Power is indeed the central, order-related event.

—Edward Shils, *The Constitution of Society*, 1982, 128

Power enforces the terms on which things *must* be done at the most everyday of levels.

—Derek Sayer, *Everyday Forms of State Formation*, 1994, 375

The State Being Compromised

In a modern society, the state is the creator, guardian, and enforcer par excellence of political order. Positioned as the main claimant of the largest share of a national community's material, coercive, and symbolic capital, the state uses that capital strategically to invent, justify, and maintain political order—the arrangement of public life and the disposition of political power in the manner willed by the sovereign force of the day. Under different regime contexts, a sovereign will can be mandated by royal fiats issued from the throne, resolved at conclaves of the Politburo, or voiced by the ballots of the people. Yet regardless of regime type, history has shown that neither the existence nor the proper functioning of the state as the guardian of order is to be taken for granted; on many occasions, the state has been shown to be a rather precarious institutional form that can succumb to various centrifugal forces and external shocks. Even a highly institutionalized, long-naturalized, and immensely routinized state may become "temporarily or situationally weak because of internal antagonisms, management flaws, greed, despotism, or external attacks" (Rotberg 2004, 4).

A state's being compromised, however unexpected in each individual case, is not an unusual political phenomenon from a historical view.[1] A rotten legitimation base weakens the state's claim to the right to rule and makes it more difficult for the state to justify its policy lines. A fundamental shift in the allocation mechanism of a society's scarce resources (such as opportunities for upward mobility), or a significant increase in the size of reckoned stakeholders who are eligible to claim a share of the governmental coffer, endangers the state's ability to reward conformity and punish defiance. A hampered regulatory infrastructure in the public sphere places the state in a disadvantageous position in its ongoing competition with rival suppliers of authority in public life and organizational activities. With a waning ability to influence social actors, the state becomes less capable of enforcing its preferred rules, maintaining political arrangements tailored to its will, or undertaking developmental projects according to its design. As Stephen Skowronek argued, commenting on antebellum state reconstruction in the United States,

> In the course of a nation's development, an impasse may be reached in relations between an established state and its society, an impasse in which the most basic political and institutional arrangements structuring state operations are no longer pertinent to the task of maintaining order. . . . Vindicating the state's claims to control under such conditions would require a reconstruction of the foundations of official power within the state apparatus and a redefinition of the routine mode of governmental operations. (1982, 13)

In this book, I call a state that is in a substantially weakened position in terms of signifying its own legitimating narrative, competing for control in the public space, and regulating social actors' behavior, a compromised state. The bureaucratic structure and coercive machinery of a compromised state may be largely intact, yet under the impact of domestic shocks or foreign influence, the justifiability of its right to rule decreases, its instruments for regulating social life become less effective, and state-social links are mutilated; thus, the state may not be able to defend against societal challenges to its authority, coordinate state-society interactions, or forge society-wide loyalty to its own advantage. The use of state violence in solving societal uprising itself is an indicator of the compromise of the state. Among the possible causes of a state being compromised, political crises—especially those that feature entrenched, emotional, hostile, and ideologically charged confrontations between the state and society—are particularly conducive to the rapid deterioration of a state's symbolic, regulatory, and incentivization capacity. A compromised state needs to manage its own salvation.

However, a compromised state is not a failed one. "Nation-states fail when they are consumed by internal violence and cease delivering positive political goods to their inhabitants," wrote Robert I. Rotberg (2004, 1). He thus recommended that a performance criterion be used to distinguish strong states from weak states, and weak states from failed or collapsed states (Rotberg 2004). Here, performance was defined as the levels of the state's effective delivery of the most crucial political goods. Internationally, a failed state suffers from "the formal loss of control over foreign policy making to another state" (Fazal 2007, 1). Combined together, a failed state is most often defined by the loss—to varied extents—of its state infrastructural power: the institutional capability of the state apparatus to perform basic public functions and provide basic public goods.

But a compromised state is different. First, a compromised state does not lose control over the territories under its rule, although its capability to project power and achieve its policy goals has been substantially weakened. Whereas today's failed states are "incapable of projecting power and asserting authority within their own borders, leaving their territories governmentally empty" (Rotberg 2002, 128), a compromised state still firmly holds its territorial borders, maintains its basic bureaucratic structure, and remains integrally sovereign. Nevertheless, its compromised ability to effect political signification, contest for control in public life, and regulate the behavior of societal actors leaves the state's authority in limbo and its future uncertain.

Second, a failed state often has a vacuum of governmental authority and rampant criminal violence, whereas a compromised state still maintains proper social order, narrowly defined, which ensures human security, the preservation of physical infrastructure, and the provision of necessary public goods; it allows people to continue their everyday routines. Nevertheless, a compromised state's ability to nurture political consensus, overhaul policy, carry out national projects, conduct political bargaining, wage wars, and deal with large-scale social resistance may be seriously compromised. Given the lack of proper political instrumentality, at the end of the day, a compromised state often has no choice but to maintain order by implementing martial law or conducting pervasive criminal prosecutions against actual and potential rebels. A compromised state cannot integrate civil society into the cooperation, negotiation, and dynamism of national politics, and its society experiences political alienation and apathy.

Third, a failed state falls apart after it has lost its ability to win competitions with other authority centers for control and domination over the nation's public life. However, even though a compromised state may not be able to maintain its old power status and regulate social actors as effectively as the reigning elites would have wanted, it remains an active, strategic, and sufficiently autonomous participant in the battle for power. A compromised state that has begun to decay institutionally and politically may nevertheless maintain a strong resolve and clear intention to secure an advantageous position against competing social centers of authority.

Unlike state failure, state compromise is reversible. Because the compromised state still possesses considerable capacity to provide basic public goods, project power, exert rule, and maintain social tranquility amid trying circumstances, with the proper design and execution of institutional reforms and the effective use of statecraft, it can revive itself as a fully functional and competent state on new terms. Yet the root causes for a state being compromised are found within the state apparatus itself. Violent state-society confrontation leaves the legitimating footing of the state dwindling with postcrisis uncertainties; from there, the state has to reinvent new and updated baseline political rhetorics. Whereas the old ways of dominating the society are scattered into pieces by the new social normalcy, the state is compelled to use its remaining institutional capacity to build up new institutional edifices of control from the remnants of the obsolete and archaic. In public life, the state also concentrates its staying capacity to reestablish its advantage in its competition with rivalry suppliers of social, political, and organizational authority. New tool kits are needed to maintain a remodeled incentivization infrastructure that effectively shapes people's behavior, induces compliance, and deters open defiance. Instead of looking for salvation from elsewhere, the compromised state has to reinvent itself from within itself.

State Reinvention in the Everyday

How a political order is created, effectuated, and maintained is one of the central concerns in studies of modern states. Immensely insightful as they have been, however, existing studies have overly focused on elite-level coalition building and strategic statecraft; insufficient attention has been devoted to how a compromised state can reinvent itself within itself and from itself after overcoming the critical moment of vulnerability. In other words, rather than emphasizing a state's founding moment, political research should focus more on the process through which a compromised political order rebuilds itself from within.

Institutionalized Political Order

The state is itself the materialization and embodiment of a territorially demarcated and institutionally defined political order. As Samuel P. Huntington (1968) argued, "the most important political distinction among countries concerns not their form of government but their degree of government" (1). However compromised or weakened, the state provides the principal dynamism behind the formation, sustenance, and evolution of the institutionalized figuration of a national community. The core of compliance, order, and control in the phenomenal experiences being lived in the modern political world is embodied in and maintained by the state (Acemoglu and Robinson 2019). Indeed, "an understanding of how societies persist and change must start with the organizations that exercise social control, that subordinate individual inclinations to the behaviour these organizations prescribe" (Migdal 2011, 48).

While the state is preeminent among all rule-making, life-shaping, and law-giving entities in people's everyday lifeworlds, two points are critical before we discuss the reinvention of statist order. First, state power is a multivocal and multifaced concept; it is never uniform or monotonal. In this book, I define power as one party's influence over another party to reduce the unpredictability of the latter's choice of action in a direction that is congruent with the former's preference. Statist power is most discernibly manifested in its structuring of people's everyday experiences, as the state reduces their unpredictability in the direction of its own preferences. Power is an everyday process that continuously generates order by restricting the number of options that are otherwise available to people in historically concrete scenarios, and the exercise of state power is bound to be complex, quotidian, and nuanced, being reckoned not only in the grandeur of state-made spectacles but also in the most mundane details of everyday lifeworlds. After all, even the most majestic power is "at its most intense and durable when running silently through the repetition of institutionalized practices" (Giddens 1987, 9).

Second, the state exercises power on competitive rather than monopolistic terms. At the beginning of the twentieth century, Max Weber defined the rational-bureaucratic state as "a compulsory association which organizes domination" that "has been successful in seeking to monopolize the legitimate use of physical force as a means of domination within a territory" (1946, 82–83). The post-Weberian scholarship, largely based on subsequent human experiences, questioned this monopolistic concept; they increasingly saw the state as just a competitor—albeit a strong and capable one in many cases—with nonstate actors and organizations (Migdal 2011), or as a "cage of norms" for the power to shape, regulate, and control people's everyday life experiences (Acemoglu and Robinson 2019). There is an intrinsic discrepancy between the state's "image of a coherent, controlling organization in a territory" and "the actual practices of its multiple parts" (Migdal 2011, 16): it has been well established that the state must compete for social control with multiple centers of power and authority within its claimed territory. The modern state has to operate on competitive terms to assert control and maintain order in a fragmented and pulverized social reality.

Institutionalist studies of political order in the past two decades have broken important ground. In the narratives these influential works offer, the state emerges from the background of a messy social arena as an automatic, quasi–rule-based, and even self-constrained center of power. States are no longer seen as structures of suppression that simply operate at the pleasure of a dictator; rather, they are perceived as a systemic political order that has its own operational logic, institutional attributes, historical continuity, and sociopolitical fixations. As research has progressed, perceptions of the state have gone beyond the muddy chaos of despotism, court conspiracies, coups d'état, and bloodshed. States have crystallized into recognizable institutional entities that political scientists can study and explore, identifying their common logics of operation.

Over the past two decades, scholars have proposed various theories of how institutionalized political order is created and maintained, or how institutions help forge elite coalitions, shape elite-mass interactions, or prevent intra-elite coups d'état from taking place (for example, Herbst 2000; Bellin 2005; Schedler 2013; Pepinsky 2009; Ginsburg and Moustafa 2008; Schedler 2013). Institutions with some degree of "democratic" appearance have received particular attention (for example, Gandhi 2008; Brownlee 2007; Magaloni 2006; Lust-Okar 2005; Meng 2020; Svolik 2012). Specific institutional devices may be helpful for states to maintain institutionalized political order. For example, some regimes use a unique institutional structure, administrative mass organizations, which are modeled on conscript armies, to effectuate and maintain political order, supplemented by the deployment of naked state violence against the most determined opponents. In such a "conscription society," the organization controls its members through shaping their everyday experiences in a multitude of ways, including material dependency, time consumption, loyalty rituals, conferring honors, the organized used of supporters, and self-directed local participation (Kasza 1995, 52–53). Institutionalist studies on the state have provided more than functional-institutionalist theories; comparative historical institutionalist studies have also examined the importance of timing, sequence, critical junctures, and other path-dependent factors in effectuating and maintaining institutionalized political order, thus linking the institutional aspects of the modern state with the complex historical landscape (Geddes, Wright, and Frantz 2018; Levitsky and Way 2022; Slater 2010; Greitens 2016).

However, prior theories share two common shortcomings. First, most theories treat the invention and maintenance of an institutionalized political order in the form of the state as a unidimensional process that takes place in one single institutional field; they overlook its multivocal and multidimensional nature. As this book demonstrates, control and order are both dynamic processes involving cognitive, regulatory, and incentivization parameters. The cognitive parameter refers to the society's explicit and implicit acceptance of and submission to the state's significative narrative. Once it is widely accepted by society, such a narrative, controlled and manipulated by the state and its agents, becomes the legitimating basis for and baseline political rhetoric of the national community. The regulatory parameter refers to the state's contentious position in its battle for domination in the public space and associational life with alternative or would-be centers of authority, which include but are not limited to societal, academic, spiritual, and foreign sources of authority and influence. The incentivization parameter refers to the state's competency, through the deployment of positive and negative sanctioning devices, to punish defiance and correct delinquency, to encourage and reward obedience, and to defy heterodox societal beliefs and behavior. These tripartite parameters work simultaneously in the compromised state's order-building project.

Second, most theories on the modern state have a strong elitist bias—they tend to overwhelmingly stress the importance of elite coalition, buying-off tactics, or co-optation strategies. They also tend to concentrate more on the high politics occurring in the grand halls of the state or within powerful cliques, paying less attention to the ways in which the state shapes, regulates, forges, and naturalizes itself in the everyday rhythm and temporal-spatial structure of the lived experiences of ordinary people under its rule. This omission has led studies on institutionalized political order to miss the important component of the state's engineering to create and maintain its command over the political everydayness. Echoing recent calls for recognition of the importance of the political everyday lifeworld under non-Western regime settings,[2], this book argues that the pervasive infiltration of state power into the everyday life of the critical social groups and the state's capacity to reform these groups is essential for our understanding of any institutionalized political order.

The People and the Space

Scholars have detailed the steps for resuscitating political order when a state has failed, but scant attention has been given to the process of reversing a state that has been compromised. To remake political order after state failure, it is believed, for example, that a crucial step is restoring the "utility" of the state (i.e., making the state usable to major interest groups) and reinventing "stakes" for societal actors (i.e., those with deep interests held in the state) (Meierhenrich 2004, 153–69). Disbarring and demobilizing insurgent groups and reintegrating members of these groups into a normalized society is also considered a necessary move (Colletta, Kostner, and Wiederhofer 2004, 170–81). Reestablishing the rule of law (Rose-Ackerman 2004), building effective trust (Widner 2004), revamping a functional civil society (Posner 2004), restoring the economic functioning of the state (Snodgrass 2004), and transforming the institutions of war (Lyons 2004) are also essential in such a situation. Moreover, as opposition parties offer a "clear, plausible, and critical governing alternative," building robust political opposition in the postcrisis era can often induce the ruling political party to "moderate their behaviour, create formal state institutions, and share power" and thus help "inadvertently build the state" (Grzymala-Busse 2007, 1).

Undertaking different remedies naturally leads to divergent outcomes of state remaking, yet all these prescribed antidotes to state decay and breakdown are less applicable to a compromised state such as China after the 1989 Tiananmen Movement. Unlike a completely dysfunctional state, the post-Tiananmen Chinese state maintains a functioning bureaucratic skeleton that includes a judiciary capable of adjudicating civil disputes and criminal charges, preserving the established social fabric (although the need for new negotiations for societal cooperation has become compelling), and possessing the competence to keep domestic tranquility and control crime. In addition, with the old state institutions remaining largely intact in the compromised state, the multiparty competition and populist political mandate that usually follow a regime collapse do not exist. Yet domestic calamity and radicalized political confrontation precipitated the state's loss of legitimacy, and loss of control over the country's critical social groups and social spaces, including educated youth. The state even faces challenges in justifying its own existence.

The compromised state appears feeble in its efforts to justifying its own existence, sluggish in its attempt to generate society-wide compliance to its rule, and vulnerable in its battle with would-be centers of power in public life, which may see opportunities to strike. The Chinese state immediately after the crackdown on the Tiananmen Movement in 1989 is a quintessential compromised state suffering from an array of deep-seated issues: the state's weakened legitimation base makes the prevailing political rhetoric, featured by a teleological vision of an egalitarian utopian future and a revolutionary altruism morality, dubious and fake. The invalidation of old instruments of control under the shockwaves of rapid marketization leaves an increasingly large portion of the society out of governmental command, and the state's rival suppliers of authority in public life, such as parallel organizations, religious solidarities, and civil society networks, are not only possible but flourishing. With the fading away of Maoist mass movement and the associated participatory enticement, the state loses its ability not only to incentivize loyalty but to monitor compliance.

Overall, in the era after 1989, the undermined governability of the compromised state poses a fatal threat to the reigning regime of China. To survive, the compromised state is impelled to undertake a complete overhaul of the state order—rather than a mere jump-start of old engines. To remain in power, the post-Tiananmen Chinese regime sets out to reinvent a state within and from itself—only on new terms. The aim is to reestablish an institutional structure that facilitates the state's reach into social fabrics, reinvigorates the legitimation footing that justifies the state's right to rule, reasserts the state's regulative capacity over the public sphere, and revitalizes an outmoded infrastructure that engenders incentives for political compliance. In undertaking to rebuild the institutional order, the compromised state has a list of priorities (Eisenstadt 2017, 3). Yet, to manage its own salvation, a compromised state's foremost concern is always to reestablish control over the country's critical social groups (*zhongdian renqun*) and reenact regulation within critical social spaces (*zhongdian chusuo*). In a similar vein, when commenting on the effectiveness of Mao Zedong's "mass line" tactics, Dimitar D. Gueorguiev (2021) wrote that "the whole of mainland China was arguably too large and too complex for the CCP to fully grasp. As a result, the CCP was forced to target its control function within urban centers and production corps, and toward specific population groups" (56).

Critical social groups—such as the technical intelligentsia in the Soviet Union, or tenant farmers in the British Raj—live on the margins of the radiant network of state control and have subjectivities that may diverge hugely from the state's hegemonic cultural influence and political will. The relationship of these groups with the ruling clique of the day is precarious at best. Neither their loyalty nor their conformity is written in stone, and foreign, external, and communal influences can claim their sympathy given the right circumstances. From time to time in history, such critical social groups are imbued with strong antisystem potential and a proven capability to provide alternative or even revolutionary imageries for the future.

In the postcrisis context, critical social groups are ostensibly comprised of citizens who share a similar socially or naturally forged identity, who suffered the most in their everyday lives prior to the crisis, and who endured the largest collective loss during the crisis. However, these groups are not merely a product of the ex post contingencies of a national crisis; their existence is a priori. Members of a critical social group maintain a close internal network of solidarity that is based on shared professional commitment, religious bonds, or collective memories. Moreover, they usually have an intentionally or unintentionally different diagnosis of the sociopolitical reality and have aspirations and plans for the future that run afoul of those advocated by the state. Sharing a discordant worldview and value system, they maintain behavioral autonomy, albeit constrained by the state's legal and political devices, by associating with each other in a communal manner and preserving a spatiotemporal structure that tries to escape from the reach of the state.[3]

Members of critical social groups inhabit and live their everyday experiences in critical social spaces. Within this socially produced spatiality, mobilizational networks, political symbolism, or a shared sense of belonging may be nurtured, and activities deemed harmful by the ruling political order may take place. These spheres usually have physical boundaries (such as university campuses, public squares, dissident bookstores, underground churches, and jungle camps of guerrilla fighters), but their more important dimensions are the symbolic meaning, interpersonal bonds, and socializing effects that are generated, maintained, revived, and disseminated. As William H. Sewell Jr. argued, "it is a space that is used, seen, and experienced" (2001, 53). The high concentration of people with similar social attributes within a critical social space enables the inhabitants to maintain a lively public life. These spaces are thus turned into meeting places for the crucial social relationships and connecting nodes for different historical periods, where the legacies of foregone eras can be most easily found and observed; these legacies may still exert influence on the contemporary narrative, the symbolic order, and individual behavior.

Critical social spaces are containers for specific practices, actions, networks, and identities that an order-seeking state seeks to monitor, regulate, and govern. Critical social groups and critical social spaces meet in people's everyday lived experiences. For instance, on the university campus, the everyday lives of students provide both the duration and the territory for social forces to take effect, for political discourses to take shape, and for the most powerful of the competing centers of authorities to take command. Space is always lived and continuously transformed by the minute practices of the everyday (Lanza 2010, 7). Lived experiences give life and form to the otherwise docile and formless spatiotemporal structure of political order; they offer a handle and pathway for the order-seeking state to exert its influence on the everyday-ness in the social sphere.

The political everyday is the confluence point of institutional dynamism, societal networks, and state imperatives. As David W. Lovell (1984) argued, what "fired Marx's enthusiasm for the Paris Commune" was "its fostering of politics as an activity integral to man's existence, not separate from him as under the system of 'alien politics' embodied in the existence of a state" (69). As this book shows, in the university, the transmutation between time and space in the everyday brings political order into focus and is one of the chosen sites for the compromised state to begin its project of rebuilding a political order.

Understanding the state's domination in the political everyday is thus of central importance for understanding the state's overall restorative undertaking to reassert control. As Anthony Giddens argued, "all social reproduction and . . . all systems of power are grounded in the 'predictability' of day-to-day routines. The predictable—that is to say, regularised—character of day-to-day activity is not something that just 'happens,' it is in substantial part 'made to happen'" (1987, 11). The silhouettes of the political everyday reflect the contours of state order. For the rebuilders of a state, it is essential to keep critical social groups at bay and critical social spaces under control; in this field, the state simply needs to win the day.

Infrastructures for Statism

The post-Tiananmen Chinese Communist Party's project to salvage the compromised state and reinvent the infrastructures of statism essentially operates in distinct fields with different concerns, strategies, operational contrivances, and reservoirs of instruments. Divergent theories about the making of state order suggest that probing the multivocal process in which order is invented and preserved in the political everyday remains a crucial undertaking for students of the state in all its variants. For example, as Margaret Levi (1997) argued, perceptually, a citizen's compliance with state order comes from her conception of the government as "trustworthy and she is satisfied other citizens are also engaging in ethical reciprocity" (19). And "the more a government is capable of credible commitments and the more its procedures meet prevailing standards of fairness, the more trustworthy that government will seem" (Levi 1997, 21). How this perceptual foundation for state order is being formed has to be discovered in the political everyday.

Behaviorally, the stability of a political order may depend on the range of continued and repeated interactions between rulers and subjects in terms of testing each other's boundaries of tolerance. As Barrington Moore (1978) argued, "what takes place . . . is a continued probing on the part of the rulers and subjects to find out what they can get away with, to test and discover the limits of obedience and disobedience. . . . The more stable the society, the narrower the range within which this testing and discovering take place" (71).

Studies on the invention and maintenance of colonial order or foreign occupation have provided particularly valuable insights into the multielement structure of state order that exists only within the political everyday. Mahmood Mamdani (1996) found that to ensure compliance and order, a colonial state in its "mature stage" often deploys a governing structure that he termed the "bifurcated state" to address the "native question" of how a tiny foreign minority can "rule over an indigenous majority" (16). This bifurcated mode of state formation features a combination of direct rule prevailing in urban areas and indirect rule in rural areas, signifying tribal authority. Under the colonial state, the former urban practice excludes the native population from civil freedoms, but the latter incorporates natives into a state-enforced customary order. Thus, Mamdani showed that to maintain control and order, the colonial state must wield dual forms of power under a single hegemonic authority (18).

The British Raj, the colonial state established by the British Empire in India, features "an orderly control in which force . . . had to learn to live with institutions and ideologies designed to generate consent" (Guha 1997, 25). To establish and maintain order in India, the colonial state had to fall back on the traditional Indian concept of *danda* to exert coercive force, and to use a combination of discourse on improvement and dharma (i.e., virtue, moral duty)—both in the nuanced political everyday—to exercise persuasive power (Guha 1997, 25–35). Even an alien ruler can maintain a legitimate rule "to the degree that rulers effectively produce the right kinds of collective goods, and allocate these goods fairly to the ruled" in the latter's everyday experiences (Hechter 2013, 3).

Timur Kuran (1995) argues, "Individuals routinely applauded speakers they disliked, joined organizations whose mission they opposed, ostracized dissidents they admired, and followed orders they considered nonsensical, unjust, or inhuman, among other manifestations of consent and accommodation" (119). While the Soviet political order was capable of maintaining itself where "the perception that society is at least publicly behind the Party" was reinforced by society's "preparedness to conform to the political status quo" (123), in this theory, the origin of this prevalent culture of "falsification of preference" in favor of political conformism remains obscure. While Kuran (1995) convincingly demonstrated that it was a "culture of mendacity"—the pervasive conformism of the people to state-mandated activities—that sustained the Soviet political order in the everyday, in his theory, the origin of this prevalent culture of "falsification of preference" in favor of political subjugation remains obscure. This book shows that, in post-Tiananmen China, conformism is the outcome of a coordinated and multivocal state project that engineers stability with the aid of the infrastructures of statism.

For the modern state, establishing order and control has become a complex business, where the state may increasingly need to deploy a full set of nuanced, normalized, and layered instruments to secure an organizational and ideological grip over society. This demands more synthetic and analytical frameworks for understanding state order and state power, going beyond the "power debate" that focuses on how a powerful party can win in a war over policy preferences or agenda setting. (Machiavelli 1513 [1998]; Schattschneider 1960; Arendt 1969; Bachrach and Baratzm 1970; Gaventa 1980; Lukes 2005).

The critical project undertaken by the state rebuilders is upheld by the reconstructed institutional, significative, regulatory, and incentivization infrastructures: the basic structural-functional components of statism.

Each of these basic infrastructures also represents a crucial aspect of the state's capacity to extend control over the social realm. It is worth noting, however, that the different infrastructures of statism are interconnected processes and social spheres, rather than separate structures of fixed spatiality. I use Joel S. Migdal's (2011) concept that these processes refer to "the ongoing struggles among shifting coalitions over the rules for daily behaviour" and they "determine how societies and states create and maintain distinct ways of structuring day-to-day life" (11).

The institutional infrastructure provides an overall structure through which the state can organize the critical social groups, arrange the critical social spaces, reassert its control over the social realm, and rebuild state order to the will of the incumbent regime. The institutional infrastructure gives the sprawling social spaces a tailored form in the image of the state itself, a hierarchical central-periphery structure based on reckoned political loyalty and an institutional web that weaves the state's presence into people's everyday experiences (Whyte 1974; Koss 2018). The institutional infrastructure connects the state and society, in fact mingling the two into one inseparable entity with strong significative, regulatory, and incentivization capacities. Also, by replicating the state's political practices at the micro level and in the everyday lifeworlds, the institutional infrastructure spreads out the institutional form of the state, colonizing a sprawling civil society by hollowing out the latter's autonomous form, and thus holding sway again over an increasingly independent social sphere in the postcrisis era. As Hillel Soifer and Matthias vom Hau (2008) argued, "the ability of states is . . . crucially shaped by the organizational networks that they coordinate, control and construct" (222).

The significative infrastructure facilitates the renewal and update of the meta-narratives that can justify the state's right to rule after its devastating political clash with dissenting social forces, ensuring that the renovated baseline political rhetorics of the state meet the new demands on fresh terms in the postcrisis era. By deploying the significative infrastructure, the state blends its legitimation message into the discursive fabrics of the people's daily lives, rendering the state's baseline political language, symbols, and meaning a natural, repetitive, and tedious presence in people's everyday lifeworlds. As Lily L. Tsai (2021) argued, in the two millennia of recorded history, the Chinese state has always sought to portray "itself as the creator and enforcer of a value system that provided social order and meaning to the everyday lives of ordinary people" (77). Obviously, this task can only be accomplished with the aid of a robust state significative infrastructure. With this infrastructure, the state strives to establish and maintain a symbolic order that masks, decorates, and upholds the reigning power structure of the day. By deploying the significative infrastructure, the state's baseline goal is to maintain the society's submission in form to the symbol, ideology, founding myth, and official discourse being advocated by the political regime; its ultimate goal is indoctrination—the genuine belief in and autonomous internalization by members of the society of official symbolism and discourses propagated by the state.

The regulatory infrastructure rectifies organizational life, manages interpersonal communications, organizes collective activities, and governs the socialization processes taking place in everyday lifeworlds, looking to securing the state's decisive edge in combating rival suppliers of authority in public life. With the regulatory infrastructure, the state competes with various kinds of centrifugal forces that drag social actors away from state order and with alternative power centers that attempt to establish parallel influence in the political everyday. By deploying the regulatory infrastructure, the state's baseline goal is to remain competitive in a market of competition for control over the subjects; its ultimate goal is to dominate the field, and it holds a forcefully advantageous position in shaping the subjects' preference in that field.

The incentivization infrastructure is also established to properly reward loyalty, punish defiance, and deter the formation of oppositional forces. For this purpose, a refurbished surveillance framework is also put in place so that compliance can be measured, monitored, created, and enforced. With the incentivization infrastructure, the state seeks to establish and maintain a disciplinary order, by which it attempts to sanction overt defiance, correct behavior irregularities, detect and tackle hidden resistance, and ensure all-around conformity in the terrain it seeks to control. In using the incentivization infrastructure, the baseline goal of the state is to forge behavioral obedience; its ultimate goal is to create a disciplinary regime based on voluntary assent, willingness to collaborate, and self-motivated submission to rules that shape not only people's behavior but their ways of thinking, their preferences, and their attention.

Anchoring the Political Everyday

"The everyday is simultaneously the site of, the theatre for, and what is at stake in a conflict between great indestructible rhythms and the processes imposed by the socio-economic organisation of production, consumption, circulation and habitat" (Lefebvre and Régulier 2013, 82). The everyday political life under an institutionalized political order is a meeting place for state forces and societal dynamism. The spatial-temporal structure of the everyday is both shaped by and reflects the interaction between grand statecraft and on-the-ground negotiation, the synergy between elite vision and mass imagination, and the convergence of high politics and subaltern networks. To effectuate and maintain an effective political order, the modern state is always concerned about shaping, controlling, and structuring the everyday. As Fabio Lanza wrote, politics lies in "the ability to produce a space in which a new everyday can be experienced, new relationships formed, and alternative lives can be lived. Space is not simply the stage of events but truly the stake of political struggles" (2010, 7).

Regional studies on states in various cultural contexts have a rich tradition of exploring the rhythm, rhetoric, and structure of the political everyday. Students of the modern Chinese state have long been interested in discovering the political structures embedded in the everyday experiences of the "ordinary and obscure individuals who lived in the shadow of great architecture and great men" (Strand 1989, xii). By doing so, they have sought to decipher the political foundation, operational principles, and networked societal dynamism underlying the political order of the body politic (Strand 1989; Duara 1988). Scholarly interest in the everyday political life of ordinary Chinese in the communist era has not faded, and new insights continue to emerge from scholars' persistent exploration of the traces of the Chinese state's various initiatives to create order through shaping and regulating people's everyday lifeworlds (e.g., Henderson and Cohen 1984; Walder 1984). Beyond China, a growing cohort of scholars of the state have also theorized about the hidden everyday groundwork for institutionalized political order (e.g., Wedeen 1999; Blaydes 2018; Khoury 2013; Bayat 2013). With that, successful resistance movements in the Middle East have contested the many forms of domination that "clothes itself in the guise of normality, of routine, of a presence that need not be questioned because it is so much part of the 'natural' order of things" (Tripp 2013, 2). These insightful studies demonstrated that, to understand the institutionalized political order disguised as normalcy, we must discern how the state structures, commands, and shapes the spatiotemporal structure of the everyday experiences lived by different social groups in different social spaces.

Three points are salient. First, a nuanced understanding of the everyday rhythm in these crucial social spaces helps the authors accurately identify the pulse of the institutionalized political order in operation as lived experience. For instance, by studying "the characteristics of everyday life in factory settings," Andrew G. Walder (1984) illustrated the communist neotraditionalist image of the Maoist political order.[4] Also, the collusion between state and societal forces in bolstering state rule as well as the "seepage" of the regime's security mandate from one policy area to another can only be found in a careful examination of the rhythms of the political everyday (e.g., Wallace 2014; Rithmire 2015; Mattingly 2020; Pan 2020; Ong 2022).

Second, the relevance of nuanced subjectivity and the diversified experiences of the people who live under an institutionalized political order is central to our understanding of the foundational importance for state power of controlling people's everyday lifeworlds. Scholars have asked that attention be devoted to the richness of the local "folk" variants of political processes and to the lively negotiation of state rule that takes place on the everyday level. They found revolutionary and postrevolutionary state formation to be a "culturally complex, historically generated process" that was "embodied in the forms, routines, rituals, and discourses of rule" (Joseph and Nugent 1994, 5, 20). Political and cultural understandings of the state's efforts to effectuate and maintain order in the everyday rhythm of people's lived experience are conceptually and empirically indispensable.

Third, state power exercised and manifested in the political everyday and through people's quotidian lifeworlds can exert a strong shaping effect on the social realm. In the twentieth century, Japan's state-directed campaigns of "social management" are "a powerful pattern of governance in which the state has historically intervened to shape how ordinary Japanese thought and behaved." These intrusive state campaigns undertook to mold the everyday mindsets, habits, and practices of ordinary Japanese, reflecting the "unrelenting drive by a transcendent state to control society as a whole"—a "state in everyday life" (6, 16).[5]

As Derek Sayer (1994) contended, "power enforces the terms on which things *must* be done at the most everyday of levels" (italics original); essentially, power is "an organisation of the times and spaces within which individual life is lived" (375). To grasp these "most deeply buried structures of the different social worlds" (Bourdieu 1996, 1) that build up the institutionalized political order, we must go back to the point of origin and sphere of ultimate power: the political everyday. In Michel de Certeau's words, there is a pressing need to rescue the operational combination (*les combinatoires d'opérations*) of everyday practices from obscurity and make it explicit (1984). Only by anchoring in the political everyday can we fully grasp the "real" operative logic of the social and political world in which we live.

Visibility of the State

The state establishes and maintains political order by manifesting itself as "an effect of detailed processes of spatial organisation, temporary arrangement, functional specification, and supervision and surveillance" (Mitchell 1991, 95). However, when the state operates to produce order and exert control, it does not always make itself visible in all the political fields. Sometimes, the state's presence in the political field is announced, overt, and even heavily propagated; on other occasions, however, the state operates in secret. The visible state is not only present in spectacular ceremonies, rituals, and grand projects, but is woven into the everyday experience of the social groups under its rule. When the state chooses to be invisible, its political operations are disguised behind administrative, scientific, or moral narratives and are often implemented behind a civilian façade by intermediary organizations, brokerage institutions, or secret agencies. Robert Nisbet (1975) quite accurately noted, "What has in fact happened during the past half century is that the bulk of power in our society, as it affects our intellectual, economic, social and cultural existences, has become largely *invisible*" (italics original) (178). To understand state rebuilding, it is crucial to understand this often-nuanced alternation between state visibility and invisibility.

By nature, the state has an abstract side, and it has been deemed by some as a subjective, conceptual, and cognitive construct: "an abstraction in relation to the concrete-ness of the social" (Nisbet, 96). Yet despite its occasional invisibility, the state remains an essential and discernible entity. The essentiality of the state is embedded in the lived experience of the political everyday. As Timothy Mitchell (1991) wrote,

> A construct like the state occurs not merely as a subjective belief, incorporated in the thinking and action of individuals. It is represented and reproduced in visible, everyday forms, such as the language of legal practice, the architecture of public buildings, the wearing of military uniforms, or the marking out and policing of frontiers. (81)

The state's visibility is effectuated by (a) the institutional operation of the state bureaucracy, (b) the public exercise of state violence, (c) state ceremonies, celebrations, rituals, and other spectacles, (d) symbolism embedded in state-invented cultural codes, and (e) the state's official narrative maintained through propaganda, historiography, and education. Compared to primitive and traditional states, modernity increases the visibility, mobility, and intrusiveness of state power in the everyday life experiences of the citizenry, and the state's visibility and invisibility have a dialectic relationship.

The state chooses to be invisible for a variety of reasons. Antonio Gramsci (1971) argued that hegemony and dominance by the ruling class can be effectuated through the intelligentsia, who serve as the dominant groups' "deputies" and exercise the "subaltern functions of social hegemony and political government." Gramsci emphasized that the intelligentsia do not serve the dominant social group directly; instead, their actions must be "'mediated' by the whole fabric of society and by the complex of superstructure" (1971, 12). In the Gramscian sense, the pervasiveness of such efforts to effect hegemony make the domination of the state both invisible and indirect.

Empirically, studies of the federal and state governments of the United States have provided enlightening reasons for state invisibility. The contradictions between an antistate American political culture and the development of a strong national identity and a strong government make symbiosis and interdependent relationships between the state and civil society organizations the best solution to advance the American welfare state (Clemens 2017). Culturally, "Americans preferred that the national government enable rather than command" (Balogh 2009, 3). Responding to that particular cultural trait, the American state has intentionally shaped people's perceptions of what are state actions and what are not: "their underlying structure remains constant, but subjective perceptions of them vary over time" (Mayrl and Quinn 2017, 62).

Scholars have also critiqued the invisibility of the American welfare state, the "submerged state," worrying that it may undermine the democratic values and practice of the public and worsen the unpredictability, vagueness, and clumsiness of public policy (Mettler 2011). Christopher Howard (1997) used the metaphor of a coral reef to describe the advantages and potential risks embedded in the invisible welfare state:

> The coral reef lies beneath the surface, hard to see unless one knows exactly where to look. Each reef plays host to a fascinating combination of flora and fauna. . . . More importantly, coral reefs grow at varying rates and in unforeseen directions depending on water temperature, clarity, and salinity, as well as hurricanes and disease. (1997, 188)

The state is by nature both visible and invisible. Scholars have provided theoretical insights by ascribing one or the other of these characterizations to particular nation-states, but they have rarely been considered together in reference to one country. In this book, by exploring the post-Tiananmen Chinese state's efforts to rebuild order and control in the university—a critical social space for institutionalized political order—I argue that visibility and invisibility are strategic choices the state made in the process of effectuating and maintaining institutionalized political order. Such decisions are largely contingent on the field in which the state seeks to operate. In the field of signification, the state operates more openly to project symbolism, propagate state narratives, and solicit ideological conformity. In the field of contestation, the state makes a calculated choice between visibility and invisibility based on the circumstances of its competition for domination with other power centers. When the state has a clear edge, it tends to be visible; if not, or if it perceives itself to have a disadvantageous position, it tends to be invisible in its operation. In the field of regulation, the state is more likely to operate covertly.

The Reinvented State

The process of building the new political order that the post-Tiananmen Chinese state has sought to reinvent also showcases an intraregime, incremental change process I call "state reinvention," which is manifested through a paradigm shift in how the state maintains order and asserts social control. Study of political regimes to date has focused on either the backsliding of democracy or transitions across regime types (such as democratization); much less attention has been devoted to the paradigmatic change within a regime, because there have not been many such cases. Yet intraregime mutation is not a new discovery. In his 1968 treatise on political development, Samuel P. Huntington describes the process of institutional decay caused by a mismatch between the level of institutionalized political participation and the demand for such participation from newly emerged social actors who press to have their voices heard. In his studies of the Third Wave democracies, Huntington (1991) studied the phenomenon of a "reverse wave" of democratization: the rapid deterioration of both the stability and quality of rule in nascent democratic regimes. Francis Fukuyama (2014) discussed "political decay" in the sense that state institutions cannot adapt themselves to changing circumstances and demands, such that competent state agencies start to malfunction. The democratic back-sliding literature tasks itself with scrutinizing how democracies break down and extending the research into exploring the compromised institutional health of democratic systems, unsubstantiated democratic rights and liberties, or a generic "deterioration of qualities associated with democratic governance" (Waldner and Lust 2018, 95).

"Conceptualising intraregime changes is no easy task" (Waldner and Lust 2018, 95). The state reconstruction project taking place in post-Tiananmen China provided a valuable opportunity to discern the Chinese state's paradigmatic change in terms of asserting control over the social realm. From 1949 and the communist victory in China, to 1976 and the end of the Cultural Revolution, the Maoist paradigm of control based on mass mobilization had prevailed in China. After the 1989 Tiananmen Movement, the Chinese state started to build up a substantially different paradigm of control. The Maoist control paradigm differed from the post-Tiananmen paradigm in terms of institutional structure, operational strategy, methods of control, reserves of resources, and the respective effects of these factors on the subjects of control. This paradigmatic change of control signifies the process of state reinvention. Interestingly, David Stavasage (2020) argued in his treatise on the decline and rise of democracy that "in the end, rather than seeing China as a deviation from a standard route for political development set by Europeans, it is instead simply an alternative route for governance and a very stable one" (26).

After its national military victory in 1949, the Communist Party swiftly demolished the old state machinery and established a new socialist order of control across China. This new order was firmly rooted in an ongoing ideological mobilization of the masses. Under such a political order, control comes from mobilization: when members of society are activated to devote themselves to the revolutionary cause and join the ranks of practicing revolutionaries, they integrate the individual into the collectivity of the revolutionary state. The task of state control is completed automatically through this integration. This paradigm of control saw its pinnacle in practice during the heyday of the Cultural Revolution from 1966 to 1976, but its primitive form was nurtured much earlier than that, ostensibly with the Yan'an Rectification Movement of the early 1940s (Selden 1971).

The Maoist paradigm of control seeks devotion based on the integration of and congruence between the collective and the individual, rather than compliance and quiescence through imposed regulation and immersive discipline. It sees members of society as a "mass" that can be educated, indoctrinated, and subsequently integrated into the Party-state's political and ideological agenda. For such an effort of mobilizational control, mass alienation is not a premise but rather something that the control mechanism strives to prevent. In a way, the Maoist control paradigm relies on large-scale societal participation, popularly based subjectivity, and a dynamism radiating from societal activism instead of the one-way projection of state power. To the contrary, the power of the social, unleashed by the state, takes the lead in the operation of the Maoist control model.

The abrupt elite reshuffling after Mao's death in 1976 precipitated not only a change of leadership but a paradigm shift in its model of governance. The demise of the ancien régime came about from its chronic dysfunction, starting with the Cultural Revolution, which was an organizational manifestation of Mao Zedong's distrust of the entire Party-state bureaucracy and his belief that the revolutionary "old guards" had reduced themselves, postvictory, to nothing more than a corrupted new class of elites endlessly pursuing privileges and perks. From the Maoist perspective, the task of destroying a corrupted Party-state apparatus in the making is achieved by launching a vehement attack based on mass mobilization toward the state machine.

The new post-Tiananmen order, however, relies on state force ahead of societal activation. In the dichotomy of state versus society, orthodox Marxist theorists emphasize the revolutionary potential of the latter against the former. For Marxists, the instrumentality of the state in the progress of history can only be materialized through the mobilization of the power of the most revolutionary class. The Maoist order of control follows this rationale; even the judicial, coercive, or categorizing powers that conventionally belong to the state are effectuated through societal channels. As this book demonstrates, the Tiananmen Movement of 1989 becomes a watershed for the old order. Under the post-Tiananmen order of control, the responsibility for maintaining political stability, effectuating control, removing threats, punishing defiance, and deterring potential rebels is shifted from armies of societal mobilizers toward a more bureaucratic state apparatus. Hence, the new order appears to be more stationary than dynamic.

The new order of control is no longer predominantly "thematic," pedagogical, and agitated; rather, it is quotidian and everyday—mingling in the daily activities undertaken by the critical social groups and in the critical social spaces. The primary target of control is the structure and rhythm of the everyday, where "political power . . . embeds itself, and becomes absorbed into the social edifice, which it supports and by which it is in turn supported" (Poggi 1990, 18). Periodic campaigns with a designated theme are still carried out, but only for very specific policy purposes and with much more limited societal impact.[6] Conformism under the new order of control comes from the routine and formalized operations of the state, with the aid of modern technologies and scientific knowledge at the disposal of state rulers. Meanwhile, the power of control is exercised through a rigid institutional architecture rather than through an energetic, passionate, radical, and at times disordered mass movement. It is interventionist in terms of the state's heavy involvement through brokerage institutions, agents, and norms into the basic fabric of social life. The new order of control is preemptive rather than instructive, with a focus on negating potential delinquency or defiance rather than usurping moral or virtuous behavior. The new control mechanism aims to prevent antiregime thoughts and behavior rather than constructing role models for others to follow; it is about deterrence rather than imitation.

The postcrisis state rebuilding in post-Tiananmen China is a process of regime self-reform. With the completion of the state-rebuilding project, the Chinese state in the post-Tiananmen era represents an overbearing type of governance that goes beyond the "transitology" terminology of the 1990s. In this book, I argue that this unique form of state is not some fleeting and "in-between" form of governance but rather represents a peculiar model of manifested state power, from which rulers of many of the world's developing countries have started to learn. I call this new form of state the "reinvented state." At the core of the reinvented state is an institutional order of control that is routinized, silent, quotidian, and seemingly casual, yet carefully designed and implemented.

The order that the reinvented state seeks to establish derives from the structuring of people's everyday lives. In this process of effectuating and sustaining control, the state has two methods of operation. At times, the state is loud and highly visible, vigorously declaring its presence, injecting its ideas and performing its spectacles to targeted social groups and rallying its loyalists in the open. On other occasions, the state elects to remain out of sight and submerged in the everyday taking-care of the routines of life; it then operates silently and is often disguised by a normalized, bureaucratic, scientific, or mundane facade, strategically downplaying the political side of the undertaking in question.

The state may also engage in a mixed mode of operation, in which its activities are hidden behind a nonpolitical mask but its essential presence and authority loom large in the background throughout the process, recognizable and detectable at least by the subjects concerned. The coded message "you know it" (*ni dong de*), used by Chinese netizens to indicate the state's omnipresence in and surveillance of virtual spaces, represents a response to such an intentional obscuring of state operations. The combination of visible and invisible modes of operation forms an important element of the state's project to reinvent order. As this book argues, these intriguing undertakings constitute a concrete state-directed social engineering process through which subjects are proactively integrated into the rules, norms, mores, and structural regimentation of the reigning regime—indeed, the "regulation of the body politic" (Turner 2008, 142).

Statist Order and the University

"Universities, like cathedrals and parliaments, are a product of the Middle Ages" (Haskins 1923, 1).[7] Originating from a society of masters and scholars and as the "lineal descendant of medieval Paris and Bologna," the university has never been free of the influence of state politics. In fact, as an institution, the university has managed to flourish under the persistent shadow of the state. Shaped by remarkable continuity and longevity, unlike those of most human institutions (an exception being the Universal Church), the university has an inseparable bond with national politics and has always been a politically charged battlefield central to the state's efforts to establish order. Interpretations of the political nature of the modern university are also full of controversies and contradictions.[8]

The university "held a central place in the formation of subjects for the nation-state, along with the production of the ideology that handled the issue of their belonging to that nation-state (culture)," and it becomes modern only when "it takes on responsibility for working out the relation between the subject and the state" (Readings 1996, 53, 167). Modern states are conscious of the political weight of the university. University students on campus are a principal target group of the modern state's efforts to build and maintain control over the society. Regardless of regime type, the university is the training school for every nation's professional class, military officer corps, and other elites-in-waiting. For the state, however, the university's functionality presents a contradiction: the university is an arena in which occur the production and reproduction of official symbolism, codification, discourse, and narrative, which constitute the legitimating foundation of modern autocracies; yet the university is also the generator of the most advanced scientific knowledge, technological know-how, and ideas for innovation, which drive socioeconomic development. As Sergei Guriev and Daniel Treisman (2022) argued, while the postindustrial economy relies on the imaginative power of an educated labor force, "the problem . . . is that higher education is intrinsically linked to freedom of thought" (174).

Striking a right balance between the two sides constitutes a formidable challenge to the state's maintenance of regime stability. Schools of higher learning produce a class of "state nobility" who possess symbolic power, are affiliated with the state's secular authority, and uphold the state's principal supporting pillars (Bourdieu 1996). This resembles John Connelly's (2000) observation in his study of the sovietization of East European universities: "universities were key to making the states in which these people lived socialist because they produced not only national histories and ideologies, but also elites, or, in the words of East German ideological chief Kurt Hager, 'commander[s]'" (3).

The university is also an "arena of action" in which "the rules of academic life and the rules of the new (state) power coexisted" (Jesse 2005, 248). The intellectual, social, and communal spaces demarcated by campus walls comprise a unique, relatively independent, yet neatly networked field. The multivocality of the university as a social space is best described by James I. McDougall, who works in southwest China as both a teacher and university administrator: "[T]he space occupied [by] higher education represents a multiplicity of social purposes" (2020, 1014). At the end of the day, the university is a meeting place of all kinds of social networks, and all kinds of existential social inequality, dominant hegemony, social miseries, class suppression, political corruption, and state coercion are mirrored in the students' everyday experiences. The university holds the "promise of being a microcosm of the nation-state" (Readings 1996, 167). The critical political importance of the university lies in the fact that it is culturally shaped and socially embedded.

For the state, the university is a politically precarious field, posing a constant threat to the entire establishment. The university provides a critical space in which alternative ideologies, narratives, discourses, imaginaries, and action plans may be proposed and discussed in partial freedom from state control and influence. This implies the possibility of a public sphere operating in parallel with the state-endorsed associational space. As an arena imbued with the force of inquiry, the "clear and unmistakable" historical continuity of the university has created a unique space for it to allow, accommodate, or even facilitate political activities that are out of the state's immediate reach (Haskins 1923, 24).[9] With its unique nature, under different circumstances, the university has the potential to nurture centers of authority that compete with state power, including academic authority, fraternity authority, hierarchical authority in student societies, corporate authority (when students engage in career development activities), parental and family authority, and prevailing social norms. To dominate the political everyday on campus, the state engages in a never-ending competition with such rival suppliers of authority and strives to maintain its own advantage. In the university, as in all such critical social spaces, the state contests, competes with, and even fights against alternative rules, norms, habits, and informal institutions to create and maintain its domination, control, and order.

Most modern universities in China are creations of the state. Nonetheless, as institutions of higher learning and a foundational component of the state's cultural project, they continue to be a major base for revolutionary mobilization. In modern China, universities are base camps for China's urban revolutionary movements; their revolutionary heritage, identity, and potentiality render university campuses some of the most critical social spaces for the order-seeking Chinese state (Wasserstrom 1991; Schwarcz 1986; Mitter 2004; Perry 1994; Calhoun 1994). For the modern Chinese state, high tension persists between the university, with its threatening revolutionary potential, and the state's efforts to create and maintain an institutionalized political order that operates on rational bureaucratic terms. However, this does not mean that the state-university relationship has always been antagonistic. Also, universities are occasionally used when the ruling regime seeks to deploy social forces to attain specific policy goals.[10]

Three features of Chinese universities—some of which are also applicable to universities in general—explain their centrality in the political processes of making and remaking an institutionalized political order. First, the alien cultural identity and value principles of the modern Chinese university make it a foreign force in the institutional arrangements advocated by the Chinese state. "To most underdeveloped countries, the university was a foreign institution with few or no indigenous cultural roots" (Zhao 2001, 96). The culturally alienated nature of the university renders it a representation of a kind of cultural "otherness," a rebellious enlightening device and an exogenous shock to the cultural "integrity" so ardently protected by the Chinese nation-state.

Second, the unique temporal-spatial structure of everyday experiences within campus walls makes the university organizationally a likely source of social upheaval. Prominent studies have found that the "ecology" of the university is conducive to social mobilization (Zhao 2001, 239–66). Scholars exploring the genesis of the 1989 Tiananmen Movement have agreed that various features of university life in China, including the network of solidarity of classmates and friends; the public space formed in dorm life;

the strong interpersonal links across institutions; the structured collective lifestyle; the instruction on alternative ideologies, discourses, and narratives in the university public spaces; and the active associational life in student societies and organizations, jointly created a unique urban space offering favorable conditions for the mobilization of a cross-cleavage student movement on a national scale.[11] The unique organizational structure of the everyday life of university students creates "'free spaces' outside immediate state control" and "a wealth of organizational resources" at the level of face-to-face relations, in addition to personal networks that were later available for anti-regime collective action (Calhoun 1994).

Third, the modern Chinese university is a hazardous and highly unstable political field filled with intrinsic contradictions and misbalances. The contradiction between a class-levelling ideal and a bureaucratically controlled hierarchical reality was manifested in the turbulent political history of the university (Andreas 2006, 2009). The fierce competition between holders of cultural capital and of political capital made this elite Chinese university a hotbed of political warfare and human suffering, where animosity and strife "transcended . . . old inter-elite conflicts and reflected the extent to which political and cultural capital had coalesced" (Andreas 2009, 130). The precariousness of China's universities also comes from the uneasy contradiction between what Susan Shirk (1982) termed a "virtuocracy" that is still rampant in Chinese institutions of education[12] and the gradual yet significant turn toward operations that run on more realistic, materialist, and professionalized terms, as depicted in Jérôme Doyon's (2023) latest study of student cadres in the Communist Youth League of Chinese universities.

Going from bad to worse, at the micro level, the internal dilemma of China's top university students presented them with a constant politically, morally, and emotionally difficult choice between their desire to separate from their parents (and metaphorically, by extension, from the state) and their moral obligation to make sacrifices to repay that parental care (Bregnbæk 2019).[13] As a recent the *New Yorker* article describes, the "shared reality [with the outside society makes] . . . many students at [Chinese elite institutions] feel . . . anxious, stressed, overworked, trapped in a status race," highlighting the coming-of-age of China's "involuted" generation (Liu 2021).[14] These embedded contradictions, tensions, and uncertainties have created in many students—the primary inhabitants of the Chinese university campuses—a constant state of doubt and fragility, as they struggle to find the best way to deal with a patriarchal state and with their own moral obligations (Havránek 2005).

Conclusion

Today, compromised states are prevalent in global politics, especially in the vast developing world. In contrast with a failed state, a compromised state still has largely intact state machinery and the capability to maintain basic law and order; however, a compromised state suffers from a weakened legitimation footing, a lack of instruments to regulate citizens' behavior, and a compromised position in its competition for domination with other centers of authority in the nation's public life. States can often be compromised in the aftermath of a traumatic national political crisis that entails entrenched, confrontational, emotional, and ideologically charged animosity between the state and society. If such issues are not addressed, a compromised state has a high likelihood of becoming a failed state, which would pose a grave threat to both domestic welfare and international peace. As Francis Fukuyama argued, "state weakness is both a national and international issue of the first order" (2004, xi).

A compromised state has to manage its own salvation, reinventing a state within and from itself. In a compromised state's efforts to rebuild political order and reassert control over the society, one of its priorities is to reestablish control over the critical social groups and critical social spaces. Critical social groups and critical social spaces meet in the political everyday. It is the state's capacity and efforts to shape the temporal-spatial structure of the political everyday that cement the foundation for an institutionalized political order to be established and maintained. Turning scholarly attention from the "high" politics of autocracies to the down-to-earth operations and the operational logic behind maneuvers on the ground helps enrich our understanding of state building, regime maintenance, and people's lived experiences under the power of the state. If the state is to live, it must live in the political everyday.

The Tiananmen Movement of 1989 was a national crisis that was ended only by a year of militant confrontation between society and the state, which significantly weakened the latter's ability to uphold order. The university, a traditional field of politically charged state influence, has become a crucial social space for the Chinese state's efforts to reestablish institutionalized political order. As discussed in this chapter and in the following pages, the best way to understand the process by which the state overhauls its control over a critical social space is to examine the rhythm of the "political everyday"—that is, to determine how the state can effectively regain its strength, signify its legitimation narratives, reclaim an advantageous position in the competition with rival suppliers of authority in public life, and reinvent an incentive infrastructure that rewards conformity and punishes defiance. In this process, the infrastructures for statism with institutional, significative, regulatory, and incentivization parameters are reconstructed. This exploration also includes the ways in which the state overhauls its crisis monitoring and processing system, which ensures that the state will not easily succumb to domestic or foreign shocks. The state alternates between visibility and invisibility along the way. The university provides an unusually valuable glimpse into this process.

TWO

Concentric Circles

The Institutional Infrastructure

School is the state school where young people are turned into state persons and thus into nothing other than henchmen of the state. Walking to school, I was walking into the state.

   —Thomas Bernhard, *The Old Masters*, 1989, 27

The more static, standardized, and uniform a population or social space is, the more legible it is, and the more amenable it is to the techniques of state officials.

   —James C. Scott, "Seeing Like a State," 1998, 82

Mobilization, Dependency and Classification

After its military victory in 1949, one of the pressing priorities for the Chinese Communist Party, which had been based in China's vast rural areas since the late 1920s, was to take over the country's urban superstructure. Given the importance of the higher-education sector in modern China's revolutionary history, universities were central to the "urban revolution" through which the CCP aimed to build an entirely new political order. After the closure of missionary universities across China and a major state-directed merger of institutions of higher learning,[1] the Maoist Party-state turned its attention to designing and imposing a novel system of internal control on China's now reorganized university campuses and the vast student population.

51

During the state-building process, successive mass campaigns, in the form of either "thought reform" or "youth movement," became the most important tool for the communists to solidify the revolution into an embryonic regime. In the Maoist state, the effectuation and maintenance of political control over university students involved three pillars. The three arms of state power—mobilizational power, dependency power, and categorizing power—secured the Maoist variant of state order. The first was the ideological-political congruence between students and the state continuously forged and consolidated through mass movements. Mass movements in Maoist universities served various political purposes for the nascent state—providing a utopian imaginary for the future, a participatory channel into national politics, a dynamic platform for ideological indoctrination by practices, and a venue for pledging loyalty to the Great Helmsman himself.

The second pillar was the strong dependency of university students on the state and the cadre-dom. The Maoist regime is a centralized command structure, in which the state monopolized most of the economic, political, social, and symbolic resources that in other systems would have been routinely shared by the state and society. In particular, under the prevailing "work unit" system (*danwei*), students were considered part of the nomenclatura of their respective universities. The communist neotraditionalist dependency relationship—à la Andrew G. Walder—was prevalent on the Maoist university campuses, too (Walder 1984). The students relied on regime-approved representatives of the revolutionary line—first the Communist Party organizations, then the rebellious factions, and eventually the revolutionary committees—to compete for educational, political, and career opportunities, and also to acquire the numerous administrative permits needed for their everyday activities and life events. This systemic control over the life experiences of young university students made compliance a rational option.

The third pillar was an unusually strong categorizing power of a dominant Party-state, which assigned significantly different rights, entitlements, and obligations to different categories of the populace, including university students. "Modern states routinely classify the populations they seek to govern" (Loveman and Colors 2014, 3). Categorical identification is the foundation of the legal-rational power of the Weberian state. However, whereas democratic states usually classify the population according to naturally defined attributes (such as gender, race, and age), the Chinese state under Mao exercised its categorizing power mostly along political lines. University students were categorized by their family background and political performance. Those who were categorized as "red" and "revolutionary" received significantly better treatment in terms of educational resources, job opportunities, financial assistance, and other advantages. Students lived under the shadow of the Party-state's categorizing power and the everlasting fear of being assigned to an unfavorable category.

The end of the Tiananmen Movement of 1989 and the ensuing political alienation and apathy that became pervasive throughout the 1990s significantly compromised the Chinese state's capacity to mobilize societal resources. On university campuses, the new forces of marketization, globalization, and opening up to the West did not facilitate state control. The three pillars of Maoist control failed to survive the nationwide engagement with a globalized market economy. In particular, marketization and the flourishing of the private sector effectively ended the Party-state's monopoly over upward mobility, significantly undermining its control over the career paths of the younger generation. With market forces at work, the neotraditionalist dependency structure between the state and students was crumbling, too. Under these unprecedented and yet mostly self-made circumstances, the Party-state was circumvented; the traditional pillars of its control of educated youth were swept away by the force of global capitalism. An alienated student population, and politically "defenseless" university campuses (in the eyes of the communist apparatchiks), threatened to make universities the weakest link in the state edifice. To reinvent a state order in the Chinese university, the first task for the Communist Party, obviously, was to rebuild for itself an all-powerful institutional infrastructure of control on campus.

Reinventing the Machinery of Control

The Centralization of Student Control

As Pierre Bourdieu argued, to understand the state as a "field of power," it is important to first grasp the "division of organizational functions associated with the different respective bodies" (2020, 20). The institutional fabric of the state assigns functionalities to state agents, facilitates cross-cleavage coordination, and sets the stage for the everyday activities involved in order building. The institutional contours of the state do not only prescribe its functionalities and thus determine its capacity; more importantly, the institutional design of the state at a given time reflects the foundation, purpose, and essential nature of the political order that the state seeks to establish.

The institutional skeleton gives form and structure to the otherwise form-less everyday lives that take place within a critical social space.

The post-Mao communist leadership struggled to demobilize the student population and restore a functional and institutionalized bureaucracy of control. The ending of the 1989 Tiananmen Movement pushed the state to accelerate this process. As a result, a triple-layered structure of control was imposed on university campuses, which included the Communist Party System, the Communist Youth League System, and the Student Work System (*xuegong xitong*).[2] Unlike the more decentralized system of academic authority that exists in parallel on campus, this triple-layered system of control is highly centralized and is accountable only to the Party secretary of the university. Moreover, this structure extends beyond the university walls and serves as part of the larger control framework headed by the Party's central or provincial "Committee on Higher Education Work" (*gaojiao gongwei*). Figure 3 demonstrates the organizational structure of the student control system in a typical Chinese university.

The most salient feature of the post-Tiananmen student-control system is its emphasis on the state's reach into every corner of student communities and its design that allows the Party-state to structure banal quotidian details of the students' lived experience on the campus. For example, political counselors,[3] as lower-level but essential components of the student control apparatus, have an around-the-clock presence in the everyday lives of university students. More precisely, as one Chinese researcher noted, "Political Counsellors should have a real-time knowledge of the conditions of student thoughts . . . and provide education and guidance in a timely manner. They should try their best to solve any antagonism and clear potential factors of instability" (Xu 2007, 239). In some universities, political counselors are required to maintain regular residence in student dormitories, keeping non-stop watch over the daily activities of university students.[4]

What the post-Tiananmen student-control system seeks is a state-directed, normalized, and routinized reorganization of the student population. With the introduction of a Western-style academic credit system in the 1990s, the separation of political authority and academic authority, the debut of an academic degree system, and other changes, university students became more free-floating in the campus public space and were able to gradually distance themselves from the direct influence of political power. The post-Tiananmen era witnessed a return of the Maoist method of organizing the student population into small units. University students were again organized into a quasimilitary structure extending all the way from basic-level classrooms (*banji*) to the year-cohort (*nianji*). Several units at the lower level constitute one unit at the higher level, with the entire

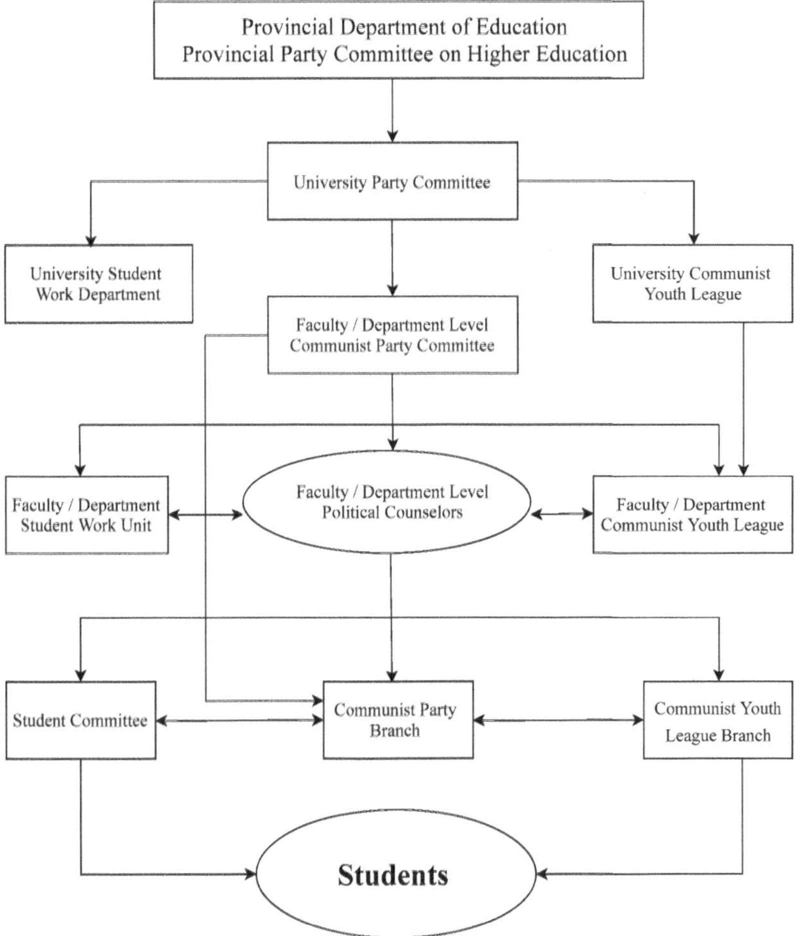

Figure 3. Organizational structure of the student-management system at a provincial university in central China (Wuhan, China).

organizational architecture tied together by the Communist Party's supervision and leadership.

A Grid-like Web Structure

The return to a quasimilitary organization of the student populace probably defines the post-Tiananmen Chinese university.[5] Unlike their Western counterparts, who form groups from sororities and fraternities to sports teams based largely on their own choice, Chinese students are assigned

Figure 4. New students attending a class (Wuhan, China).

by university authorities to rigid, immovable, hierarchical administrative units—"grids"—from day one. The lowest organizational layer, *banji* (class)—the basic level of such units—contains from 20 to over 100 students, who are normally in same-year cohorts in one specific major of study. *Nianji* (year cohort) is the higher level of organizational unit, comprising students from the same faculty or school who enter the university in the same year. Higher than the "year cohort" (*nianji*) is the collective unit that contains all the undergraduate students of different year cohorts who belong to the same faculty, college, or school (*yuan/xi*, or "school cohort") within the university.[6] At both the "class" and faculty (college or school) cohort level, the Communist Party Branch, the Communist Youth League Branch, and Student Administrative Committees (student unions) are in place. These neatly demarcated organizational structures frame students' lives on campus and shape the dimensions of their sociality.

Martin King Whyte (1974) has discerned several strategies featuring primary ties that control-oriented state elites may adopt to deal with social groups. The elites may ignore those ties, appeal directly to the individuals, "draw individuals away from their primary groups," or "break up and disperse existing groups," such that a new order might be established. Yet for Whyte, the final and most ambitious strategic choice is to "create new primary groups in which to encapsulate individuals, thereby gaining control over group norms and using them to reinforce higher demands" (10). In the post-Tiananmen era, the rationale behind the Chinese state's decision to install a grid-like web structure has several dimensions. First, this arrangement of people and space—which denotes the grouping of socially homogeneous subjects or the demarcation of socially homogeneous spaces into small, parallel, yet interlocking units—facilitates the state's reach into each small human or social unit, streamlining the reproduction of a consistent pattern of control and operation over identical groups of subjects or demarcated social spaces. This significantly reduces and simplifies the state's workload in keeping critical social groups and spaces in order, compared with managing a "flat" society that includes many diffusive, interactive, and multicultural elements.

Second, the grid structure increases the legibility of each demarcated unit of the social space and its inhabitants, facilitating the state's surveillance at both the holistic and the everyday levels. Moreover, the institutional, spatial, or temporal boundary between grids puts up barriers to cross-sector or cross-institutional information flow and knowledge formation, leaving the entire space and group under stable monitoring and control conducted exclusively by the state.

Third, the institutional structure in each grid is made in the image of the state—the identical institutional structure of each unit makes the everyday operation of the entire system a natural reproduction of the overall institutional culture. The accumulative effect of this repeated institutional practice, which mirrors the overall political operation of the regime, helps to consolidate the political order in its quotidian exercises. For example, in the grid-like web structure of the Chinese university, each parallel grid, or *banji*, features a dual structure of governance comprising a prerogative Party organ along with a normative administrative organ, the Student Committee. This structure resembles the dual-state structure of the Chinese communist regime; its operational principles, assignment of work flow, and everyday practices also resemble those of the Party-state.

Figure 5. First-year students in compulsory military training (Wuhan, China). *Note*: Each class cohort (*banji*)—the basic organizational unit of students— sits together in a "grid" formation.

The repeated institutional practice within each gridded unit habitualizes the regime's political concept, political principle, and institutional practice in the world of university students. A sense of conformism can be gradually forged through students' participation in the collective life of their own community and from as early as the very first day of their university life.

The Miniature State in the Everyday

Under this grid-like web structure, most Chinese students consider their "class cohort" (*banji*) to be a home base throughout their entire university life. They tend to study and socialize with peers in the same class cohort, to which they are assigned on enrollment. Campus accommodation is usually arranged based on this organizational structure, which thus shapes the main domain of students' everyday activities. Students from the same "class cohort" live together in the dormitories designated for their college or school. Students from the same "year cohort" often occupy the same block in a dormitory building. One senior university official explained:

This kind of arrangement is put into place in order to facilitate the university's monitoring of student activities and their everyday lives; but the most important reason is that it prevents students who belong to different faculties or departments from "mingling and interacting" (*chuanlian*, literally, liaison and connection) with each other. We have to remember that [a] cross-faculty solidarity network among the students [was] a crucial instrument of mobilisation in the (1989) Tiananmen Movement and the Party has striven to prevent that same situation from "taking place ever again."[7]

The rigid accommodation arrangements further strengthen the arbitrarily "grid-like" web structure that organizes China's vast university-student populace.

The resemblance between the micro institutional structure of control within each basic unit of students and the larger political system of the state is considered essential. In each class cohort (*banji*), the Student Communist Party Branch is the main source of leadership. Similar to the country's Communist Party apparatus, the Student Party Branch serves as the invisible prerogative authority that deliberates and makes decisions only in exclusive internal meetings; however, the decisions it makes are the most consequential ones. For instance, the Student Communist Party Branch is responsible for vetting the "political performance" (*zhengzhi biaoxian*) of each student every year—an important form of political categorizing mandated by the Party-state. It also determines the principles for selecting the recipients of scholarships and awards, the granting of Communist Party membership to noncommunist students, and the distribution of other benefits. Also, the Student Party Branch operates as a formal monitoring agency in parallel with the "political counselor"—the communist cadre-teacher—assigned to the unit; both institutions report directly to the higher-level Communist Party Committee, and neither is accountable to the other. Thus there are implicit checks and balances between the political counselors and the Student Communist Party Branches, preventing either from deviating from their responsibilities.

The composition and operation of the Student Party Branch resemble those of the larger Party-state apparatus outside the campus as well. The Branch, whose membership comprises all of the student Communist Party members in the unit, is led by a committee of a party secretary and two commissars, one in charge of propaganda and the other of organization. All of the cadre students are either elected at a general meeting of all student

Party members or appointed by the supervisory Party Committee. The Student Party secretary oversees the operations of the Party Branch and is usually considered the most senior-ranked student cadre of the entire unit.

The commissar in charge of propaganda is responsible for assisting in ideological education; the commissar in charge of organization oversees the admission of new Party members and the training of student activists, and initiates disciplinary action against any student Party member for political offences. The commissar in charge of organization also accepts "reflective journals" or "reports of thoughts" (*sixiang huibao*) on behalf of the Communist Party from noncommunist students, who want to establish good political records that may lead to the Student Party Branch's favorable consideration in major personnel or welfare decisions, or when it considers admitting new Communist Party members. These journal reports vary in content and length; their core function is to examine and confess one's current political thoughts and activities—in particular those that are politically problematic or sensitive for the Communist Party. These reports also serve occasionally as an information source about irregular events, discussions, or debates taking place in the student community. "Reports of thoughts" are kept, read, and recorded by the leaders of the Student Party Branches—and whenever they deem it necessary, individual reports may be transmitted to higher-level Communist Party committees for further perusal.

Just as in the larger state system of China, in each "class cohort," the Student Party Branch is assisted by a Communist Youth League (CYL) Branch, which includes almost all of the noncommunist students in the unit;[8] in the rare cases of students who are not CYL members after entering college, the CYL admits them immediately after the *banji* is formed. The CYL—as a major institutional component in the Party-state machinery to organize and educate youth—is much more visible in the students' everyday life. It organizes leisure activities and group events, from student chorus to hikes. The top position of the secretary of the CYL is always filled by a student Communist Party member.

In addition to the prerogative authority exercised by the Student Party Branch, there is also a normative authority in each "grid"—the Student Administrative Committee (*banwei hui*, SAC). The SAC is a nominal self-governing entity. Its responsibilities are often mundane and sometimes trivial, including managing any collective funding for class events, or maintaining the hygiene of student dorms. As in the larger Party-state structure, the SAC does not have substantial decision-making power; in most scenarios, it just implements or formally announces any decision made by the Student Party Branch. For instances, the annual competition for scholarships and student awards is nominally operated by the SAC, yet in reality, the vetting and selecting process is performed by the Student Party Branch behind closed doors.

In most places, the Student Administrative Committee is led by a "class head" (*banzhang*), with members in charge of sports, welfare, mental health, women's rights, and academic studies. In some universities, the membership of the SAC overlaps with that of the Communist Youth League, but it rarely overlaps with membership of the Student Communist Party Branch. Describing the administrative duties of the SAC as follows, one political counselor commented,

> The Student Administrative Committee is the body that governs the student community of the "class cohort." . . . It is like the "government" of the student community—you see in Beijing, the Party Center makes decisions while the State Council implements those decisions and runs the national economy. The logic is same here.[9]

Tension between different institutional bodies may also arise on campus, as in the larger Party-state apparatus. For example, within a "class cohort," the relationship between the Communist Youth League and the Student Administrative Committee can be contentious, given their overlapping responsibilities. One student said, "the power status and relative weight of them entirely depends on the personal influence of the student leaders. If the Class Head is aggressive and active, the Communist Youth League Secretary can be relatively weak in power; and vice versa." However, under the ultimate leadership of the Student Communist Party Branch, this kind of institutional competition can be managed. As the same student said, "if their conflict is very serious, they will resort to the Student Party Secretary to mediate or make the final decision. Ultimately, we all know it is the Party that calls the shots!"[10]

Compared to the Student Communist Party Branch, the Student Administrative Committees are more accountable to the student community. One student said, the Student Committee serves the students, while the Student Communist Party Branch acts more as a "bridge" between the student body and the Communist Party organization on campus.[11] In recent years, the Student Administrative Committee (*banji*) has been elected via an open campaign and competitive election organized by the students.[12] This demonstrates a synchronization between the political climate on campus and the national experiment with more direct democratic elections for lower-level People's Congresses. Nevertheless, it is evident from other students' accounts of the process that the Communist Party still has an enormous influence on the "election."[13]

In the everyday life of a university student in post-Tiananmen China, an organizational structure that resembles the larger Party-state apparatus forms the basic institutional foundation of a grid-like web structure that students belong to and must deal with on a daily basis. Within the student community, the Student Communist Party Branch, despite its habitual invisibility, firmly holds on to the core leadership role and makes the most important decisions for the student community. From this resemblance between the micro structure of control in the basic organizational unit of university students and the overall institutional culture of the state, a "social engineering" process silently produces an institutional, cultural, and bureaucratic environment in which the university students are accustomed to, and indeed habitually conform to, the large political system through repetitive and quotidian everyday practices. Through daily engagement with and participation in the miniature power structure of their own community, these immersive experiences integrate students into the norms, mores, and culture of the ruling regime. This silent political integration is a powerful tool the temporarily broken state used after the 1989 crackdown to regain its capacity and reestablish order in one of the most critical social spaces under its rule—the university.

Political Counselor

"The state finds expression in those individuals who act on its behalf," argued James N. Rosenau (1989, 19). Political counselor (*zhengzhi fudao yuan*, or simply *fudao yuan*) is the most basic post in the hierarchy of the student-control apparatus.[14] This position was established in an instruction issued by the Ministry of Education (MoE) on October 28, 1952, shortly after the founding of the PRC, mandating that a political counselor be present in every class in every university in China. The system was abandoned during the Cultural Revolution, as a remnant of the institutionalization efforts of Mao's opposition, but revived in the 1990s when the Party bureaucracy returned to power.

In July 2006, the MoE issued Instruction No. 24, which promulgated a new "Regulation on the Construction of Corps of Political Counsellors in Ordinary Institutions of Higher Education." According to this new document, "Political Counselors . . . should have a dual identity as both a

Figure 6. A political counselor chairing a class meeting (Wuhan, China).

teacher and a Party-state cadre," and such counselors are also "the primary working force for moral and ideological education of university students." "They are also," the document goes on, "the organiser, implementer and supervisor of the daily ideological education and political management of university students" (Ministry of Education 2006). The dual identity of the political counselor manifests clearly the essential nature of the student-control apparatus in the Chinese university—an extended arm of Party-state power.

Although the institutional settings of the post-Tiananmen Chinese university make a silent social engineering process possible, equally important is the corps of personnel who implement the daily task of establishing, effectuating, and consolidating state order on campus. Within this corps of personnel, political counselors, student Communist Party members, and

TABLE 1: Number of full-time and part-time political counselors in China

Year	Full-time Counselor	Part-time Counselor	Total
2005	48,692		
2006	69,198	36,000	105,198
2008	91,818	29,329	121,147
2015	About 130,000		
2016	About 130,000	About 50,000	About 180,000
2020			About 200,000

Sources: Zhou 2021; Yuan 2009; Xinhua News Agency 2021; Xiao 2008; Chen 2015; Chai 2016.

the student cadres form a series of centripetal forces that support the control apparatus on the university campus. Among the three teams of collaborative forces, the position of political counselor represents the key formal and institutional point of liaison between the Party-state machinery and the university student populace of China.[15]

Political counselors are usually appointed from the university's recent graduates by the Organization Department of each university's Communist Party committee. Normally, three criteria are used for selection. First, with very rare exceptions, political counselors must be Communist Party members. As one senior cadre working at a national university put it, "political counselors are supposed to help the Communist Party to manage the student population and their loyalty is essential for doing the job well; you cannot recruit any troublemakers—however talented—into this workforce." Second, the selected candidates must have enough prior experience working as student cadres in college; the argument is that, if they don't, they will be unfamiliar with the nature of the task of student control and the relevant policies and work procedures involved. Former student cadres are also considered to have better skills in dealing with university students and to be more loyal to the Party-state in moments of crisis. Third, the selected candidates for political counselorship have to be both committed and devoted to a career path as a political official for the Communist Party. To keep the Party's workforce stable, they are supposed to remain in their position for quite a long period of time, barring the rare opportunity for early promotion. After political counselors are appointed, they are trained by the university's Communist Party Committee.

The central Party-state has clear regulations and rules for the construction and maintenance of the political counselors work force. The MoE requires a "ratio of political counselors to students (of) 1:200" (Ministry of Education 2006). More specifically, the central government requires that, of the entire team of political counselors on any university campus, 70 percent must be full-time Communist Party cadres on the state payroll, and no more than 30 percent can be part-time cadres appointed from the ranks of former academic staff or senior-year postgraduate students.

The university's Communist Party committee and its subordinate working departments issue periodical internal briefings to political counselors, sharing important state instructions, talking points, and intelligence about potential student unrest. Political counselors are required to monitor students' social media accounts so that they have real-time updates of students' "thought condition" (*sixiang zhuangkuang*) and can immediately detect if anything is about to go wrong. Overall, as a senior university Party official described it,

> Political counselors are at once the "eyes, ears and hands" of the Communist Party; they should know everything taking place in the student communities and understand clearly what should be done in various situations, including efficiently and appropriately dealing with political emergencies in consultation with senior Communist Party representatives.[16]

Political counselors also act as the shepherds of the collective everyday life of university students. From orientation camps for freshmen to the eventual graduation ceremony, political counselors work with students from the beginning through the end of their university lives. They approve, coordinate, and oversee group events and serve as guardians of students' community activities. Political counselors also endorse recommendations for scholarship applications, financial aid requests, and petitions to change majors, and address complaints about dormitory assignment and similar issues. Such trivial matters, which are usually considered procedural niceties in Western universities, are placed in the hands of political counselors in Chinese universities. In a way, a university student's everyday life on campus is inextricably linked to the power of the political counselor assigned by the Communist Party to the student's grid unit.

Meetings are an important instrument for structuring the everyday rhythm of the Chinese university. Regular meetings break up students' spare time, restrict them via spatial confinement, increase group cohesiveness, facilitate the Party-state's ideological education efforts, and foster students' political compliance. It is an important part of the job of a political counselor to hold regular political meetings for students. At one provincial university, for example, political counselors hold weekly meetings for the group of students they supervise. Known by the student as *ban hui* (literally "classroom meetings"), these compulsory gatherings are usually held on Sunday nights, and a roll call is periodically conducted to keep a formal record of attendance. The content of the meetings varies; frequently, however, they are reading and sharing sessions for discussing topics in the official newspapers. Sometimes political counselors use classroom meetings to brief students on the latest state policies; alternatively, such meetings may become sessions in which students report their thoughts and activities in the past week.

On other occasions, classroom meetings are discussion sessions on a book about the Party's revolutionary history assigned by the Central Propaganda Department—an activity termed "reading red books" (*du hongshu*). At times, the political counselor may guide students to discuss the latest controversial social issues along the "correct" line designated by the Party-state. The purpose is to provide proper guidance for the students to understand the "dark" side of Chinese society (i.e., unpleasant political or social occurrences) and prevent more critical opinions on these inadequacies from emerging. Aimed at shaping students' understanding of social reality, this sort of "thought guidance" (as it is described in the official discourse) attempts to nurture a sense of "social awareness and political responsibility" (however state-manipulated) among the student populace, and has become increasingly important for the regime's stability maintenance efforts in light of the mounting social grievances outside the ivory tower. Students who have shown signs of "irregularity" in thought or behavior are usually kept behind by the political counselor for individual conversations.

Given the nature of their daily work, it is all the more important for political counselors to keep a close and friendly relationship with the student communities for which they are responsible. These cadre-teachers are charged with the obligation to show a "humane" face of the power of the state. As one former student recalled,

> For undergraduate students, political counselors were more like an elder brother or sister who took care of their junior siblings. Most of them were kind and friendly—although a few were indeed ill-tempered and harsh. When I was at the university, I could call my political counselor whenever I had a question or needed some advice—the feeling was just like having an elder college friend whom you could always turn to for help. Therefore, although we all knew that political counselors were assigned by the state and they were meant to monitor and discipline us, this tension could hardly be observed in our daily campus life.[17]

Nonetheless, political counselors are also motivated, indeed incentivized, to use coercive means to discipline the student populace whenever needed. Political counselors work under considerable pressure arising from peer competition in terms of the vetting of their work performance. One important component of the job evaluation system for political counselors is a horizontal comparison of key indicators among different student units in terms of the level of political stability, the number of newly admitted Communist Party members, the number of applicants for Party membership, group honors, the students' attendance at official activities, the frequency of political meetings, etc. Given the pressure, political counselors are not only on high alert around the clock for any sign of student unrest—any protests would be a permanent black mark on their performance records—but also keep a close eye on how neighboring units are doing in terms of political education and control, to get an edge in the competition.

In their daily operations, political counselors have various instruments at their disposal to establish their authority among students. Opportunities for graduate studies, quotas for public and private scholarships, and slots in state-sponsored overseas exchange programs are in the hands of political counselors. As one student said,

> If you work with the [political counselors] and demonstrate your loyalty and compliance, you get a lot more opportunities and a "competitive edge" in various aspects of your life. For instance, you may be admitted into graduate school with a waiver (of the extremely competitive national graduate school entrance examinations), get exchange opportunities, obtain scholarships, etc. These resources are all accessible through the political counselors, who are obviously more favourable to those [students] who have a closer relationship with them—but I consider this a normal part of human nature.[18]

Student organizations, hobby clubs, and societies are under the control of political counselors, too. Before such a request for university funding or the use of space or other resources can be submitted to the university organizers must obtain a recommendation from the political counselor.

The Communist Party's institutional heritage from the revolutionary period still plays a significant role in its effort to rebuild order and state control on the post-Tiananmen university campus. For instance, political counselors remain in control of students' personnel dossiers—confidential sets of files that record individuals' life events, political evaluations, and other personal data. These files are only accessible by Communist Party organizations at all levels. The records formally start with a person's entrance into college and accompany that person throughout his or her entire professional life. In the university, political counselors are the principal cadres authorized to compile records and evaluations of each student's political performance, and include them in the students' personnel dossier. When the students graduate and are hired, these dossiers are transferred by special post for classified Party-state documents to the Communist Party organization at their new employer's workplace. The general awareness of the existence of these records makes political counselors quite powerful. In short, in dealing with university students, political counselors shoulder the most important responsibility on behalf of the Party-state. As state agents, political counselors structure the students' everyday experiences in a tender, largely unnoticed, communicative way. However, the threat of political coercion constantly looms in the background, and cannot be ignored.

Student Party Members

For state rulers—always a minority in number—to exercise their authority and exert control over a vast population, more often than not they choose to build a solid "ruling coalition" that comprises the regime's most loyal and trustworthy subjects. This inner circle of political loyalists is encircled by a larger group of politically "friendly" members of the population, who vary in their degree of support and willingness to assist with governance. The popular base that supports these two circles is an even larger collective of "nonantagonistic" members of society at large, who either remain uninterested in state politics or passively comply with the political regime in power. Different layers of this stratified structure have different levels of access to the regime, enjoy different forms of privilege, shoulder different obligations, and incur different corresponding personal costs in the case of systematic collapse. Figure 7 demonstrates the structure of political stratification among the student population of a typical Chinese university, which mirrors the larger political stratification under the Chinese state.

In the Chinese university, a major force supporting the Party's edifice of control is student Communist Party members. As Daniel Koss argued, "regime party can provide the organisation infrastructure that allows a state to project authority throughout the realm" (2018, 3). With perhaps only a brief interruption during the Cultural Revolution, the Communist Party has remained the sole source of authority, privilege, and power on the university campus since 1949. The dominant position of the Commu-

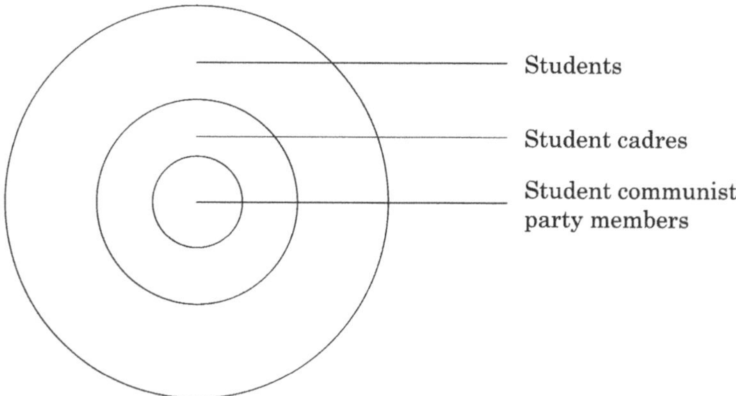

Figure 7. Political stratification in the student populace.

nist Party in everyday work and life on campus was affirmed and elucidated by the Central Committee in a document issued on 16 March 1996, which for the first time specified that university presidents in China are responsible for managing their institutions "under the leadership of the university's Communist Party Committee" (*dangwei lingdaoxia de xiaozhangfuzezhi*). The 1996 document assigns extensive power to the University Communist Party Committee.[19]

Given the position of the Communist Party at the top of the institutional power pyramid, the extremely selective group of student Communist Party members are naturally seen as "elites" on the university campus. Student communists constitute the inner circle in terms of power stratification in the student populace and remain the most important element of the Party-state's power coalition in the university. Political stratification directed by the state manifests the categorizing power of the regime and serves as a major vehicle for overall governance and control. In the Chinese university, this inner circle of the state's "golden boys and girls" consists exclusively of student Communist Party members, who are presumed to be politically more loyal to the Party-state than to competing sources of authority.

The number of student communists, as the designated "elites" on campus, has to be kept at a level that ensures the group's continuing selectivity. Figure 8 shows the nationwide number and percentage of Communist Party members in both the undergraduate student populace and the entire populace of students in higher education in China from 2004 to 2019. In 2004, only 5.85 percent of college and university students were

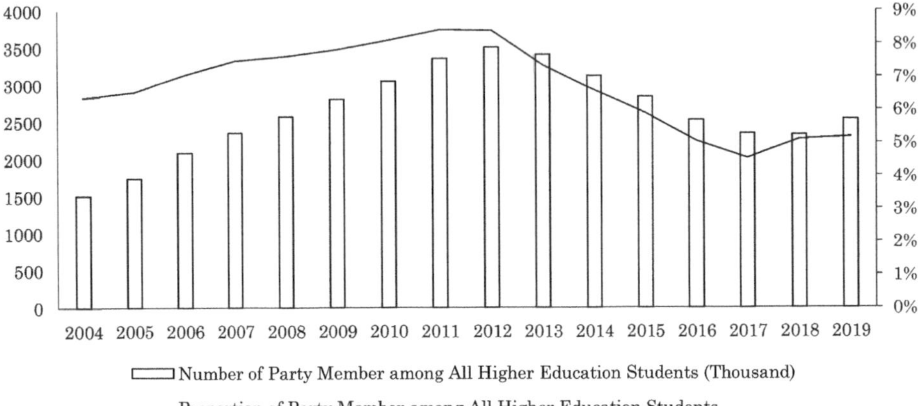

Figure 8. The number and percentage of Communist Party members in the university student populace in China (2004–2019).
Note: Here, "undergraduate students" only include students enrolled in normal courses. Communist Party members among higher-education students only include students enrolled in normal courses, short-cycle courses, normal courses provided by Adult HETs, short-cycle courses provided by adult HETs, normal and short-cycle courses provided by web-based programs, short-cycle courses provided by web-based programs, as well as doctoral and masters students. In contrast, higher-education students include those enrolled in postgraduate courses, advanced degree programs, or persons in employment, state-recognized credit programs provided by nonstate/private HETs, registered viewers/auditors of programs provided by RTVUs, classes run by nonstate/private HETs for students preparing for state-administered examinations for self-directed learners, college-preparatory classes, in-service training, as well as foreign students.

Communist Party members; in 2010, this percentage rose to 9.17 percent. After 2010, the percentage of Communist Party members in both groups dropped dramatically; in 2019 it was only slightly more than 5 percent. Despite the Communist Party's claim to have engaged in proactive recruitment campaigns on university campuses in the past decade, student Party members still represent a tiny portion of the student population, maintaining their privileged status as an exclusive group of the regime's most trustworthy supporters in China's higher-education sector.

The elite nature of the corps of communist students on campus is reflected in the lengthy and tedious yet also highly selective and competitive processes of identifying, evaluating, and admitting university students to the Party. In the post-Tiananmen Chinese university, Communist Party membership is highly sought after within the student community. A quantitative study by Xin Guihua and Zhang Yangyang revealed that 75 percent of the surveyed students had submitted an application for Communist Party membership at some point during their undergraduate years;

85 percent of these students submitted the application during their freshman year (2016, 49). Our interviewees also reported that the number of applications for Communist Party membership is particularly high when members of the freshman class arrive on campus after completing their prematriculation military training. In the Party's selection of new members from among university students, three criteria are considered. The first is political performance (*zhengzhi biaoxian*). With the decline of its capacity for ideological mobilization, the Party-state now relies more heavily on vetting applicants' attitudes toward the current Party leadership and the supreme leader. One student Party member responded as follows when asked to define political loyalty:

> Political loyalty is something you cannot define in concrete terms—it is more of a sentiment. It is the way you feel about the Communist Party. In fact, I can tell you that . . . our generation [note: the interviewee was born in the 1990s] does not feel the relationship between us and the Communist Party is as close as our parents felt; but I think I had full loyalty to the Party before I became a member. Why? I remember at that time, whenever I heard someone talking about the negative side of the Party leaders, I would feel very uncomfortable. I think all of the political parties in the world are problematic but eventually they can become better (and thus criticism of leaders is groundless). I use my own example to show why I think political loyalty is a kind of sentiment. And when I review new applications on behalf of the Party, I always take this as a criterion.[20]

In a separate interview another student Party member of the same age seemed to agree:

> I guess I judge someone's political attitude by the criterion of how they feel about the Party. . . . I think Communist Party membership is an indicator of your political identity, which you should feel proud of. Like last time, when I was watching a TV programme [in which the Party celebrated the impressive selfless deeds of model Communists], I strongly felt that being a Party member is glorious. . . . My generation has never experienced a China without the Communist Party, so we take the rule of the Party for granted and as a natural phenomenon. There is of course sporadic negative news about the Party—but I always feel that there is nothing wrong with the organisation itself, even if a few of its members may commit crimes. I

think this is also the kind of political belief we would like to see in applicants for Party membership.[21]

Political loyalty is hard to measure, and outright defiance is rare. Thus, the frequency of reporting on anyone's state of mind, of attending official events and meetings, and of contributing information on the student community, as well as the willingness to perform the duties of a student cadre, are taken into consideration. In a few cases, a background check of a candidate's parents becomes necessary. For students whose parents have been convicted of a crime or engaged in antiregime activities, the scrutiny may be stricter. On the other side, the offspring of "revolutionary martyrs"—whose deaths have been officially recognized by the Party-state as glorious examples of devotion to the Revolution—find it much easier to pass the recruitment review for Party membership. Overall, following the overall demobilization of Chinese society, the Party today uses increasingly bureaucratic criteria to measure political loyalty, with a focus on the candidate's support for the current communist leadership rather than ideological purity or class identity, which was stressed in the past.

The second criterion in the selection of new members from among university students is academic performance. Given that the Party claims to be the "vanguard" of the Chinese people and Chinese nation, one of the major legitimizing narratives for the rule of the Communist Party lies in the supposed "advanced" nature (*xianjin xing*) of its membership, which requires that Communist Party members be not only politically loyal but professionally talented. In the recruitment of new Party members in the Chinese university, this is manifested through criteria for academic performance in the vetting process. At the leading universities, to be admitted to the Communist Party, a student needs to at least reach the top 30 percent in terms of academic performance in the class cohort (*banji*). In smaller or lesser institutions where the quota of new Communist Party members is more limited, a student has to reach the top 5 to 10 percent of the class cohort to be eligible for consideration. At some institutions, even a student's performance in the National College English Proficiency Test held by the MoE can become a factor in the selection of new Communist Party members.

The third criterion considered is the candidate's popularity among peers and influence in the student community. Since its years of revolutionary warfare, the Communist Party of China has stressed the importance of maintaining a popular power base through Party members' daily activities in the community. *Qunzhong guanxi* (relationship with society)—defined as feedback on the candidate's personality and moral character from her peers and the extent of her devotion to community service—is a very important criterion for the Communist Party. A ruling party that is gradually losing its ideological power from the revolutionary era naturally holds more tightly to the "moral" high ground to claim legitimacy. One student Party member said:

> To get into the Party, we even have to sweep the streets (as volunteers), go to Party School classes on the weekends, help fellow students in extraordinary ways—as your image in the community and people's evaluation of your character mean a lot in the application process. Community service and good interpersonal relationships are almost indispensable if you want your dream (of getting into the Communist Party) to come true. I'd say that the sacrifice a student has to make to obtain Party membership can be tremendous.[22]

Student cadres who make a significant contribution to political education events and official activities and who serve as informants for the surveillance apparatus are guaranteed priority treatment. To ensure that new Communist Party members are popular among their peers, potential candidates in the university almost all need to go through a process termed "mass recommendation" (*qunzhong tuijian*) or "democratic referral" (*minzhu tuixian*)—a secret poll conducted by questionnaire among all of the noncommunist students in the same grid unit as the candidate, investigating how popular the candidate is in the community. Negative results in such a poll will almost certainly kill an application.

Naturally, the chance of getting into the Communist Party also depends on the quota issued to each basic grid unit of students. For example, in a class cohort of about 60 students at a provincial university, only two can be admitted to the Party each year beyond the second year of study, whereas four can be admitted in the fourth (and final) year of study, right before graduation. The quotas are much more generous for China's prestigious national universities. A special quota is allocated to officially endorsed student organizations in favor of the principal student cadres who operate those groups. This kind of extra quota sometimes leaves room for manipulation, nepotism, rent-seeking, and outright corruption. Even more importantly, because it circumvents the mass monitoring of character within small "grid" units, the extra-institutional channel for accessing the Communist Party becomes a useful perquisite that the Party can trade for support, loyalty, and collaboration from politically ambitious but unpopular student cadres.

Yet overall, to maximize its utility in securing order and control, the Party regulates the quota for admitting new members very carefully. The Party sets annual quotas and merit-based criteria for the initial selection of potential candidates, which guarantees that new admissions are students who have demonstrated outstanding political and academic performance and a record of devoted community service. This measure aims not only to maintain the selective nature of the Party's membership, but to ensure that only the most loyal and outstanding candidates are recruited. As one university Party secretary said, "in terms of recruiting university students to the Communist Party, our policy is that it is better to leave a deficiency unremedied than to deal with it poorly—in Chinese, this is called *ningque wulan.*"

Students who finally become Communist Party members enter an elite group of loyalist students on campus. They enjoy a wide array of privileges, ranging from easier access to the university or faculty leadership to more career opportunities on graduation. For the politically ambitious, Communist Party membership is itself an admission ticket to the all-powerful Party-state establishment and the officialdom of the People's Republic. Given their enormous stake in the future, student Party members constitute the primary force supporting the order and control that the state seeks to reestablish on university campuses. Student communists serve as the principal student cadres, run the Communist Youth League, report on activities and irregularities within the student community, and assist in the operation of various ideological training programs, political education projects, and official Party-state ceremonies. The state relies on them to establish, effectuate, and maintain its reach and control on the university campus and in the student population.

Student Cadre

In the political landscape of the Chinese university, student cadres (*xuesheng ganbu*) represent a special case. Unlike student Communist Party members, who are at the center of the political stratification structure, student cadres constitute the outer layer in the concentric circles of forces that buttress the political order that the post-Tiananmen Chinese state seeks to reinvent. Broadly defined, the concept of "student cadres" covers a wide range of student leaders and activists who work at different levels of the institutional pyramid on campus. Members of the corps of student cadres are dispersed in the Communist Youth League, student unions, student administrative committees, student organizations, and interest clubs and serve as student assistants or helpers for Party or state agencies on campus.

From the university-wide Student Union to the basic grid unit of the class cohort, student cadres are a community of selected students who run an array of activities for the student populace and implement instructions issued by the Party-state. Although not as trustworthy as student Communist Party members in the eyes of the Party-state, student cadres play a supporting yet indispensable role in the operations of state control on the university campus. Good student cadres are rewarded with political incentives and material perquisites, and as their loyalty has been tested in their service to the Party-state, they may receive fast-track admission to the Communist Party. Ultimately, student cadres are a critical buffer group between the state machinery and university students.

Compared with student Communist Party members, student cadres are recruited on a more democratic basis. One political counselor said:

> After the students arrive on campus and the basic organisational "grids" are established, we face the issue of selecting student cadres. . . . What I feel is that it is necessary to respect the students' collective choice. As this is also a screening process for us to find a pool of potential Communist Party members and the backbone [*gugan liliang*] of our student control apparatus, the selection process has to be freer and more open, rather than narrow and closed.[23]

With this mindset, the selection of student cadres is usually conducted through open, quasidemocratic competitions. Most posts have a one-year term, and selection polls are held annually. However, the Communist Party still exercises considerable influence in the process. One student described the election of the president of his school's Student Union as follows:

> Student cadres are produced by open voting. For the presidency of the student union, the election involves a candidate speech and subsequent voting by all of the students. But officials from the Communist Youth League occasionally intervene in the election process. For example, last time, a male student was elected. However, the Communist Youth League cadres indicated that a female candidate might be better, as it is a tradition of our school to have a female Student Union president; the male student was eventually forced to withdraw from the competition. This came as an enormous surprise to us all, as no one had even mentioned the existence of such a tradi-

tion in the past. Eventually, we learned that the female candidate was the favourite pick of the Party, as she had contributed a lot to the Party's official activities and had a close relationship with political cadres. They feared that the male candidate might be a little "out of control" if he were elected.[24]

In other cases, political counselors might encourage and advocate the candidacy of students who are considered to have the potential to join the Communist Party, as taking up a student leadership position is considered a major credit in the competition for Party membership. For senior positions in the student organization hierarchy, the list of candidates must be scrutinized and approved by the Communist Youth League before they can be put on the ballot. Students who are favored and supported by the Party but lose in the open voting are very likely to be asked to serve in less important cadre posts for which a formal election is not required.

Once selected, student cadres have to attend strict, sometimes tedious political education and training sessions organized by the Communist Party. After all, the formation of a reserve of student loyalists is one of the principal purposes of the institutional arrangements of student cadre-dom itself. Political training has larger purposes, too. It involves introducing the Communist Party's internal and unannounced rules and regulations for managing the university student community. It also covers basic knowledge about the internal chains of command within the Party apparatus, the content of inner-Party disciplinary codes, and rules about how to respond to natural or political emergencies (such as a sudden outbreak of student protests on campus). Obviously, this kind of political training does not merely aim at ensuring the student cadres have a safe experience in their leadership post; more importantly, it can be seen as the Party-state's initial reaching out to the country's future professional, community, or state leaders in a holistic way. The exclusive live-in political training program is a rare opportunity for Communist Party representatives to examine each student cadre up close and vet their loyalty, capability, and character. The group training also provides a venue for the student cadres to socialize with each other and form a social group comprising only student loyalists—a group closely affiliated with the political establishment and serving as one of its principal supporting pillars on university campuses.

The corps of student cadres on campus is a hierarchical infrastructure. Both its internal institutional structure and its daily operating methods resemble those of the larger Party-state apparatus. Jérôme Doyon (2023) also found "behavioural homogeneity" between the CYL student cadres he studied and the formal Party-state officials—the kind of congruence that is believed to be an important part of the basis for the student cadres' eventual commitment to the incumbent Chinese regime. The operation of this student hierarchy is highly bureaucratic, with student cadres at the top of the chain of command deciding on matters in closed-door meetings, and student cadres at each level in the bureaucracy possessing absolute authority over their subordinates. This may itself be a means to demobilize a corps of potential student movement leaders on campus. As Sara M. Evans and Harry C. Boyte (2003) contended, commenting on the changes of social movements in America, "as social movement leaders over time became distanced from the communal foundations of democratic revolt, and adopted dominant categories and vocabularies . . . they often [hastened] the process of bureaucratization and incorporation of protest into the language and terms of modern, centralized authority" (264).

Similar to other spheres in the everyday rhythm of the Chinese university, the life experiences of student cadres can be also seen as a process of synchronization of the students' political attitudes, behavior, and philosophy with the larger Party-state system operating outside the campus walls. This involves processes of education, indoctrination, habitualization, and internalization in which the political rationale and principles of the Party-state are integrated into the mindsets and senses of self of university students. According to research on Arabic politics, "for a regime to be stable surely implies that the structures in place are to some extent internalised in the minds of the citizens," and people are not "necessarily [compliant] simply because they are coerced" into it (Wegner 2007, 94). A similar logic is applicable to China.

Conclusion

The nationwide marketization and opening to global capitalism in the 1990s seriously weakened the three powers—mobilization, dependency, and categorization—that had supported the Chinese state's edifice of control over the university and its population of students during the previous era. With the Maoist strategy of "control via mobilization" fading into history, the Party-state endeavored to construct a routinized, normalized, and bureaucratic system of surveillance and control in the university, and a concentric structure that aimed to stratify and organize the student populace in order of political trustworthiness. Within this critical social space, "the expectations, roles and attitudes are internalized, corresponding to what is demanded and foreseen" by the new normative structure (Germani 1978, 16).

This institutional infrastructure for control has three significant features. The first is the highly bureaucratic nature and the decidedly hierarchal formulation. This structure operates a pervasive network comprising Communist Party officials, political counselors, student Party members, student cadres, and other activists and informants. It extends into the students' lived experience, structures the everyday rhythm on campus, and positions the Party as the supreme source of authority in this critical social space. The second feature is the grid-like web structure and quasimilitary framework that organize university students into parallel administrative units. In such a closed space with crowded (and layered) means of control, the compliance and order sought by the regime is habitually internalized by students through everyday practice and the endogenous dynamism of the student community, even with little forceful state intervention. Third, the concentric stratification structure of the student community serves as a supporting framework for the order the Party-state seeks to reestablish. Sorting university students into groups based on their perceived political loyalty and performance is a good example of the state's revamped categorizing power. With these labeling and stratification processes, the regime is not only able to locate its most loyal supporters among educated youth, it can create a pyramid of incentives to attract university youth to align themselves with the political establishment.

THREE

A Torrent of Encounters

The Significative Infrastructure

"The State" never stops talking.
  —Philip Corrigan and Derek Sayer, *The Great Arch*, 1985, 3

Great power announces itself by its power over order. It discovers order, creates order, maintains it, or destroys it. Power is indeed the central, order-related event.
  —Edward Shils, *The Constitution of Society*, 1982, 128

The State's Signification Project

The state has never been a mere coercion-wielding organization in the Weberian sense, and it is not "'formed' once and for all" (Steinmetz 1999, 9). The production, perpetuation, and projection of the state's power of symbolism, signification, and mystification have always been essentially constitutive components in both modern and ancient states. As Pierre Bourdieu argues, "one of the major powers of the state is to produce and impose . . . categories of thought that we spontaneously apply to all things of the social world—including the state itself" (1999, 53). With effective signification of its tailor-made legitimating narratives, the state makes the society accept the official order as not only justifiable but also natural and purposeful. Signification can be used to establish the state as a "coherent, controlling organisation in a territory" (Migdal 2011, 16–17). Indeed, an integral part of state formation is the state-directed goal of "normalising, rendering natural, taken for granted, in a word 'obvious,' what are in fact ontological and epistemological premises of a particular and historical form of social order" (Corrigan and Sayer 1985, 4). The state's strategic significative efforts anchor the very existence of the state itself, making people "forget that it issues out of a long series of institution (in the active sense) and hence has all the appearance of the natural" (Bourdieu 1999, 56).

The state's signification project involves establishing and promoting a mega-narrative that justifies, rationalizes and naturalizes its control over the social realm. This mega-narrative usually includes a legitimation discourse, a founding myth (historiography), a visionary anecdote to substantiate the state's political lines of the day. By tactfully deploying the discursive devices it has at its disposal, the state constructs its desired social reality and directly combats all opposition to it. Moreover, this mega-narrative places the state's political order within a larger order, thus justifying and signifying its *raison d'état* from a broader perspective (e.g., by fulfilling a historical mission to wash away a national humiliation), or within a spatial sphere that reaches beyond the Westphalian nation-state (e.g., by contributing to a human community that shares a common fate in peace and prosperity), or both. In a "realpolitik" sense, the state's mega-narrative is designed to explain away social grievances, tensions, and even atrocities, to encourage personal sacrifice, to legitimize the incumbent political order, and to present a visionary statement for the national community.

The state's signification project has visionary value in that it provides a higher meaning and purpose deriving from a larger outlook for the political world, and a teleological justification for that outlook acquired from a historiography tailored by the state. The availability of a justifiable statement of purpose has long been an important foundation for all forms of states, from Babylon under the reign of Hammurabi to the states of the twentieth century. Chalmers Johnson contended that in any revolutionary ideology, a "goal culture" and a "transfer culture" can be identified. Whereas the "goal culture" is the revolutionary state's "image of the ultimate utopia, its idealized contrast to the present," the "transfer culture" provides a path to the promised future and legitimates the present reality (Johnson 1970, 7). The state's provision, justification, and signification of a visionary statement not only attributes a grander meaning to the everyday sacrifices that people make in reality, it also provides a teleological rhetoric that facilitates the rationalization of the current political order. For those who experience a quotidian reality, the state's mega-narrative provides a bond, a teleological confirmation of meaning, a solemn assignment of purpose, and—all together—a red thread knotting events and occurrences into a defined order in which every person can be identified, interlinked, and made a part of a larger cause. The state's significative power thus becomes a centripetal force that connects the seemingly disintegrated temporal and spatial particulars of the everyday into strong support for the control and order that the state seeks to effectuate and maintain.

Multivocal Signification

The state's signification project—namely, the forging, projecting, and solidifying of a mega-narrative—is multivocal, involving a variety of channels, arenas, and forms. The university is by nature a critical site where the state can carry out its signification project. While "the contemporary University is busily transforming itself from an ideological arm of the state into a bureaucratically organised . . . consumer-oriented corporation," the grand narrative of the university "centered on the production of a liberal, reasoning subject" of the state still firmly holds (Readings 1996, 9, 11). The uniqueness of the university as a critical space for state building hinges on the fact that it integrates pivotal yet parallel existent contradictions.

The university is both an institution of education that prioritizes the pursuit of knowledge, and a precarious arena for potential societal mobilization over which the state seeks to exert control. It combines the functionalities of learning and disciplining. As the producer of national "professional elites in waiting," the university must at the same time nurture expertise and allegiance, talent and obedience, quiescence and innovation, and indoctrination and enlightenment. The university is a microcosm of society, where social networks meet and the structural defects of human society, such as economic inequality, are manifested. Moreover, in the eyes of the state, opposing ideologies, discourses, and agendas are always hidden under the university's "facade" of free inquiry into truth. It is one of the most formidable strongholds that the reinvented Chinese state seeks to conquer to win control over the social realm and secure its supremacy.

Obviously, coercive instillation and assertive propagation do not produce the conformism that the state needs for its future professional elites. Imposition of the state's official discourses increases the difficulty of naturalizing the political order and building a cognitive foundation for self-motivated compliance. This situation is similar to other scenarios in states where forced indoctrination creates passivity, resistance, and counter-reaction rather than the much-desired voluntary conformity. Since the demobilization of Chinese society following the 1989 Tiananmen Movement, therefore, the state has striven to rebuild a new infrastructure through which a state-directed experiential signification project can be implemented.

Three mechanisms have thus become central. First, the state's significative operations are increasingly embedded in the temporal and spatial fabric of the student community to ensure that students' contact with the state's baseline political rhetoric is constant, nuanced, and carefully woven into their everyday experiences. The official political rhetoric can thus eliminate alternatives from the structured life experiences of the targeted social group as much as possible. Second, effectuated signification is realized through a combination of passive training and active participation. Encounters with the state in various forms of participatory activities prevent the official narrative from becoming a lifeless doctrine with no meaning in university students' temporal and spatial present. Third, the effectuation process entails constant surveillance over the political everyday lived by the student population. Monitoring quotidian details in both the personal and public spaces provides the state with a safety net, helping it to maintain an edge in its competition with alternative mega-narratives, rival suppliers of authority, and alien forces that enter the social space it seeks to command.

Given the intricacies of the university as a social space, whereas the state's signification project on campus appears to have adopted an open and direct approach, the form of the state's operation remains task-contingent and scene-specific. The official story is told in various formats and through numerous avenues, and the high visibility of the state throughout the signification process proclaims to the audience the inviolability of its mega-narrative, deterring any competing rhetoric. The state's significative activities in the university permeate everyday campus life. Through repeated exposure to the state's discursive framework, which often takes the form of scientific discussion, administrative rationality, or educational proceedings, students are expected to learn that the explanatory framework, which hinges on the social reality constructed by the state, is the only valid system of signification.

A New Significative Infrastructure

The tidal wave of marketization and global capitalism of the 1990s posed grave challenges to the legitimacy and capacity of China's state. Almost overnight, the state found that its ability to maintain political order had broken down. With tensions high between the state and society, the regime's old legitimizing discourse—stressing a revolutionary spirit and "blood and flesh" bonds with the subaltern classes of China—was no longer effective. The rapid accumulation of wealth by China's nouveau riche made the Maoist mission of achieving a class-leveled society not only infeasible but also undesirable. Marketization fundamentally weakened the state's monopoly over the allocation of scarce resources and career opportunities. If unaddressed, these intrinsic contradictions could consume the state. The Chinese state is not hesitant to undertake a complete overhaul of its significative infrastructure.

In terms of content, in the post-Tiananmen era, the state's old mega-narrative, which is based on the concept of perpetual domestic and international class struggle and positions the Chinese version of communism as the antithesis of Soviet "revisionism," has lost much of its appeal. The Party's mission to level China's class-based social inequalities, which is central to the visionary statement in that old mega-narrative, has even become detrimental to the long-term interests of a stability-seeking and development-driven state. The nascent market economy and the entry of global capitalism have brought a new agenda and a new imagery for the state, yet both further compromise the credibility, authenticity, and allure of the Party's long-held ideals. The state overhauls its signification project by injecting new elements that are more China-specific, identity-based, nationalistic, and development-oriented to meet the ideological needs of a state that only marginally survived the political trauma of 1989 and has since sought to repair its ability to signal its own existential value to the population amid economic, social, and cultural transformations occurring at breakneck speed.

Facing a demobilized Chinese society in the post-Tiananmen era, the state's significative operation has undergone reform on three fronts. First, the demobilization of Chinese society requires a new signification project that is normalized, routinized, and suitable for mundane bureaucratic management. Second, without devoting time and energy to mass movements, the new style demands a combination of overt politico-ideological education and subtle activities to fill the temporal and spatial structure of people's everyday lives. Third, a demobilized society and the state's compromised legitimation base necessitate that state signification provide a submerged and quiet experience for the target audiences—university students in particular. The new state project, compared to its Maoist counterpart, appears to be diffusive, experiential, noncentralized, and integrated naturally into the everyday experiences of the people. By implementing the new state signification project, the post-Tiananmen Chinese state strives to prove that, even in this completely new era driven by globalism, capitalism, and the power of the internet, the Party remains the master of the fundamental truth about China's future and the champion of its destiny to achieve national rejuvenation.

The State Signification Project on Campus

Since the 1990s, immersive and pervasive state-directed significative operations have become a strong driver of the renewal of the cognitive, perceptual, and legitimation foundation for securing a largely obedient and quiescent student population. In the new routinized, quotidian, and immersive signification system, the state remains visible at the center of the arena. The new significative infrastructure includes three essential components: a political education curriculum, significative activities, and mandatory military training—each representing a primary device for the state's significative operation on campus, namely formal education, immersive experience, and formation training.

The Formal Curriculum

Formal classroom teaching had not been the favorite form of politico-ideological education for Mao.[1] Classroom instruction in Marxism, Leninism, and the Mao Zedong thought violated Mao's philosophy that one can only develop a truly revolutionary spirit by participating in real revolutionary movements, not by studying state-designated textbooks in the classroom. It is unsurprising that in 1957 and 1966, Mao himself abolished all formal politico-ideological curricula across China (Xu 2013).

It was not until the end of the Cultural Revolution that the Party-state's more bureaucratic instrument of signification and ideological training, a formal politico-ideological curriculum, returned to the classroom.[2] In April 1978, only one and a half years after Mao's death, the Ministry of Education (MoE) issued the "Opinion on the Strengthening of Marxist Education in Institutions of Higher Learning," in which the Ministry stressed the following:

A curriculum on Marxist theories must be mandatory for all kinds of socialist institutions of higher learning. Whether a curriculum on Marxist theories is on offer is a key difference between universities of the New China and those of the Old China, and between socialist universities and bourgeois universities. All teachers must teach well, all students must learn well and leaders at all levels must manage (this curriculum) well. (Feng 2009, 16)

In June 1978 and July 1980, the Ministry issued further national guidelines covering issues from the publication of textbooks on the politico-ideological curriculum to the pedagogy for these now-mandatory courses (Feng 2009, 16). In August 1985, a complete set of newly designed mainline courses for the politico-ideological curriculum—"Revolutionary History of China," "China's Socialist Construction," "Basic Theories of Marxism," and "World Politics, Economy and International Relations"—was endorsed by the state and offered in colleges and universities across China (Feng 2009, 16–17). In these four mainline courses, instructors taught students the Party-state's official version of historiography dating to the Opium War of 1840, the Communist Party's political narratives since the founding of the PRC in 1949, the basics of Marxist philosophy and political economy, and discourses on China's position in the world and justification for its foreign policy. These courses were the first attempt of the post-Mao state to theorize, standardize, and streamline the content of the state's signification project on university campuses. They served as de jure politico-ideological training for China's professionals-in-waiting until the Tiananmen Movement in 1989.

The suppressed uprising of 1989 and the ensuing tension between the state and Chinese society were a shock to the political elites that motivated them to reevaluate the style, format, intensity, and effectiveness of the politico-ideological education being provided to the country's educated youth. In the wake of the bloodshed of 1989, the communist leadership blamed inadequate politico-ideological training in Marxist theories and the incompetence of educational institutions in communicating the Communist Party's mega-narrative effectively to their students (Li 1992). In March 1991, China's rising new leader, Jiang Zemin, wrote to the State Commission of Education (SCE, later renamed the Ministry of Education, MoE) requesting that an enhanced course of instruction on China's revolutionary history be included in the curriculum at every Chinese educational institution (Jiang 2021, 479–80). From then on, the state endeavored not only to redesign the curriculum per se but to provide a routinized, immersive, and well-rounded learning experiences for politico-ideological education nationwide. The process was, to use Stanley Rosen's term, "a massive infusion of political 're-education' in an attempt to forestall a recurrence of the turbulence and, more ambitiously, to win back the hearts and minds of Chinese youth" (1993, 310).

To create such an immersive educational experience, the state deemed it important that the politico-ideological curriculum takes up a certain amount of the credit-bearing learning time in university studies. In the wake of the Tiananmen Movement, on 3 August 1991, the SCE significantly increased the credit-bearing learning hours for the politico-ideological curriculum:

> [It has been decided that] the teaching hours designated for the politico-ideological curriculum need to be increased. For undergraduate students enrolled in a four-year program, those who major in the arts and social science must complete 350 teaching hours and those who major in the natural sciences, engineering, agriculture and medicine 280 teaching hours. . . . These designated numbers of teaching hours must be guaranteed (by the university administration). No university or individual administrator shall reduce or reallocate any of these designated teaching hours for other purposes. (Department of Ideological and Political Work, MoE 2008, 161)

These courses are usually taught not by regular academic faculty members but by a corps of teachers who belong to a specific teaching unit set up for "Thought and Political Education" (*sixiang zhengzhi jiaoyu*) in the university. In recent years, most of these special teaching units have been incorporated into or directly managed by the School of Marxism at each institution.

The politico-ideological education courses are usually conducted in a completely academic format, with all of the typical educational components in place, such as weekly lectures, tutorial discussions, term papers, final examinations, and occasional field trips. The state also mandated the precise division of the designated teaching hours for political-ideological courses among these different educational modules. The standardization of the format and content of the national politico-ideological curriculum after the Tiananmen Movement reflected the state's novel efforts to further theorize the Party's mega-narrative and communicate it to university students in a systematic manner. To forge universal syllabi for these courses, a simpler version of an introductory Marxist curriculum inherited from the 1950s has now been developed and expanded into a comprehensive, holistic, and organic educational program whose main trunk includes four mandatory courses of instruction that reflect the major aspects of the state's renewed political narrative.

The foundational course in this curriculum is "Introduction to the Basic Theories of Marxism," which focuses on the basics of the "sinicized" versions of Marxist philosophy and political economy. It aims to teach students the state's philosophy, with the formation of a correct worldview and epistemology as the most important goal. The course covers entry-level Marxist concepts with heavily simplified explanations of topics ranging from dialectical materialism to political economy terms such as "surplus value," "exploitation," and "class struggle." The textbook concludes with theory about the inevitability of communism's replacing capitalism worldwide and why socialism with Chinese characteristics is the only route to reaching that ultimate goal (Editorial Group 2010c).

The course "Introduction to Modern and Contemporary Chinese History" surveys China's modern history from the Opium Wars of the 1840s to the most recent National Congress of the Communist Party, focusing on the ongoing endeavor of the Communist Party to lift China out of poverty, instability, and subordination to Western powers by leading the Chinese people down the road toward modernization. The course's primary mission is to outline and elaborate on the state's official historiography. It seeks to legitimize the state in the historical context of modern China and justify to students that the state is the only choice for China, a nation seeking to reclaim its dignity and greatness (Editorial Group 2010a).

The course "Introduction to Mao Zedong Thoughts and the System of Theories on Socialism with Chinese Characteristics" introduces and justifies the Communist Party's political platform and policy lines—in the words of the authors of the course's textbook, "the historical process and theoretic achievements of the sinicisation of Marxism." The course delineates the major ideological discourses of the state since 1949, including Mao Zedong thought, Deng Xiaoping theory, Jiang Zemin's "Important Thoughts on the 'Three Representatives,'" and Hu Jintao's theories on scientific development. Since 2018, Xi Jinping's "Thought on Socialism with Chinese Characteristics for a New Era" has also been included. The main purpose of this course is to provide a systematic overview of the Communist Party's major national policies and a theorization of the Communist Party's substantially different political lines across history as a holistic and organic whole, thus showing the Communist Party's resilience, adaptability, and infallibility—in a word, why the Party is fit to lead (Editorial Group 2010b).

The course "Moral Education and the Basics of Law" completes the politico-ideological curriculum by sketching out the state's official moral codes and providing basic knowledge of China's legal system. The moral education component of the course covers the "socialist value system." The official textbook identifies the core socialist values to be observed in various areas: the guiding moral principles of Marxism (placing the "public" over the "private"), the moral codes required to construct socialism with Chinese characteristics (stressing individual citizens' patriotic devotion to the needs of the state), public virtues (observing civility in the public space and upholding public order by being a law-abiding citizen), traditional family values, and professional ethics in the workplace (Editorial Group 2009). This last textbook ends with a call to action:

> The future of the motherland will be incredibly beautiful and the future of the younger generation unprecedentedly bright and promising. The youth can only flourish in their sincere devotion to the state and the people. Your life will only shine by mingling it with the grand endeavours of the state and of the nation. Let the youth shoulder the responsibility. Let responsibility guide your life. Let us together synchronise with the pulse of our time, share the fate of the motherland, work hard with the people, and create an eternal young age that belongs to us forever. (Editorial Group 2009, 251)

Standardized courses of instruction, disguised educational procedures, and carefully designed course content have all facilitated the establishment of the Party-state's desired discursive milieu in the critical social space of the university. In this ideological theater, both the Party and the state display a high level of visibility, operate openly, and play the salient roles of commander, instructor, and narrator in the campaign to promote the state's baseline political rhetoric to educated youth. Yet classroom instruction is only one device. To reinvent and maintain the political order, other activities outside the classroom setting, both voluntary and mandatory, are also necessary for the state to fill the vast temporal and spatial gaps in everyday student life.

Political Training Activities

Obviously, in the university, classroom teaching alone cannot provide a sufficiently immersive educational experience. To more closely structure and shape the students' everyday experiences on campus, the state undertakes to extend its signification project from the classroom to the everyday fabric of campus life through political training activities.

The Party-state appears to be highly strategic in designing and implementing such activities. Via its youth work arm, the Communist Youth League (CYL), the Party-state assigns content and designates activities to different sectors of the country's youth. "Document No. 17," issued by the Central Committee of the CYL in 2010, categorizes Chinese youth into four major groups—university students, peasant workers, professional youth, and rural youth—and states that political training activities specifically should be tailored to the needs of each group and be implemented in certain ways.[3]

For university students, the Party-state has much grander aims and more intensive political training activities than it does for the other groups of youth:

> For university students, we should focus on guiding them to acknowledge the great achievements our country has made in her socialist construction and modernisation endeavours under the leadership of the Communist Party, making sure they have a correct understanding of the current situation of the world, the country and the Communist Party, convincing them that patriotism, socialism and the Communist Party's leadership are organically and consistently linked to each other. (Chinese Communist Youth League [CCYL] 2010)

The document mandated that all institutions of higher education "shall explore innovative methods and forms [of ideological training activities] that are welcomed by the younger generation and that effectively propagate the Party's ideology and discourse among them" (Chinese Communist Youth League [CCYL] 2010). Table 2 lists all of the ideological training activities discussed in Document No. 17.

Political training activities are implemented at three levels in Chinese universities: national campaigns, everyday activities, and political rituals and ceremonies. At the highest level, the Politburo or Central Committee of the Communist Party periodically implements nationwide political, ideological, and rectification campaigns. Universities all over China must participate in these national campaigns. For example, in February 2021, the Central Committee launched a nationwide campaign to promote the study of the Communist Party's history, with a focus on the Party's historical achievements as it celebrated its centennial. On 25 June 2021, Xi Jinping and the entire Politburo visited the Red Building on the old campus of Peking University in downtown Beijing for an exhibition on the Party's revolutionary activities in its early years. In an article published shortly

TABLE 2: Forms of innovative ideological education activities mandated by the Central Committee of the Communist Youth League

Category	Forms of Activity
Face-to-face	Party/CYL school seminars, keynote speech, discussion sessions, workshops, debates, study groups, individual consultations
Experience by Practice	Site visits, social surveys, field trips, internships, volunteer work
Media Propagation	Mass mobile phone text message, themed website, mini-blog or blog, online discussion groups, traditional news media (including newspaper, public radio, magazines, and TV channels)
Culture and Fashion	Singing contest, performance, film, ceremonies, and fashion activities (i.e., the use of fashion products, discourses, and stars in ideological education activities)
Exemplary Cases	Awards for exemplary individuals, promotion of the moral deeds of exemplary individual, themed conferences

Source: "Notice on the Work of Classification and Divergent Guidance Work for the Youth," Chinese Communist Youth League, Zhong Qing Fa [2010] No.17, November 19, 2010.

afterward, Qiu Shuiping, the Communist Party secretary of Peking University,[4] described the immersive politico-ideological training experiences:

> Peking University pays high attention to the best and strategic use of "red" historical resources of the university in carrying out the study of party history campaign. We will closely integrate the study of party history into endeavours of implementing the moral education for our students. We will strive to form a lively situation at our university where everyone talks about party history, in every corner people learn about party history, people know about party history and love the Communist Party, and people understand the national history and love our motherland. (Qiu 2021)

Regarding the implementation of this national ideological campaign as an experiential signification project, the article stated,

> We must promote the integrated construction of [the] politico-ideological education curriculum with practical learning across [China's] vast society. Every summer, our university shall allocate financial resources and send our students to the old revolutionary base areas, to the urban cities and the countryside, to the farming land of China to carry out experiential teaching and learning [about the Party's history]. We will send our students to the battle-

field against the COVID-19 pandemic to help them understand the grand spirit of fighting and to the main ground of reform to help them sense the power of development. Ultimately, we will make sure that China's educated youth are equipped with strong minds, pure Communist beliefs and adherence to the doctrine of "four self-confidences" from their own first-hand experiences. (Qiu 2021)

National campaigns specifically designed and carried out for the nation's younger generation have been fairly frequent. For instance, in 2011 alone, at least three national political education campaigns designed for university students were carried out in Chinese universities under state mandate. The schedules for these national campaigns are usually extensive and exhaustive; they occupy a large amount of students' time on campus.

Everyday political training activities also take up a sizable portion of university students' time, especially for students who anticipate a career in the public sector or who seek Communist Party membership. These activities vary in format and include regular class meetings (*banhui*), CYL meetings (*tuanhui*), reading sessions (*dushu hui*), and Student Party Branch meetings (*danghui*), in ascending order of importance. At almost all of these mandatory meetings, much time is devoted to reading aloud important articles published in the Party's mouthpiece newspaper and journals, or paragraphs taken from the latest central documents. The reading is followed by a discussion in which every participant is expected to express support for the official lines and pledge personal allegiance. Such reading and discussion sessions may seem odd in the internet age, especially given that the content of the Party's documents and newspaper is readily available online, yet the tedious reading of often very long texts remains an important political ritual for university students in China.

In addition, university administrations periodically organize various forms of political training activities, often public seminars or public lectures where senior communist cadre members or officially endorsed scholars from outside the university are invited to deliver keynote speeches on policy or political issues relevant to the student population. On each university campus, a Communist Party school serves as an important center for the ideological training of student activists who are hand-picked by the Communist cadres that oversee student affairs at all levels.

On other occasions, mandatory political study sessions can be crisis-response measures to prevent students from participating in anti-regime activities off campus. Since 1989, it has almost become the norm that whenever an extraordinary political situation arises, Party organizations at all levels on campus are required to hold urgent political study sessions. Such gatherings are also used to release relevant information to students, to pacify them if they are agitated by the situation, and to limit their mobility amid a growing social or political crisis. For example, in spring 2011, when antiregime websites outside China called on Chinese students to launch a "Jasmine Revolution"—a Chinese form of the "Colour Revolution"—university students were immediately required by university administration to attend special political study sessions scheduled for the designated day of protest, a measure obviously meant to prevent the student body from mingling with or being co-opted by domestic or foreign oppositional forces.

Rituals and Ceremonies

A ritual is a "formalised collective performance, usually combining movement and both visual and verbal discourse" (Gill 2011, 15). At the individual level, rituals and ceremonies express "some deeper ordering of political and social relations" through the "clothing of power" (Wilentz 1985, 1). "Participation in ritual can give individuals a sense of continuity, belonging, and an affirmation that all is regular and in accord" (Gill 2011, 15). At the collective level, rituals and ceremonies are important instruments for building a stable sense of community membership, which "is so much more resistant to change than beliefs [are]" (Kertzer 1988, 67–68).

Scholars have identified two key ways in which rituals and ceremonies are valuable to state rulers. Functional-instrumental theories focus on the ability of rituals and ceremonies to strengthen state legitimacy, display state might, define national identity, and meet the physiological needs of the population (Podeh 2011). Rituals and ceremonies also have an essential-existential value well beyond the functional convenience provided by the "ordering force of display, regard, and drama" (Geertz 1980, 121). As Clifford Geertz argued, rather than exogenous instrumentality, the "hierarchical, sensory, symbolic, and theatrical" dimensions of the state are part of its intrinsic nature—the cultural form and display of the state are, ontologically, the state (Geertz 1980, 124–25).

The Communist Party and the state understand well the important role played by political rituals and ceremonies in bolstering state order, state control, and state legitimacy. In the Communist Youth League's terminology, political education through participation in rituals and ceremonies is "education by rites" (*yishi jiaoyu*) (Chinese Communist Youth League [CCYL] 2010). For a Chinese university student, participation in political ceremonies and rituals organized by the Communist Party or the state consumes a considerable amount of time outside the classroom.

From the public oath-taking ceremony for new student Communist Party members to the solemn memorial service for the "revolutionary martyrs" who lost their lives in revolutionary warfare, China's political rituals and ceremonies are significant events. These rituals and ceremonies can be classified into three main types. *Loyalty-nurturing rituals* are designed to cultivate and strengthen students' political loyalty to the regime. Only the most politically privileged students on campus can participate in these rituals, which include oath-taking ceremonies for new Communist Party members, the opening ceremony of the Student Party School, inner-Party award-conferring ceremonies, and annual political training camps for student cadres.

Regime-identifying rituals are intended to enhance students' identification with the regime through the festive display of, ceremonial exposure to, and participatory observation of the signification and celebration of the Communist Party's mega-narrative, historiography, and political lines. Attended by more common students, these rituals include the annual memorial service held at the graveyard of the "revolutionary martyrs," the annual chorus competition of revolutionary songs, and the national flag-raising ceremony held on every university campus in China.

Punitive rituals are more special. Students have nicknamed such rituals the "political guillotine" because they usually include quasitheatrical displays of criticism of members of the student community who have been deemed to have made political or moral mistakes, as well as self-criticism by such members. Such rituals include, in descending order of severity, public criticism sessions (*xuesheng dahui*), public announcements of disciplinary penalties, and sessions of "criticism and self-criticism" to "help" politically wayward students to return to "correct" ways of thinking and behaving. Despite their highly unpleasant nature, punitive rituals are mandatory events, serving not only as public sanctionings of "wrongdoers" but as deterrents to others.

On special occasions, political rituals organized by the university administration might go beyond the campus walls. For example, on 1 July 2003, the first anniversary following the national SARS crisis of the founding of the Chinese Communist Party, Peking University held a grand ceremony in Tiananmen Square at which participating students were instructed to collectively pledge their allegiance to the Party as a sign of approval of the regime's performance in fighting the deadly pandemic over the past half year. At the ceremony, after observing the raising of the national flag by the honorary guards of the army, the students stood in prearranged lines, wearing university uniforms and chanting slogans such as "Keep Our Heart with the Communist Party" and "Rebuild Our Glorious Achievements" (Guan 2004). This unusual ceremony was a public display of elite university students' political loyalty to the Party-state following a devastating medical crisis that had initially been mismanaged by a number of senior communist cadre members.

Military Training

Military training for university students has appeared periodically in modern China since the late imperial era, the product of a nascent Chinese state that gradually proclaimed itself as having been founded on rational, scientific, and modern principles, instead of Confucian moral codes. As early as 1902–1903, radical institutions that served as student protest centers in Shanghai—such as the Patriotic Academy (*aiguo gongxue*)—had adopted military training to educate a new generation of modern Chinese citizens with a patriotic mindset. The students in such radical institutions formed themselves into "student armies" composed of small brigades (*xiaodui*) whose "avowed purpose was to prepare to defend the nation's sovereignty" (Wasserstrom 1991, 40).

After the founding of the communist regime in 1949, military training for university students declined. The emphasis of such training on a rigid organizational nature, absolute obedience to the chain of command, and the stringent control of a military bureaucracy went against Mao's desire to foster a permanent revolutionary spirit in the country's youth. The culture of mechanical obedience sought by a military training program did not fit with Mao's vision for spontaneous youth activism that would self-organize against any revisionist Party-state leadership that might arise.

The intensification of military training on university campuses after 1989 was first introduced as an insulation measure to prevent the members of the incoming freshman class in 1989 (who were scheduled to matriculate in September of that year) from mingling with students in other year-cohorts, many of whom had participated in the Tiananmen Movement. But on the other hand, mandatory engagement in institutionalized activities has long served as an effective instrument of social control, and particularly of regulating the social behavior of youth (such as required apprenticeships for young vagrants in sixteenth-century England) (Mizruchi 1983, 13). Thus, at the same time that the special long program was implemented in two universities renowned for their influential arts and social sciences disciplines, shorter military training programs (typically seven to fourteen days) of varying intensities were implemented in all institutions of higher education in China.

On April 28, 2001, China promulgated the first "National Defence Education Law," which requires that "institutions of higher learning . . . shall carry out national defence education to the students through [a] combination of classroom teaching and military training" (Standing Committee of the National People's Congress 2020). A joint instruction issued by the State Council and the Central Military Commission in June 2001 (Document No. 48) specified that universities, colleges, and high schools that had not incorporated military training into their curricula were to do so in a coordinated manner so that student military training could be implemented all over China (State Council and the Central Military Commission 2001). According to the *People's Liberation Army Daily*, the mouthpiece of the Chinese military, in 2018, more than twenty million university students in China attended military training (Shi 2018). Most of the faculty advisors assigned by the university administration to accompany the students and oversee the military training program were Communist Party members. In 2020, 84.1 percent of the 107 faculty members who oversaw the military training of students at Peking University were Communist Party members (Education and Publicity Group of Peking University 2020 Freshman Military Training Corps 2020).

Military training programs for university students in China usually have three areas of focus: physical training, collective life training, and ideological training. Physical training involves a rigid daily timetable from dawn to midnight, emulating the exercise and training routines of an ordinary soldier in the Chinese army. An instruction jointly issued by the State Council and the Central Military Commission (Document No. 76) emphasized that students should receive "combat readiness training, training in defensive tactics, basic combat training and military sports training." It also encouraged universities and schools to promote "simulation training . . . such as shooting with a light weapon system" and, for institutions with the necessary capacity, to hold "training in basic navy sailing skills" (State Council and the Central Military Commission 2017). Table 3 displays the basic elements of the ten-day military training program for students at Sichuan Agricultural University in 2013.

Collective life training focuses on the organization of students into gridlike units and nurtures students' ability to live a collectivist life in cohorts and to collaborate with team members to accomplish military tasks. In an instruction issued in May 2017, the Ministry of Education emphasized the importance of managing collective life rhythm in the implementation of military training in universities. The instruction required that during

TABLE 3: Basic elements of a provincial university's ten-day military training program

Summary	Contents of Training
1. Study of the Common Regulations of the PLA	Study of regulations on routine service of the People's Liberation Army, the regulations on discipline of the People's Liberation Army, the regulations on formation of the People's Liberation Army; routine service setup and competition
2. Formation training	Stand at attention, stand at ease, parade rest, face to the flank, face to the rear, steps and marching, salute and review
3. The tactics training of defense and attack in catch and grapple	Combination attack, the use of army daggers, the use of a police baton
4. Shooting practice	Theories of shooting, including the introduction to frequently used light weaponry, practice shooting, preparation for shooting
5. Cultural activities	Learning to sing revolutionary songs, university battling songs, barracks singing competition
6. Military theories	*The university will invite experts to teach.*
7. Seminar on national defense	*Regiment for military training will implement the teaching.*
8. Emergency response	*The military will organize the teaching.*

Source: "Implementation Plan for the Military Training of the 2013 Freshman Class," Sichuan Agriculture University
https://bwc.sicau.edu.cn/info/1004/1022.htm, accessed 9 September 2021.

the period of military training, students' everyday life must be managed according to the "Regulations on Routine Service of the People's Liberation Army," which rigidly structures the everyday lives, work, and training of soldiers in PLA barracks (Ministry of Education 2016).

Ideological training involves studying the revolutionary history of the Communist Party and the military, reading party and military newspapers, discussing current affairs in society outside of the barracks, singing military songs, and carrying out criticism and self-criticism sessions (State Council and the Central Military Commission 2017). In many universities, the Communist Party's student branches take full advantage of the symbolic nature of military training to promote the ruling party to members of the freshman class. In Sichuan Agricultural University, student party members moved their Party membership initiation program to the training field. Student Communist Party members in the senior cohorts set up water and snack kiosks on the training field and provided help for new students requiring medical attention or other assistance. The university's news website reported,

"Buddy, here is hot water and over there is cool water, please line up to get what you need." "Classmate, get some bread and don't let yourself faint due to low blood sugar." Today, the freshman class military training officially kicks off under the scorching sun. The Communist Party Service Team of the School of Economics had set up service kiosks on the training field by dawn. During the day, they were busy arranging "Communist Party member service spots," distributing free breakfasts, preparing a glucose sugar solution (for students who might need treatment for low blood sugar), accompanying students who had heatstroke to the medical clinic. . . . They were practising what the Communist Party requires of her members, and they made every effort to attract freshman to the Chinese Communist Party. (Sichuan Agricultural University [SICAU] 2017)

Political rituals and ceremonies are abundant during military training. For example, on 18 September 2009, students at the Ocean University of China who were undergoing military training observed a moment of silence with military officers in honor of the victims of the September 18 Incident, which marked the beginning of the Japanese invasion of China in 1931. The university news website reported the occasion using the emotional title "Don't Forget the National Humiliation: I Am a Chinese National":

At 3:30 in the afternoon, with the three long whistle sounds, all of the military trainees belonging to the Third Battalion immediately stood in attention. At the command of the training officer, all of the students took off their army caps and observed a moment of silence. There was suddenly pervasive silence on the training ground. Perhaps the students' [military] posture was not yet accurate, but they all bore a sad facial expression. On that evening in 1931, a permanent scar was imprinted in the minds and hearts of countless Chinese—it was a national humiliation that cannot and shall not be forgotten. . . . At the end of the ritual, the sound of gentle weeping was heard from the corps of trainees—a few female students were crying and even some boys seemed on the verge of tears. (Ocean University of China [OUC] 2014)

"People often think of the army as an instrument of coercion . . . but the army is also an instrument for inculcating cultural models, an instrument of training" (Bourdieu 2020, 157). Military training occupies a block of time during which freshmen's activities are rigidly structured by the state and familiarizes them with heavy state control and intervention in their subsequent college years. This military training also provides intensive exposure to the state's baseline state rhetoric through the various activities organized by both the military and the university's Party organizations. More importantly, military training furnishes the students, at the outset of their university life, with officially sanctioned exemplary model soldiers and officers of the People's Liberation Army. The martial spirit of the soldiers and officers, the neatness of barrack life, the devotion of the military to the Communist Party, and the display of bravery, commitment, service, and sacrifice are not only essential to the state but also attractive to the young students, the majority of whom have embarked on independent lives free of parental control yet marked by obstacles and uncertainties. Juliette Genevaz argued that at this pivotal juncture in students' transition to maturity and to "social" life, the Party-state "uses the [army] to structure social relations" and "crafts an image of the soldier as the embodiment of (the ideal of human) personal quality" (2019, 466). These experiences have a long-lasting impact on young student trainees.

The Threat Posed by Fundamentalist Students

The state's immersive signification project has had some specially strong impacts on the minds and hearts of a small group of university students: the young Marxists. The surprising rate of growth and the unusual vigor of the fundamentalist Marxist groups on Chinese university campuses in the past decade has become an unintended externality of the Communist Party's decade-long compulsory state-sanctioned ideological education. The radical leftist student groups in the elite Chinese universities are a product of the state's indoctrination into Marxist ideology, and their political confrontations with the state and the state's crackdown on them are among the most bizarre occurrences in the state-student relationship.

Student Marxist groups in the Chinese elite universities were originally state-endorsed academic and propagandist societies. Although they were gradually alienated from campus life following the reform and opening-up period, these groups maintained a tradition of researching Marxist doctrines and propagating them not only to the university community but to wider society. However, they began to cause problems for the state in 2015, when some of these groups started to raise concerns over the labor rights of workers in their universities. For example, at Peking University, the Marxist Society released a comprehensive report on campus workers' mistreatment by the university administration in December 2015. This report, written by sixty-one students from nineteen faculties and departments, noted that campus workers were often back-paid and lived in substandard accommodations. The report stated that 61 percent of the campus workers surveyed had not been provided employee insurance and 36 percent had not signed an employment contract. It also noted that the workers often worked excessively long shifts: 79 percent worked for more than eight hours a day and 32 percent worked for more than twelve hours a day. The publication of the report led Peking University to promise a "self-check" of labor conditions on campus (Wu and Sha 2015). At Renmin University of China, an elite institution of education in the social sciences, a leftist student society called the New Light Society for the Development of Common People organized a night school for campus workers from 2011 to 2017. In these night classes, the students befriended young migrant workers employed by the university as janitors, cooks, drivers, and other support staff, helping them to improve their work conditions, fighting for their rights as employees, and assisting them in gaining new skills and knowledge (He 2017).

Equipped with Marxist teaching and educated to have a strong belief in the power of the proletariat, the students' concern was naturally not limited to the campus; many joined forces with the burgeoning labor movement in China, which brought these leftist students into conflict with the state. The triggering event was a small local labor movement by workers for Jasic Company at a manufacturing factory in Shenzhen. In 2018, when the workers at Jasic tried to organize a labor union to fight for better employment terms and improved labor conditions, they came to know the leftist students at Peking University. Within a matter of months, the leftist students had joined forces with the workers to fight not only Jasic's management but also the local government of Shenzhen, which sought to suppress the labor unrest through coercive measures. In a way, the elite students of the Marxist Society followed in the tradition of the Communist Party's revolutionary labor movement of the 1920s and 1930s (Perry 2012). However, for a state that had shifted its priorities to economic development and social stability, this mingling of educated youth with the impoverished labor force was politically dangerous (British Broadcasting Channel 2018a, 2018b; Xinhua News Agency 2018). As the New Year Message of the Supporting Group for the Jasic Workers stated,

To our surprise, there were many new young voices in the Supporting Group: from new generations of workers who were following in the path of Marxism-Leninism-Maoism to students from universities all over China and to youths who had abandoned their fame as elite-college graduates and stood alongside the workers. They stood together under the scorching sun of Guangdong to defend the rights and the pride of the working class. . . . One hundred seventy years ago, Karl Marx wrote down the maxim of the proletariat movement: "Workers of the world, unite!" The Jasic Worker Supporting Group stands not only for workers who are striving for a labour union but for all our comrades of the working class who are currently under suppression and exploitation. (Jasic Workers Support Group 2019)

A nationwide crackdown on leftist student societies on university campuses followed. In December 2018, Peking University removed the chairman of the university's Marxist Society, Qiu Zhanxuan, after he was detained and questioned by law enforcement agencies, and reshuffled the society's leadership. The university administration also stopped the society's memorial service for the anniversary of Mao, delayed the renewal of registration for the society, and terminated the studies of the most active members of the student organization (*New York Times* 2019).[5]

This rise and decline of the leftist student movement represented a ripple of vigor on the quiescent campuses of post-Tiananmen Chinese universities. The emergence and demise of fundamentalist students with a firm belief in Marxist doctrine are a surreal reflection of the state's signification project carried out on university campuses. The defiant students were true believers in the state's official ideology and practitioners of the state's proclaimed revolutionary heritage; yet as Dimitar D. Gueorguiev (2021) wrote, "the homeostasis of [the Chinese control system] is threatened by extremes in any direction" (199). The outcome was partly the result of an overdose of politico-ideological education and partly the outcome of immersive ideological training. When historical contingencies meet at a critical juncture, inexperienced and unsophisticated students who have been indoctrinated by the state's signification operations and ideological teachings may challenge the state for deviating from the grand theories that they have learned in the classroom.

Conclusion

The post-Tiananmen era has witnessed a paradigm shift in the Chinese state's implementation of its signification project. The memories of Mao-ist mass mobilizations rendered the "crusadic" style of state's signification operation—forging a state-society congruence based on the never-ending revolutionary fight between antagonistic societal forces—unnecessary to the post-Mao Chinese leadership. In the wake of 1989, it became even clearer for the state that, to rebuild the state's capacity and to reinvent political order, it needs a routinized, normalized, immersive, everyday mechanism that is embedded in the fabric of the political everyday lived by the critical social groups. Therefore, in the critical battlefield of the university, the state has sought to create an interlinked web of significative operation that is immersive and compelling, one that is interwoven with the students' everyday campus life.

Infusing the standardized content of the state's baseline political rhetoric into the formal educational system is not only a pedagogical goal but also a direct exercise of the state's sovereign power in the field of signification. Extracurricular political education activities permeate university students' everyday experiences and fill their timetables outside the classroom. The nationwide mandatory military training designates a time period in which students have intensive contact with the People's Liberation Army, the "military arm of the Communist Party." Training in formation, collective life, and ideological compliance is intended to instill in students state-defined morale, patriotism, and the organized, self-disciplined life required by the state. Political rituals become expressions of political loyalty, shared memories, and community compliance that shape students into professional elites in waiting for a country of 1.4 billion citizens. The impact will be long-lasting.

Eventually, the discursive landscape continuously forged by the state becomes so pervasive that students, despite experiencing occasional fatigue, nevertheless consider it familiar, natural, and instinctive. In the field of signification, the state chooses to be visible, overt, and upfront in its operations. This is natural, as the field of signification is where the state projects its baseline political rhetoric. Only by operating visibly can the state deliver a clear message and establish a well-defined politico-ideological terrain. When the state's significative activities and the content that it contrives to project are ingrained into the everyday rhythm of the university, the state's baseline political rhetoric becomes a ubiquitous part of students' social environment. This is a fundamental way in which the state establishes, effectuates, and maintains political order.

FOUR

Shaping Public Life

The Regulatory Infrastructure

[C]oncrete space is defined in relation to human occupation, use, or gaze. Concrete space is a space for some person or collection of persons. It is a space that is used, seen, and experienced.

—William H. Sewell Jr., "Space in Contentious Politics,"
2001, 53

The most important political distinction among countries concerns not their form of government but their degree of government.

—Samuel P. Huntington, *Political Order in Changing Societies*,
1968, 1

The Campus Public Space

To reinvent political order, a compromised state needs to reestablish control over the public life within critical social spaces. Given the state's nature as a public organization claiming exclusive sovereign power, its utmost purpose is to safeguard orderly public life. For state rulers, the desire for order goes beyond pursuing the functionalities of a mere "watchman state"; instead, the state competes for dominance in critical public spaces and seeks to control the sociopolitical, mobilizational, and discursive potentialities of that public sphere. In the Chinese state's campaign to reinvent political order in the university, therefore, establishing supremacy in campus public life was a priority for the regime.

The university is a unique public space that features a high density of interpersonal and communal networks; its organizational principle is that—in Habermas's phrase—"reason alone has force" (Habermas 1991, 103). It is also closely linked to the larger sociopolitical system, with its embedded inequality, injustice, and conflicts, but it offers a relatively free atmosphere for the education and socialization of youth; it is a place in which competing societal forces can contest the state and its project of maintaining an institutionalized political order. The public sphere of the university is a field in which the state commits itself to guarding against the influence of rival suppliers of authority.

The university's uniqueness as a public space is tripartite, involving its dense connectivity, its latency as an abeyance structure for youth progressing into the adult world, and its centrality to the production and projection of state ideology. First, the university is a connective structure, producing through its members' everyday interactions and exchanges a public space tightly knit together by associational networks and interpersonal bonds. The associational space comprised primarily of student societies, organizations, and clubs is a fertile ground for the growth of communal reciprocal links, and an intensive web of interpersonal connectivity powered by peer pressure, accumulating and maintaining within it a wealth of organizational resources (Calhoun 1994; Guthrie 1995). The rapid advance of campus computer networks further enhanced connectivity on the university campus and strengthened its mobilizational potential. When virtual communication on campus is boosted, the campus public space is augmented and becomes a self-multiplying space for debate and activism (Yang 2009; Han 2018).

Second, the university is what I term a "preparatory abeyance structure." Societies use abeyance structures (such as monasticism, compulsory apprenticeship, mandatory schooling, and programs hosted by the Works Progress Administration during the US New Deal) as social-control measures to manage surplus population, prevent marginalization, and maintain the status quo (Mizruchi 1983). "Abeyance" refers to "the process of holding personnel" with "mandatory engagement in institutionalised activities" (Mizruchi 1983, 11, 13). Universities serve as a special form of abeyance structure. The university holds young people together for a designated time period, during which they experience the transition from late adolescence to mature adulthood, physically, mentally, and sociopolitically. The university also uses carefully regulated campus public space and assiduously structured everyday experiences to shape students' associational life and interpersonal bonds to compete with other forms of organized influence, and thus nurture compliant, quiescent, and politico-ideologically congruent "professional elites-in-waiting." For the state, the campus public space is a critical support for the political order the state seeks to effectuate.

Third, the university is a public sphere where both the official state ideology and its counterarguments, alternative frameworks, and substitute discourses are manufactured, tested, contended with, and broadcast to society at large. The public sphere on campus is an arena for the discussion of national issues, debate on policies, and the formation of discourses about the most fundamental topics of the time. As a country's primary zone for knowledge accumulation, scientific discovery, and theoretical construction, the university is naturally an engine for the invention and reproduction of a country's prevailing ideology. The state also tends to rely on the symbolic, intellectual, and human resources of the university to produce and project its baseline political rhetoric. The relative autonomy enjoyed by the university as the island of knowledge, along with the state's practical need to preserve the innovative capacity of the scientific profession, *faute de mieux*, means that it offers room for theses that compete the state's mainline discourse. This public space, even if it is not exactly like the "little corner(s) of freedom" under the Soviet Union (Weiner 1999), is nonetheless more provocative, disparate, and heretical than the monotonous discursive landscape in the closely watched and strictly regulated mainstream public sphere outside the university walls.

To effectuate political order, states regulate any community-based public space that exists in parallel. The existence of a nonstate public sphere—*societatis civilis*—provides both the avenue and the vehicle for pluralistic and dissenting public discourses. As Craig Calhoun contended, in the public space of university campuses, members of the campus population create an alternative, parallel system of politico-ideological discourse—a "rational-critical discourse"—that aims at the resolution of public disputes (1994, 200). This system infringes incrementally on the symbolic and actual power of the reinvented Chinese state. When this plurality of heterogeneous discourses is protected by the online anonymity provided by the campus virtual space, they come to be even more powerful. At China's institutions of higher education, the state's regulatory infrastructure is constructed in four overlapping arenas of public life: associational space, virtual space, the field of the spiritual, and the institutional subculture.

Disciplining the Associational Life

Student groups are a vibrant part of everyday campus life in the university. As a primary component of the associational life of the student populace and a crucial element of the campus public space, student groups have

Figure 9. On the university sports ground (Wuhan, China).

often served as a mobilizing vehicle for revolutionary movements in modern China. The "highly organised nature of university daily life and patterns of student interaction facilitated and left their imprint on outbursts of collective action" (Wasserstrom and Liu 1995, 365). The regime party also traces its origin to the radical leftist student groups active in the early twentieth century. Since the 1990s, various kinds of student groups—hobby clubs, associations, reading groups, sports teams, or open and underground societies—continue to form a lively scene of communal life on campus, where youth form ideological affinities, fraternity-like personal ties, political alignments, and social networks. Ultimately, the associational space becomes crucial for the state's project of reinventing a stable political order in the university.

For the state, keeping a firm grip over the associational life of students is no easy task. Student groups tend to bring together like-minded friends and devoted comrades. It is easy for a student group to form a deep interpersonal commitment and sense of fraternity on the basis of shared identity. Sticking to pure principle and often holding a sociopolitical stance that is more idealistic, radical, and impatient for change than that of more mature and sophisticated social sectors, the student associational space remains a powder keg that is in constant danger of exploding, and it can be set off by even a little spark.

With the development of modern higher education in China, student groups in Chinese universities persistently contributed to the central theater of national politics. Throughout the Republican, Maoist, and post-Mao periods, student groups remained a dynamic social force that fueled radical social movements.[1] Yet before the state could take substantial steps to address the issue, amid the tidal wave of marketization and globalization, the 1990s witnessed the resurfacing of civic activism in the associational space across China—and the university campus was no exception. Meanwhile, the liberal intelligentsia—now purged from the ruling elites—became elements of a political opposition either hidden (domestically) or in exile (overseas), which shifted its attention from high politics to the grassroots associational space.

This political unrest came along with new social cleavages and a desire for more active expression among those whose private interests were violated by public authorities during the process of rapid urban development. The renewed civic activism has been reflected in the robust associational life on Chinese university campuses since the 1990s. In a survey focusing on the development of student groups, Wang Xiaojun found that, on average, in the mid-1990s, 34.37 percent of university students joined at least one voluntary student organization on campus (Lv 2012, 90). *China Education Daily*, the mouthpiece of the Ministry of Education, reported in June 2005 that another national survey found that in 2003, 72 percent of the university students in Shanghai had joined at least one of the 712 voluntary student organizations in the city. In Zhejiang Province, 142,000 university students reported membership in 1,420 student organizations, accounting for 68 percent of the total provincial student populace enrolled in tertiary institutions. The report "Student Groups: An Important Classroom for the Growth of University Students" stated that "more than 80 percent of university students in China have joined at least one student group within their respective universities, across campuses or on the Internet. . . . Student groups function effectively in self-service, self-education, self-governance and self-development, playing [an] important role in facilitating the socialization process of the students" (Tian 2005). This expansion of campus associational life over just a single decade was remarkable. Student organizations flourished in the first two decades of the new century. At Tsinghua University, only 54 student organizations existed in 1994; by 2010, the number had risen to 120, and the number of registered student members was more than 20,000. In 2017, the number of student organizations had increased to 251, with more than 33,000 registered members. On average, a Tsinghua student joined 2.6 student organizations.

In March 2004, there were 2,093 student organizations affiliated with universities in Beijing, which claimed nearly 170,000 student members. As many as 445 new student organizations were founded between 2003 to 2004 in Beijing. A survey conducted in 2009–2011 shows that, in Beijing, more than 90 percent of university students were members of student organizations, and they spent 3.7 hours on group activities each week. In 2009, there were more than 2,800 student organizations in Shanghai, which had more than 260,000 student members, accounting for 47 percent of the entire student populace of the city (Li 2017, 4). As *China Youth Daily* exuberantly announced in November 2012, "participating in student associations has become a way of life for China's Post-90s Generation" (Xie 2012b). "Post-90s generation" is a popular term widely used on the Chinese internet, referring to members of the younger age cohort who were born after 1990.

The reactivated associational space in the Chinese university, however anticipated, turned out to be a matter of concern for the Party-state. In 2005, *China Education Daily* warned that "oppositional forces in the West deem institutions of higher education a strategic focus for their campaign to divide, Westernize, and weaken the Chinese nation, reaching their evil goals of intervening in the political and economic spheres of China. Student groups have a weak capacity to defend against such influences—we should be highly attentive to such a danger" (Tian 2005). In 2004, the Central Committee of the CCP issued a document entitled "Instructions on the Further Strengthening and Improvement of Thought and Political Work Amongst University Students," ordering Party organizations to tighten the regulations governing student groups on university campuses. In 2005, the Central Committee of the Communist Youth League and the Ministry of Education jointly issued more specific guidance, entitled "Instructions on the Further Strengthening and Improvement of Work on Student Organisations in the Universities" ("Document No. 5"), which categorically set out the requirements, methods, and institutional arrangements enabling the Party-state to exert control over university student groups (Central Committee of the Chinese Communist Youth League and the Ministry of Education 2005).

Subsequently, University Communist Party Committees across the country were given the job of keeping student groups under control; the university CYL committees were responsible for managing, directing, and monitoring student groups on campus on a daily basis. In 2019,

Peking University made it clear in its regulations that "student organisations are . . . important vehicles for politico-ideological education. . . . Student organisations shall accept the regulation and leadership of the university" (Peking University 2019). Tsinghua University announced similar guidance in 2021. The Tsinghua University document said that "the basic mission of student organisations is: under the guidance of Xi Jinping Thought on Socialism with Chinese Characteristics for a New Era . . . [to] actively organise student activities that have correct political direction, healthy character, refined contents and varied forms" (Tsinghua University 2021).

In January 2020, the Ministry of Education and the Communist Youth League categorized student groups into three types: Communist Youth League organizations, Student Union organizations, and student clubs and societies. Student clubs and societies are further classified into seven categories, including political-ideological organizations, academic and scientific organizations, startup business groups, culture and sports societies, volunteering and social service groups, multi-aid and self-discipline groups, and other miscellaneous student organizations. The state implemented differing levels and forms of control and surveillance over each category, yet on the whole, the presence and power of the Party-state and its agents in everyday associational life on the university campus became pervasive.

Everyday Management of Student Groups

Among the three main categories of student groups, the Student Union is the only officially endorsed association that represents the interests of the entire student body in university administration, academic instruction, and campus life; nevertheless, the Communist Youth League, staffed by full-time communist cadres with the assistance of the student cadre-dom, holds the most powerful place among the three. Given the CYL's political status as the youth arm of the Chinese Communist Party, CYL organizations are specifically entrusted by the Party-state with advising the official Student Union, managing student groups and societies, and overseeing all group activities taking place on campus.

The main universe of the campus associational space is a wide array of student societies, groups, associations, and clubs. Academically oriented, recreational, and friendship-based groups appear to be much more popular among university students in China today. According to a survey conducted in 1996, 80.53 percent of the active student groups in Chinese universities can be categorized as "apolitical," such as academic, recreational, and educational groups (Lv 2012, 90). The motivations behind students' participation in societies or groups on campus are often pragmatic. Compared with those in the Republican or Maoist period, or even the 1980s, student groups and societies in Chinese universities are more depoliticized, pragmatic, and compliant. Yet the Party-state, having learned a painful lesson from the June Fourth Movement, has remained on high alert nonetheless. The Communist Youth League and the Ministry of Education declared jointly in 2005 that "it is essential to make sure that politically false ideas and discourses . . . are not spread via activities held by university student groups and societies" (Central Committee of the Chinese Communist Youth League and the Ministry of Education 2005).

In 2020, the regulatory codes were made clearer. Another joint ordinance issued by the CYL and MoE that year stated that "all qualified student groups must . . . establish a provisional Communist Party Cell or CYL cell, presiding over political studies and discussion of the important issues within the respective groups." It also declared, "University Communist Party Committees shall implement periodic reviews of student organizations and groups . . . [those that] have followed a false political direction or organized illegal activities must be closed down."[2]

Based on these guidelines, a comprehensive regulatory infrastructure has been reinvented at Chinese universities to establish control of the associational spaces on campus. This national regulatory infrastructure also emphasizes preventing cross-institutional and cross-regional liaisons among student groups and societies, in particular the formation of any nationwide student alliance or movement. The devices regulating campus associational life are ubiquitous, woven into the fabric of the everyday collective lives of university students and throughout the campus public space.

The state's regulatory activities begin as soon as the creation of a new student group is proposed. For example, at Tsinghua University, to found a new student organization, a proposal in writing needs to go through a five-stage application process: (1) documentation submission and review, (2) internal hearing, (3) endorsement, (4) registration, and (5) certification of the group or society leader. Strict bureaucratic requirements are set for each stage. To take one example, the submission of documents requires a "detailed list containing the personal information of the proposers, the official opinion of the affiliated faculty-level Party Committee that serves as sponsor, and any additional materials to justify the founding of a new student society must be submitted." In the internal hearing stage, all of the proposers must be present to "fully answer any concerns the CYL reviewers may have." For the few lucky proposals that pass these stages, the proposers have to prepare four additional copies of the formal application forms, which have to be signed and stamped again by the sponsoring faculty-level Party Committees. The signature of a Party cadre who endorses this proposal is required for the formal application. Once the approval is obtained, the proposers are required to go through another equally long formal "registration" process to get the "red-cover registration permit" to officiate over their new student organization. Next, the president of the new student organization is required to contact the university's CYL Committee and complete a training and certification process to officially take up the responsibility of leading this newly founded student group. The treasurer of the new group is required to go through a similar training program operated by the CYL and obtain a certificate to be qualified for the responsibility (Department of Student Societies and Clubs of the CYL Committee of Tsinghua University 2006, 13–14). Existing student organizations have to pass an annual review and registration renewal process, and groups that are deemed politically problematic—let alone oppositional—are denied renewal. Some universities, such as Peking University, require student organizations to renew their registration at the beginning of each new semester—i.e., twice a year (Peking University Center for Extracurricular Activities 2015). In its regulatory activities in the campus public space, the Party-state does not hide its preference for recreational and apolitical student organizations over their political and ideological counterparts.

The CYL's management of the associational space on campus, on behalf of the Party-state, is facilitated by its monopoly on the distribution of campus resources, such as venues, information broadcasting platforms, and funding. Student groups rely on these resources to hold activities and operate. Almost universally across institutions of higher education in China, even a fully registered student group has to apply for separate approval each time it wishes to use some of these resources. Approvals are only granted on a case-by-case basis after a review of the contents, format, and potential audience of the suggested activities. At Peking University, the codes for regulating student organizations include detailed procedures for processing requests from student organizations to use classrooms, display boards, set up information kiosks, and receive financial reimbursements (Peking University Center for Extracurricular Activities 2015, 46–57).

Financial measures are also deployed to curtail the frequency and intensity of the activities of certain student organizations, or to censor student events that are disfavored. In this process, favoritism toward the politically loyal student groups can be pervasive, and the Party-state's perception of the nature of a particular student organization might also become a factor of consideration.

Taming the Ominous Danger

The state's everyday control over the campus associational space—via its youth work arm—is nearly total. Whereas the joint instructions of the Ministry of Education and the Communist Youth League in 2005 and 2020 only banned student group activities touching on "philosophy and social sciences" or opposed to the constitution and laws, in reality, the criteria used by the CYL at each university to regulate student organizations vary widely, but tend to be much stricter. When a student drama society wanted to stage an interesting new drama depicting the "informal rules" prevailing in Chinese society (from bribery to consensual adultery), the plan was immediately rejected by the CYL censors, citing political sensitivity and the threat to "moral standards." The effort of the CYL to "purify" (*jinghua*) the campus associational space from the threat of deviant political discourses reflects the Party-state's desire to curb the potential development of an antagonistic symbolic power or organizational influence among university students. As one student said, "when it comes to student groups and societies, the Party acts like a babysitter, based on a belief that university students are immature and not to be trusted. The paternalistic state has to watch you 24/7 to make sure the kids do not 'play with fire.'"[3]

A key area where the state has reestablished control over the associational space on university campus is the management of cross-institutional student collaboration and activities. The escalation of the Red Guards Movement in 1967, the spread of the Tiananmen Movement from Beijing to the provinces in 1989, the siege of the Zhongnanhai Compound (the headquarters of the Chinese Communist Party) by Falungong practitioners from all over China in 1999—these political incidents all resulted from national alliances of like-minded people. The communist regime has learned its lessons from this history. Student activities going beyond individual institutions tend to facilitate the formation of solidarity among university students, which can further become a rival supplier of authority and organized influence to the state. Concerned about the possibility of a new cross-sector alliance in the social sphere, the Party-state has strived to keep communication, connection, and collaboration between students at different institutions to a minimum. In the first decade of the twenty-first century, most provinces in China made rules restricting cross-institutional and cross-regional student collaboration and activities (Student Confederation of Beijing 2002).

Also, the Chinese state is particularly concerned that student groups may nurture close interpersonal bonds and thus a spirit of camaraderie among their members. The Mountaineering Association of Peking University (shan ying she), founded in April 1989, is one of the earliest and best-known nonofficial mountain-climbing clubs in China. Its members share a strong commitment to mountain climbing and have tightly knit social bonds that cross age groups. Members go through harsh training and exercise together, relying on seniors to provide training to the juniors. During mountain-climbing trips, members face fierce circumstances—sometimes even life-and-death tests. Strong solidarity networks, such as the one created by shan ying she, remain a point of concern for state agents. For shan ying she, even the secretary of the University Communist Party Committee—the top communist official of Peking University—regularly meets with its leaders and members over meals for updates on the organization. The Party-state's revived regulatory infrastructure exerts increasingly firm control over the associational space in Chinese universities. Through its domination of public space and financial resources and outright censorship of students' associational life, along with the more overt operation of the state signification project (see chapter 4), the Chinese Party-state has stymied student activism and patterned the student community's everyday rhythm through a highly disciplined, formal, covert, univocal set of activities that occupy a significant part of the timetable of university students. The unique scenario of a largely quiescent and compliant public space on Chinese university campuses contrasts sharply with places without such a rigid state control apparatus, such as universities in Taiwan, where the campus public sphere remains pluralistic, energetic, somewhat chaotic, but remarkably liberal. As one former student society leader from a prestigious national university of China commented:

> People try to stay away from politics and live a "normal" life that conforms to the preferences of state authorities. We do not have the room to think of things outside of this predefined mini-structure of student life. The public sphere on campus—particularly the student groups and societies—is a part of the extensive training camp operated by the Party and the State. Through the "socialisation" process in the form of a highly controlled associational space, university students are trained into a bunch of mini-bureaucrats-in-waiting for the regime, who mechanically seek approval, obey orders and do

not even think of questioning the rationale and justification for what they do. You know, the social environment makes the person.[4]

Disciplining the Virtual Space

Cyberspace—or "virtual public space"—in the university poses novel challenges. The internet was introduced to Chinese universities in approximately 1994, when an internal computer network was created to link the campus computers belonging to Peking University, Tsinghua University, and the Chinese Academy of Science, the three major institutions of higher learning in the country. This intranet was connected to the outside world by a 64K cable connection provided by Sprint, a United States telecommunications company (Cao 2012). With financial support from the Ministry of Education, this small interuniversity network was later expanded into a national internet infrastructure, CERNET, which connects all institutions of higher learning in China and links to the global internet via data-exchange hubs located in Hong Kong, Japan, Vietnam, and the United States. At the same time, commercial internet service providers entered some campuses and offered internet connections to the student community at competitive prices (China Internet Network Information Center [CNNIC] 2013, 18–19). The high-quality network infrastructure and internet-savvy populace on university campuses provide an ideal environment for an alternative public sphere to bloom, which soon replaced traditional spaces for everyday community activities and became the primary part of the everyday public space on campus.

Due to its pervasiveness, anonymity, and instantaneity, the virtual public space on the internet is a relatively free space, providing a gateway to liberal and Western discourses, ideologies, and historiography. The internet also provides students with a cheap, private, and fast means of communication, facilitating information flow within the student community. The availability of user-friendly instant messaging services to the student populace not only enhanced interpersonal bonds but helped develop new connective structures—whether extended friend circles (*peng you quan*) or intimate groups of like-minded students who would have remained strangers prior to the internet age. The group chat feature of these messaging platforms and other readily available social media networks—such as Weibo (the Chinese version of Twitter)—has given students an effective means to forge group-based solidarity.

The perceived threat of the virtual public space in the university also comes from the fact that it gives marginalized students a platform for publishing political opinions challenging the orthodoxy of the state. The university public space can easily become a birthplace, or (worse), a national hub, for dissenting ideas, as discourses can be transmitted through the national intellectual network to the outside and override institutional barriers. For anyone who wants to initiate discussion of a topic that is politically sensitive, embarrassing, scandalous, or otherwise controversial—simply put, anything that the Party would not want to include in the country's prime-time news broadcasting—the university campus has always been the best starting point for larger-scale communication.

Fully acknowledging the mobilizing potential of the internet, the Party-state has continuously revised and redeveloped a novel regulatory infrastructure to keep its control over the campus virtual public space. As early as July 2004, the Central Committee of the Communist Party and the State Council called for more attention to the control and regulation of campus networks in a joint document entitled "A Few Opinions on the Further Enhancement and Improvement of Thought and Political Education among University Students" (hereafter Document No. 16).[5] This document required that all university Communist Party committees "proactively occupy the new frontline of online thought and political education." More specifically, the leadership stated that such a mission had to be completed along two lines. First, the Party organizations in the higher-education sector must learn to use the internet as an instrument for the ideological indoctrination and political education of younger age-cohorts. For that purpose, university leaders all over China were required to create a series of "red" websites that were correct in political orientation, rich in information, and fun and helpful to university students. Second, the instruction declared that "all necessary technological, administrative and legal measures should be adopted to strengthen control over the campus computer network, preventing harmful information from being spread via the Internet." To secure the purity of the campus internet, university authorities, the document advised, should organize a team of staff members in charge of "online thought and political education," and a mechanism should be established to regulate the virtual public space on campus. Overall, Document No. 16 sent a clear signal to communist cadres nationwide that the Party must "secure a firm grip over any initiative" in cyberspace by putting a strong regulatory infrastructure in place (Ministry of Education and the Central Committee of the Chinese Communist Youth League 2016).

The ministerial instructions issued subsequently clarified the measures of control that must be put into place to discipline the cyber public space on campus. University administrations were required to take responsibility for three major areas: online ideological education, public opinion guidance (*yulunyindao*), and information censorship.[6] For all three areas, a durable technological infrastructure is essential, but it also relies on a clear division of labor.

To manage the university cyberspace, the university administration relies on an advanced surveillance infrastructure. Chinese universities are linked to the "Great Firewall" at the national level, and have also established their own firewalls that block and censor politically harmful information. This infrastructure varies across institutions but usually includes five major components. First, access to "harmful" websites that have a static internet address is blocked. Second, the universities screen data packets that travel through the campus network with a dynamic list of harmful keywords identified by state regulators—whenever a data packet containing a specific keyword is transmitted through the campus network, it is blocked and registered at the root server. Third, domain-name hijacking is applied at the root level of the domain name system of campus computer networks, misdirecting efforts to access a "harmful" domain name to a wrong address from the list of permitted websites or to a blank page. Fourth, network content is screened and censored: whenever users attempt to publish information to the campus network (whether a conversation in a virtual chat room or a longer post in an online forum), the system automatically checks it against a list of banned content and decides whether to let it go through. Fifth, monitoring software is installed on any computer registered on the campus network, which records and monitors all activities and information flow occurring on that computer (Cao 2012, 172–73). In addition to the technological firewall, the university also manually censors online forums through an internet management center—the campus equivalent of "cyberpolice" that is staffed by Party officials and student activists.

On top of these defensive controlling measures, the state undertakes more aggressive steps to control campus virtual space, including authentication of online identity, mechanisms for instant censorship, and more proactive "opinion guiding." The first major step was the implementation of a system of identity authentication (*shi ming zhi*) for bulletin-board systems, online forums, comment sections, etc., on campus computer networks. Access was restricted to computers properly registered on the campus computer network, which also needed authentication of the university affiliation—a measure excluding members of the general public, including alumni. Notwithstanding a brief outcry from a small number of frequent users, the new system was steadily rolled out, first at Tsinghua University and Peking University and then throughout China after 2005 (Chen, Cheng, and Li 2005).[7] As a deterrence mechanism, universities also issued codes and rules for disciplinary sanctions against antiregime or politically incorrect conduct in the virtual public space on university campuses.

The state's decision to take away the anonymity previously enjoyed by campus network users was decisive. Identity authentication kept most university students away from alternative, deviant, oppositional, or rebellious public debate and discussion in the campus virtual public space. However, a side effect was that the newly installed system led some students to turn away from the virtual public space built on the campus internet infrastructure and to look for an online space outside of the university. Other students simply indulged in the consumption of online entertainment information or gaming. This trend can be seen in the sharp decline of the popularity of campus bulletin-board systems as a virtual public sphere after the implementation of the identity authentication system. Figures 10 and 11 demonstrate the decline of the campus bulletin-board systems of Peking University after the state established control over the campus virtual space: they show a sharply diminished number of posts, decreased number of visits, and significantly shortened average time of each visit (Feng, Qian, and Pan 2012).

To secure influence over everyday campus life, university Party authorities were also ordered to actively shape the discursive landscape formed in the virtual public space on campus. Operations on two fronts are involved: "opinion guiding" (*yulun yindao*) and the construction of "red websites" (*hongse wangzhan*). The ministerial guidance of 2005 demanded that institutions of higher education "properly guide public opinion in that virtual space." University Party committees were instructed to "establish a team of 'online commentators' who are politically loyal, knowledgeable, plentiful and familiar with the style and form of online language." This corps of online commentators (*wangshang pinglunyuan*) must proactively "write online posts concerning hot discussion topics," "attract university students to click and respond to their messages," and "effectively guide and shape public opinion in the campus virtual space."[8] University leadership was directed to "enrich the contents of online propaganda" and consolidate the "domination of positive discursive power in cyberspace."[9] "Opinion guiding," as an everyday operation of the state's regulatory infrastructure, carves out a compliant discursive landscape to the state's liking beyond outright censorship. "Online commentators" initiated new discussion threads by order of the Party, responded to existing discussions along official lines, and reported to the authorities any inappropriate comments made by their peer

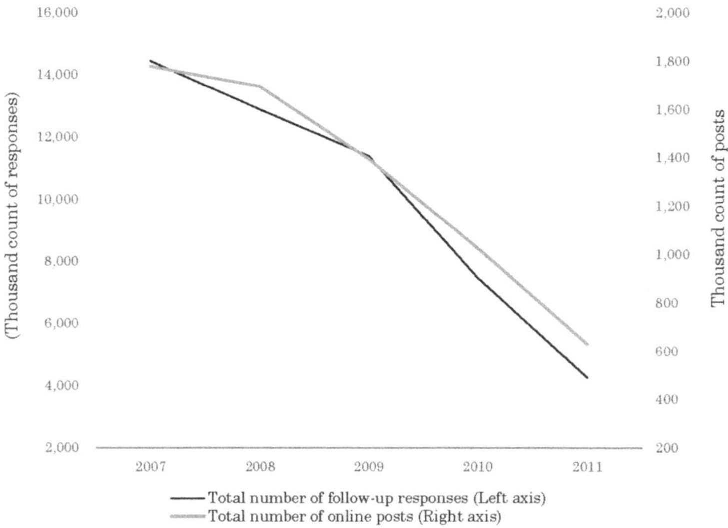

Figure 10. The number of online messages and follow-up responses posted on the Peking University BBS.

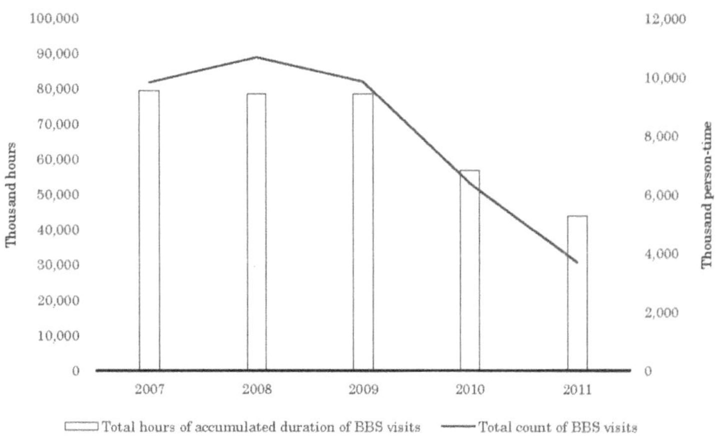

Figure 11. The total count of forum visits and total hours of accumulated duration of visits to the Peking University campus BBS.

users. The activities of hand-picked, state-paid "online commentators"—dubbed the "50-cents army"[10] by Chinese netizens—reflect the state's willingness to not only firmly control but also systematically tailor the virtual public sphere. One former student cadre from Peking University described the impact of the campus "50-cent army":

> Quite a few of my friends were recruited by the university's Propaganda Department to do this job. This kind of operation had some real effect—when a hot political issue emerged, without the "50-cents army," most of the responses might be negative and critical toward the government; but when the online commentators kicked in and wrote tons of responses, suddenly 9 out of 10 responses to that same thread would be positive, pro-state and consistent with the official line. More often than not, students who were originally involved in the discussion would just let it go in light of so many pacifying messages. And the community's attention to that particular issue is successfully diluted by such operations, to the Party's advantage.[11]

In addition, university authorities are instructed to promote political education online, primarily in the form of "red websites." After 2005, under the auspices of the central and municipal Party-state, a series of "red websites" was created on the campus network across China.[12] Despite their various names, these "red" websites disseminate the Communist Party's propaganda on all emerging issues and publish information for group political study.

The Chinese state has not neglected the role of the campus internet connection as a cheap and instantaneous means of interpersonal communication. With the rapid advance of group communication mobile platforms, chat groups of like-minded students and friend circles sprouted up everywhere. Responding to this new development, surveillance of all instant communication taking place on the campus network is conducted daily. To weave the instrument of control into everyday communicative experiences, the university authorities also implement manual monitoring, restrict certain interactive capacities of the campus network, and collaborate with law enforcement agencies to monitor outbound links from the campus network to the public internet outside the campus walls.

Due to the rapid development of the internet in China, virtual space has shifted on the university campus from a marginal terrain mainly for personal enrichment to a battlefield where the state competes with rival suppliers of cultures, ideologies, discourses, and organizational forces for influence over the everyday experiences of university students, struggling against numerous forces emanating from the broader processes of marketization, globalization, and culture wars. Instruments provided by the virtual public space significantly increased the capacity of the student community for public deliberation, interpersonal communication, and communal bonding. The advance of new information technologies, the growing availability of mobile devices, and the constant development of the network infrastructure facilitated the formation of new group identities and solidarities and the mobilization of a future student movement. Learning from the past, the Chinese Party-state has decisively strengthened its regulatory infrastructure over the virtual public space on university campuses.

Relying on advanced firewalls and a corps of censors on the public payroll, the state has established a defensive network of monitoring and censorship that screens out politically "harmful" information and filters out alternative political rhetoric, historiography, or ideologies, ostensibly defending the virtual sphere from the invasion of foreign, antiregime, or agitating content. The censorship system has been further strengthened by self-censorship by end users, due to the online identity authentication mechanism and a strict set of disciplinary rules punishing online offences. The second line of defense in the virtual public space is the construction of the "red websites" that disseminate official political information and the activities of state-paid "online commentators" who shape the discursive landscape in the virtual domain to the liking of the state. The third line of defense specifically targets the communicative features of the campus virtual space. In addition to having a monopoly over the interactive functions of the campus computer network, university authorities work closely with state law-enforcement agencies to monitor antiregime communications that virtually link the university and hidden oppositional forces in society at large. As in other fields, this regulatory infrastructure is ingrained into the fabric of students' experiences in the campus virtual space, and it ensures the state's ultimate dominance over this virtual public space.

Fighting the Spiritual

Philip L. Wickeri, an American researcher of Christianity in China, argued in 2011 that "public life is a contested space in China today, and religion has a growing importance within that space" (2011, 5). Following the fading of internationalist utopian ideology, the post-Mao Communist Party-state gradually adjusted its policies toward religious practice in mainland China in the direction of tolerance. The deepening of market reforms and the rapid accumulation of wealth provided new dynamism for the revival of religion in public space in China.[13] This resurgence naturally facilitated an increased exposure of university students to various religious practices, from traditional Buddhist liturgies to gatherings of Baha'i followers. Steadily, newly restored religious organizations, practices, and influence reached the seclusion of the ivory tower.

Although national statistics are not made public, various scholars in China have estimated the number of students on Chinese university campuses who are religious believers. For example, in a 2006 survey of 11,000 university students from eight universities located in northeastern China, Yang Xiaohui—then deputy party secretary and vice president of Northeastern Normal University—reported that 18.7 percent of the surveyed students were believers or had attempted to acquire religious belief (Yang 2006, 19). In a 2011 survey carried out in five universities in Shandong Province, researchers found that 14.11 percent of the surveyed students claimed to be believers and 16.78 percent were "not sure" (Zhang et al. 2011, 84). Another survey conducted at five major universities in Fujian Province in 2012 reported that 30.98 percent of the surveyed students claimed to have at least one religious belief (Liao and Xie 2012). Researchers from Hubei and Hunan Provinces reported that 14.4 percent and 15.08 percent of surveyed students claimed to be believers, respectively (Zhang 2012; Jia and Zhou 2012). A survey conducted among financially disadvantaged university students reported a much higher percentage of religious belief—44 percent of the surveyed students claimed to be believers (Zhu 2006, 30). Depending on the definition of "religious belief" and the method of sampling, the statistics from different localities vary; nevertheless, these numbers provide a rough sketch of the overall landscape of the influence of religion on campus public space today.

Religion is a natural enemy for any atheist political regime that seeks to monopolize the public sphere—whatever the repercussions. The mere "contamination" of students' minds and hearts by religion is a menace to the state's signification project, competing not only with the state's political rhetoric but also its efforts to structure their life experiences. More fundamentally, organized religion and the community identity it creates endanger the regime's efforts to reinvent the political order. The many students who identify with established—or worse, underground—religions have the potential for mobilization beyond the reach of the state.

For the state, links between religious students and underground religious fellowships—ranging from those within the "gray area" of the law (such as the "House Churches of China") to outright illegality (such as "Eastern Lightning")—is particularly disturbing. Ethnographic studies conducted by scholars of China have revealed the extensive networks linking the student populace and the secretive universe of illegal or quasilegal religious communities in Chinese universities. For example, in Beijing, Christian students forged a covert fellowship through regular participation in activities organized by the underground "meeting points" (*juhui dian*) on university campuses. The size of these meeting points varies from seven or eight persons to as many as thirty student believers. Often led by foreign students, teachers, or professionals residing in Beijing, participants in these underground Christian fellowships gather to study the Bible and share biblical testimonials. They also hold an array of activities—from potlucks to field trips—to develop friendship and religious community. These secretive Christian fellowships, often supported by the semiunderground House Churches of China, also have a snowball effect. Regular student participants in the secret meeting points introduce friends and classmates to them; some subsequently choose to be baptized (Zuo 2009; Xie 2010b).

Ideologically, religion posed an even graver threat to the Party's worldview, value system, and philosophy (Laliberte 2011). As a regime governed by a Marxist party, the post-Mao Party-state still sticks firmly to its ideological foundation of dialectical materialism; in fact, with the decline in the Party's more internationalist and utopian revolutionary ideology, atheism has become a crucial defining feature and shared "spiritual" identity of the rank-and-file members of the Party itself. The increased influence of religious beliefs on the university campus could compromise the philosophical legitimacy of the regime. For example, a survey conducted in Hunan Province showed that 40.3 percent of the surveyed university students completely misunderstood the Party's atheist nature by responding "true" to the statement "Even believers of a religion can join the Communist Party" (Liu and Liang 2007, 116). A later survey carried out in Fujian Province revealed that 35.59 percent of the university students surveyed did not know that "Communist Party members or Communist Youth League members should not believe in any religion." The surveyors observed that "this testified to the fact that quite a few students were only aware of the Party-state's 'religious freedom' policy but [were] ignorant of the customary rule that believers of Marxism must first be an atheist." They concluded that many university students were completely unaware of the ideology of the Communist Party, which requires that "party members should completely oppose the practice of any religious belief" (Zhou 2013, 62).

In its efforts to reinvent order and rebuild a regulatory infrastructure that shapes the campus public space, the Party-state has remained vigilant against the spread of religion among university students. Despite the increased freedom of religious practice outside university walls, the Chinese state still prohibits religious observations and connections in the ivory tower. There has also been a shift of attitude: compared to the Maoist period or even the 1980s, the Party-state has focused less on individuals' voluntary rejection of religious spirituality through atheist education, and instead insisted on mechanical compliance with the government's complete ban on public and organized practice of religion in all institutions of higher education.

The state especially attempts to prevent the growth of underground religious networks attended by university students. A particular focus is their ties with the international religious community. A research report authored by security officials from Chongqing University investigated the underground Christian advocacy network operating on Chongqing University campuses. The report found that due to China's reform and opening up to the West, and the globalization of world culture, Western Christian organizations have penetrated institutions of higher education in China; it warned that Western political organizations might take advantage of the campus Christian network to influence Chinese universities. The report asserted, "foreign religious organizations have devoted much effort to entering border regions, coastal areas and prestigious national universities—among these, universities are the most important area of their endeavours" (Luo et al. 2010, 70).

The campus religious network in China features multiple communication channels, secret interpersonal bonds, and strong ties with international religious organizations. Research conducted in universities in northeastern China showed that, despite the state-enforced prohibition of religious practices on campus, 27.78 percent of the students surveyed had received proselytizing materials in school and 77.66 percent had been preached at by religious advocates at least occasionally (Yang 2006). Take Christianity as an example. Researchers in China found that to reach out to nonbelievers, first, underground Christian proselytizing on university campuses usually relied on a multiplicity of communicative means, such as face-to-face conversation, radio broadcasting, printed materials, telemarketing, and internet platforms. Second, Christian proselytizing within the student community mostly relied on a secretive interpersonal network. According to the security officials of Chongqing University, religious advocates on campus often "hide behind" the disguise of ordinary professions, such as exchange student, language instructor, or visiting professor. They also found that Christians on campus often communicated in a "coded"[14] manner that was very difficult for people outside the network to interpret. Third, they noted that many proselytizers on Chinese university campuses were covert missionaries dispatched by international religious societies. Their activities posed a grave threat to the Party-state, because these covert missionaries were sophisticated in spreading religious belief through interpersonal networks, discreetly establishing organizational structures, and converting university students (Luo et al. 2010, 70–71).

Such perceptions of the danger of religious influence were pervasive and consequential after 1989, amid the Party-state's endeavors to rebuild order and control. To defend the university campus from this threat, the state put in place a series of measures against not only organized religions per se, but theism in general, superstition, and belief in the supernatural. Overall, political education that discredited religious belief and practice—particularly targeting antiregime sects such as Falungong—was strengthened to an unprecedented level in institutions of higher learning across China. Education in "core socialist values" was also promoted by the Party-state against the potential spread of religion on university campuses.

In provincial districts with a higher concentration of ethnic minorities with their own religion, state-sponsored education on "scientific atheism" is added to the standardized political education curriculum designed for the local university students. For example, since 2002, all institutions of higher education in Xinjiang—the autonomous region of Uighurs in northwestern China—must offer compulsory courses on scientific atheism (*kexue wushen lun*) to students from all ethnic backgrounds. The local Party-state explained the rationale behind the measure: "learning scientific knowledge per se cannot substitute for education in the Marxist concept of religion." The course on "scientific atheism" focuses on the Marxist view of religion as the opium of the people, dialectical materialism, the official distinction between religion and superstition, and the differences between religion and "evil cults" (*xie jiao*). The purpose of this mandatory curriculum—a comprehensive critique of spirituality at large—is to "guide the students into establishing a worldview based on scientific atheism and . . . thus achieve the ultimate goal of resisting . . . the infringement of the evil religions on university campuses" (Li and Ye 2008).

The Chinese state has also deployed different means to limit the rising influence of open or underground religion on university students. A research report, sponsored by the Ministry of Education and the Municipal Communist Party's Higher Education Committee of Beijing, argued that it is essential to "guide every university student into a true understanding of the authentic nature of religion and . . . make them willingly stand on the side of science and rationality" (Zuo 2009, 9). A study sponsored by the National Association of Higher Education of China claimed that 31 percent of the surveyed students who were believers converted from atheism due to "unresolvable psychological problems" (Zhou 2013, 62). To prevent more students from being converted, it was suggested that mental-health monitoring and counseling could reduce "loneliness" and "helplessness" among young university students, mitigating the driving force behind their search for spiritual comfort from religion (Hua 2010, 80).

For the order-seeking state, the associational space occupied by university students is a potential field for the spread of religious belief, and it needs specific regulatory arrangement. One of the most important criteria used by Communist Party authorities and state law-enforcement agencies in scrutinizing student groups and societies is whether a religious component is included in any of their activities. This is seen as a taboo that no student group in China should touch. Security agencies across China are also ordered to monitor activities organized or encouraged by the unofficial Christian churches on the university campus; legal sanctions are applied if the churches are found to be preaching to—or worse, converting—nonbeliever university students. In particular, the ties between underground or illegal religious associations and on-campus student groups are carefully watched by state law-enforcement agencies. University security officials must closely monitor the activities of foreign teachers and students, striving to cut off their connections with the Chinese student community to discourage potential missionary activities. To attain these goals, as one author wrote, "it is crucial to strengthen the investigative and detective work (at the grassroots) and let student party members, student cadres and political counsellors play their role in garnering and reporting information on illegal religious activities as early and effectively as possible" (Su 2009). The regime has clearly realized that its fate depends to a great extent on its ability to win on this smokeless battlefield.

Creating an Institutional Culture

Born out of an Enlightenment ideal of liberty, happiness, and the free pursuit of knowledge, universities in China have long been deemed "islands of freedom" that preserve for the nation a culture of critical thinking, a desire for the exploration of truth, and a deeply ingrained liberal idealism that goes beyond the domains of immediate regime control, inspiring in the younger generation a yearning for the betterment of the state and society. The liberal university campus is an ideal breeding ground for an oppositional intelligentsia, a parallel authority and an autonomous social space beyond the reach of state control. The unique institutional culture of the university makes it a danger zone in the eyes of the reinvented Chinese state.

The state's way to mitigate this danger of the university is to create an institutional culture that differs substantially from the ideal model. After all, institutional culture characterizes the public discourse taking place within its borders, molding individual and collective political behavior and framing social norms and moral standards. Dictating the formation of the institutional culture on university campuses improves the political atmosphere, resets behavioral codes, and shapes public opinion to the advantage of the state. Eventually, a state-sponsored institutional culture that divorces universities from liberal idealism and produces an alternate set of cultural norms and standards can facilitate the state's endeavor to secure its hold over the social space of the university without deploying outright violence or coercion.

Thus, the Chinese Party-state has increasingly attempted to construct a "positive" campus culture in institutions of higher education. The 2004 joint guidance issued by the Ministry of Education and the Central Committee of the Communist Youth League emphasized that the "campus culture of institutions of higher learning is an essential part in the advanced cultural component of socialism. The strengthening of the construction of campus culture is a crucial mission . . . for the enhancement and improvement of our thought and political education work with the university student populace."[15]

In this new institutional culture of the university, one feature has become prominent: pragmatic careerism. The institutional culture overwhelmingly emphasizes students' career prospects throughout the educational experience, at the cost of developing the student's values, such as liberalism, idealism, or spirituality. The flourishing of careerism in Chinese universities since the 1990s was a natural consequence of the overall market transition and the fading away of the internationalist utopian ideology of the Maoist past or the ardent appreciation of Western liberalism in the 1980s. It was also a result of the regime's institutional arrangements and encouragement of careerist sentiment among university students. Pragmatic careerism shifted students' attention from the abstract discourses of individuality, liberty, and democracy in the 1980s to an embrace of technical know-how, economic gain, accumulating personal wealth, and satisfying hedonistic desires (Ci 1994). In 2010, 5,754,245 undergraduate students graduated from Chinese universities; among them, 4,095,814 (71 percent) majored in science, engineering, agriculture, medicine, or managerial science. In 2019, 7,585,298 undergraduate students graduated; among them, 5,482,209 (or 72.27 percent) majored in science, engineering, agriculture, medicine, or managerial science. The choice of major for most Chinese students also reflected this cultural turn toward pragmatic careerism in the Chinese university.

New institutional changes added to the growth of careerist culture on the Chinese university campus. Abolishing the state-controlled "job-assignment" system of the socialist past robbed university graduates of job security and forced them into the fierce competition of a free labor market. Not so much an ivory tower from which the intelligentsia could criticize political authorities, Chinese universities since the 1990s have become the major supplier of manpower for the country's booming market economy—in collaboration with pervasive global capitalism. The Party-state's decision in 1999 to significantly expand the higher-education sector and increase the number of admissions to colleges and universities across China further diluted the old identity of university students as "elites-in-waiting" whose traditional duty was the betterment of national politics, even at the cost of personal sacrifice.[16] With the transformation from an "elite" to a "mass" higher education, Chinese students—no longer the "favoured sons of Heaven" (*tian zhi jiaozi*)—now had to endure intense insecurity, self-doubt, and anxiety about their future career and life opportunities.[17] Owing to these multiple pressures, it is only natural that many Chinese students chose to join not China's critical intelligentsia, but instead the much more politically apathetic and compliant professional working class. This new identity shift—from presumptive elites of the nation to "professionals-in-waiting" within a modern labor force—has had a continuing impact on Chinese politics.

Conclusion

The campus public space—in theory "a specifically political space distinct from the state and the economy, an institutionally bounded discursive arena that is home to citizen debate, deliberation, agreement and action" (Villa 1992, 712)—has thus become a major battlefield for the Chinese state to compete with alternative authorities, parallel discourses, or powerful social hierarchies for control over the university as a critical social space and university students as a critical social group. After all, a consensus-based public realm, driven only by the "unforced force" of the better argument, is against all of the principles of the reinvented state (Mendieta and Vanantwerpen 2011, 3).

In Chinese universities, after the 1989 student movement, the Party-state relentlessly reinvents a powerful regulatory infrastructure to maintain its control over the associational, virtual, and spiritual realms of the university community, and to forge on university campuses a distinct institutional culture that is apolitical, careerist, and cynical. By doing so, the state struggled to ensure lasting compliance from the student populace, and stability—or rather quiescence—across the higher-education sector. This systematic project of reinventing the political order and reestablishing control represented the reinvented state's renewed effort to subjugate the critical social space through regulating and structuring the rhythm of the everyday associational life and communal experiences of members of critical social groups. Only history will tell where this state project will lead China or whether it will eventually backfire; but at least for the moment, it has secured the quiescence of the nation's vast social group of educated youth and tamped down the most rebellious and fragmented space in the country's political landscape.

FIVE

Nurturing Compliance

The Incentivization Infrastructure

We are all just prisoners here, of our own device.
   —"Hotel California," the Eagles, 1977

A country that was hurrying into the future required colleges that
would hurry along with it.
   —Frederick Rudolph, *The American College and University:
   A History*, 1962, 110

Incentivization Infrastructure

"Discipline and compliance," wrote Andrew G. Walder in 1995, "where
they occur, must be explained" (7). The reinvention of a political order
has been no easy undertaking for the state; "one cannot simply assume
disciplined and cohesive state apparatus, just as one cannot simply assume a
compliant citizenry" (7). For the state, cultivating and sustaining a capable
and justifiable political order portends regulating the rhythm of everyday
experiences of the citizenry; to achieve that, the state has to make the effort
to shape and mold its citizens' behavioral and discursive pattern at the individual level. This entails reconstructing and deploying a revamped incentivization infrastructure by which the state can compensate compliance,
reward loyalty, punish defiance, deter away potential resistance, and keep
a close eye on the lively occurrences within the critical social space that it
seeks to control.

In this book, these contrivances and activities undertaken by the state to generate incentives for conformity, mete out punishment for trespassing, and maintain a surveillance system to measure and enforce compliance are termed the "incentivization infrastructure." The rewarding instruments create positive enticements that encourage compliance, whereas the punishment devices create negative sanctions on defiance and deter potential challengers to the state. When linked to rewards and penalties, monitoring and surveillance mechanisms ensure that the incentivization infrastructure is effective. The incentivization infrastructure serves as an institutional architecture, a cognitive lens, and a symbolic frame that shape speech and actions at the individual level, bolstering the state's internal cohesiveness and strengthening the capacity of the reinvented order.

"Institutions rest upon credible promises, of either reward or punishment" (Bates et al. 1998, 5). For a state striving to reestablish its domination on university campuses, success in manufacturing such an infrastructure is imperative. With older methods of mobilizational control withering in the new political atmosphere, the state has embraced more pragmatic means to produce incentives for compliance and secure loyalty among the nation's educated youth. Supported by the state's inherited as well as newly established command over various economic, social, political, and symbolic resources, these baseline "safety-net" arrangements to ensure acquiescence at the individual level overwhelmingly focus on the exchange of benefits, gifts, and privileges for those who display political compliance or loyalty, illustrating a salient pragmatic, quotidian, and normalized nature.

Rewarding Loyalty

To effectively shape the behavioral space at the individual level, positive incentives are an important vehicle for rulers looking to exert control over their subjects. Compared to threats or coercion, positive rewards supply more information about "what kind of behaviour is preferred" by the state (Milburn and Christie 1989, 626). Political rewards facilitate governance and simplify state control. First, positive incentives increase the opportunity cost of outright defiance and motivate a rational person to side with the state. Second, rewards dispensed in a hierarchical structure may enhance internal competition between loyal subjects and thus create peer pressure and an atmosphere of loyalty to the state. Third, rewards enable the state to establish an explicit set of norms for preferred discourse and behaviors. Rewards "often produce more predictable actions and outcomes, which are helpful for co-operation and improved relations" (Milburn and Christie 1989, 626). A carefully designed, hierarchically subdivided, and systematically enforced structure of positive incentives is a powerful weapon with which the reinvented Chinese state can create, preserve, and administer its desired political order.

States hand out perks of all kinds in a stratified structure to entice passivity and encourage compliance. The lines dividing the tiers are not always clear; however, the highest tier of positive incentives given by the state is nearly always membership in the ruling coalition. This elite membership is reserved largely for the state's most trusted subjects whose loyalty has been consistently proved and who are considered role models for their peers. Granting membership to the ruling elites is a process of both absorption and expansion, where the boundaries of the establishment are broadened as new blood is inducted into the ruling coalition.

The second tier of positive incentives is preferential advantages. To allocate scarce resources, states always set up informal procedures that operate in parallel with formal mechanisms. These secondary channels for valuable resources (which include but are not limited to materialistic resources, symbolic capital, or administrative permits) are relatively easier to navigate and less competitive than formal channels, but operate at the absolute discretion of the regime. With full control of access to such channels, the state can reward its favorite subjects and nurture in them a sense of identification with the political regime.

The third tier of rewards is earmarked opportunities. In addition to parallel and secondary channels for dispensing scarce resources, a state might set aside valuable political, economic, cultural, and careerist opportunities, making them available only to the state's handpicked loyalists.

The fourth tier, direct material benefits, is cash or other material benefits directly given to selected subjects. In contrast to the other tiers of positive incentives, direct material awards are one-off and do not have long-term effects on the recipient's career advancement or political status. The regime usually uses such benefits to reward those who are politically passive yet compliant but have demonstrated outstanding professional capability. Together, these four tiers of rewards constitute a hierarchical framework of positive incentives that regimes may use to enhance the link between the targeted social group and the political regime.

An important component of this incentivization infrastructure that is associated with all four tiers of rewards is metaphysical gratification (in Chinese, *jingshen jiangli*). Metaphysical gratification associated with receiving positive incentives from the state occurs on several fronts. First, by being among the small number of selected receivers of state rewards, recipients naturally feel a sense of satisfaction and pride among their peers. When such rewards are accompanied by a public ceremony, commemoration, or ritual of conferral, recipients' psychological fulfilment will be even greater. This is an important way for the regime to provide psychological welfare to its favored subjects. Second, rewards may nurture in recipients a sense of intimate access to a sovereign power and of being favorably connected to the establishment, which increases their identification with the ruling clique. Third, the sense of being included among the ruling elites of a state could easily lead reward recipients to develop a sense of empowerment, and some may feel a sense of obligation to the state even though they are not actually members of the *nomenklatura*. An overhauled incentivization infrastructure is a central component of the new edifice of control the post-Tiananmen Chinese state has sought to reestablish on university campuses.

Communist Party Membership

Communist Party membership is one of the greatest positive incentives that the regime can dispense to its most loyal followers on university campuses. As the Party is the dominant political authority, Party membership has been widely considered to be a ticket to join the ruling elite. The long-term benefits, privileges, and advantages of Party membership for career advancement are among the more attractive incentives for the state to garner support and followers among the nation's educated youth. However, being "an elite-dominated Leninist party" (Guo 2005, 372), the Party only offers membership to a limited number of university students. According to the Central Organisational Department of the CCP, Communist Party members accounted for about 7.33 percent of China's university student population in 2021.[1] The positive incentives associated with Party membership make identification with the ruling regime profitable and desirable for common students. The long-term prospects of becoming a part of the powerful establishment equipped with overarching power also strengthen student Party members' loyalty to and belief in the state.

More than other forms of reward, Party membership can have lifelong effects on students' career advancement and social status. Communist Party membership is required for many positions within the state apparatus and is preferred for other official posts. Despite its gradual transformation from a Soviet-style cadre system to a modernized civil service, the Communist Party has held firmly to the enshrined political principle of the "Party managing cadres" (*dangguan ganbu*), meaning that Party committees at all levels have the sole power to make decisions on personnel matters in the public sector. The Party has thus maintained its monopoly over the selection of entry-level Party officials and civil servants from university graduates. Since the 1990s, the Central Organisation Department of the CCP has made it clear that "some civil service posts may be held only by Party members" (Burns and Wang 2010, 62). Notwithstanding the thinner spread of the Party apparatus at the local level, sensitive positions in most civil servant–employing agencies remain "limited to Party members, including positions in personnel management, confidential document handling, investigations handling, Party work and sometimes financial administration" (Burns and Wang 2010, 62–63). The institutionalized preferential treatment of student Party members for junior positions in the state at all levels includes an array of political privileges that the Party provides to its junior rank-and-file student members, further enhancing their sense of elitism—and even of being "indulged"—in their everyday experiences on campus.

Even for opportunities for which Party membership is not required, such as trainee cadre membership, the majority of students understand that most Party and state agencies give priority to applicants who are Party members. As Gang Guo observed, "to prospective government employers, Party membership is a sure indication of a student's political reliability" (Guo 2005, 387). According to the student interviewees, student Party members also enjoy significant advantages when they compete for employment at lucrative state-owned enterprises (SOEs). With China's progress in market reform and the revival of traditional SOEs since the late 1990s, employment opportunities provided by these giant global corporations have become highly sought after by many Chinese university graduates. According to Xinhua News Agency, by the end of 2011, there were 144,700 SOEs with total assets valued at 85.4 trillion yuan, revenues of 39.25 trillion yuan, and profits of 2.6 trillion yuan (which accounted for 43 percent of China's total industrial and business profit) (Xinhua News Agency 2012). Since then, SOEs have become an even more profitable sector of the Chinese economy. Jobs with centrally controlled SOEs (*yangqi*)—primarily "those SOEs directly controlled by the State-Owned Assets Supervision and Administration Committee (SASAC), national banks and financial corporations, and 'media, publications, culture and entertainment companies' administered by central state agencies—were even more appealing to university graduates" (Cary 2013). In a 2009 survey conducted by the Municipal Statistics Bureau of graduating university students in Tianjin on their employment preferences, 70.5 percent of the respondents placed SOEs as their first choice (Statistics Bureau of Tianjin 2009). Thus, not only have SOEs become a crucial source of revenue for the state, but employment opportunities with SOEs have become important positive incentives to nurture and reward political loyalty among educated youth. Document 37, issued jointly by SASAC and the Ministry of Education in 2013, explicitly required SOEs at all levels to treat the recruitment of university graduates as an important way for these enterprises to fulfil their social responsibility to preserve the overall political stability of the country and to implement the political lines of the Communist Party (Ministry of Education 2013).

As the revenue-generating arm of the state apparatus, central and municipal SOEs deliberatively give priority to Communist Party members when recruiting new employees. For example, the state's mouthpiece, the *People's Daily*, reported that at the 2013 SOE job fair for university graduates in Tianjin, "various big corporations used Communist Party membership as a criterion in vetting job applications" (Zhu and Zheng 2012). In Zhejiang Province, a special job fair was held exclusively for student Party members, at which about 1,000 applicants competed for more than 900 job vacancies, a much easier competition than the normal job fair for students who were not Party members (Fang and Liu 2013). The advantages enjoyed by Communist Party members in career opportunities with SOEs are widely known to members of the university community. As one student said, "If you want to find a job in any place that is controlled by the state, membership of the Communist Party is certainly an incomparable advantage."[2] Given the rising unemployment rates and expanding university enrollment, the preferential treatment given to student Party members is widely envied. Andrew G. Walder analyzed a 1986 survey conducted in Tianjin and found that in combination with the educational credentials of a college degree, Party membership "leads to administrative posts with high prestige, considerable authority and clear material privileges" in the long run (Walder 1995, 309). This phenomenon has continued in the new century.

On top of future benefits, university Party organizations across China also deem it important to reward student Party members with privileges in their everyday campus lives. Reporting on Shandong University of Technology's efforts to consolidate political loyalty among student Party members, the university's official newspaper stated,

While [the university Party organizations] should certainly place high expectations and strict requirements on [our student Party members], we also listen carefully to their practical needs. . . . (The

Party) must help her student members to overcome personal difficulties, strengthen their belief, facilitate their efforts in making progress and ensure that they become talented people. Education and care have to be combined together—we must let student Party members feel deeply the care and warmth of their Party organisation. And through care and attention paid to them on all the aspects, we should strive to enhance their firm pursuit to the Party's ideals and beliefs as well as their unshakable loyalty. (*Shandong University of Technology News* 2011)

These everyday rewards involve a variety of benefits and privileges. For example, student interviewees reported that student Party members enjoy priority in competition for scholarships, student cadre posts, and even purely academic awards and need-based financial aid. When a point system is used in such a competition, Party membership is often worth points.

Rewards in the form of elite membership given to the state's most loyal subjects serves a number of purposes. First, elite membership and the benefits, privileges, and opportunities associated with it strengthen the bonds between the state and its rank-and-file followers. Second, rewards in the form of elite access make Party membership desirable to ordinary students, especially aspirational students who seek a promising career and a good lifestyle, and thus attract more students to behave in ways desired by the state. Third, rewards and privileges associated with Party membership reinforce the political stratification of the university student populace. The status disparity between students based on their political affiliation gives the privileged ones a sense of shared authority with the elite establishment.

Direct Admission to Graduate School

Preferential treatment in the allocation of scarce resources and opportunities is the second tier of positive incentives. This usually occurs via an informal resource allocation mechanism for the privileged that is operated in parallel with the formal allocative process accessible to the general public. In Chinese universities, a salient example of this kind of incentive is direct admission to graduate school (*baoyan*) for senior undergraduate students. Through such programs, each year, a small number of university seniors who have been selected by their respective university authorities and endorsed by the Ministry of Education receive admission offers from the prominent graduate schools of national universities, bypassing the highly competitive National Admission Examinations for Graduate

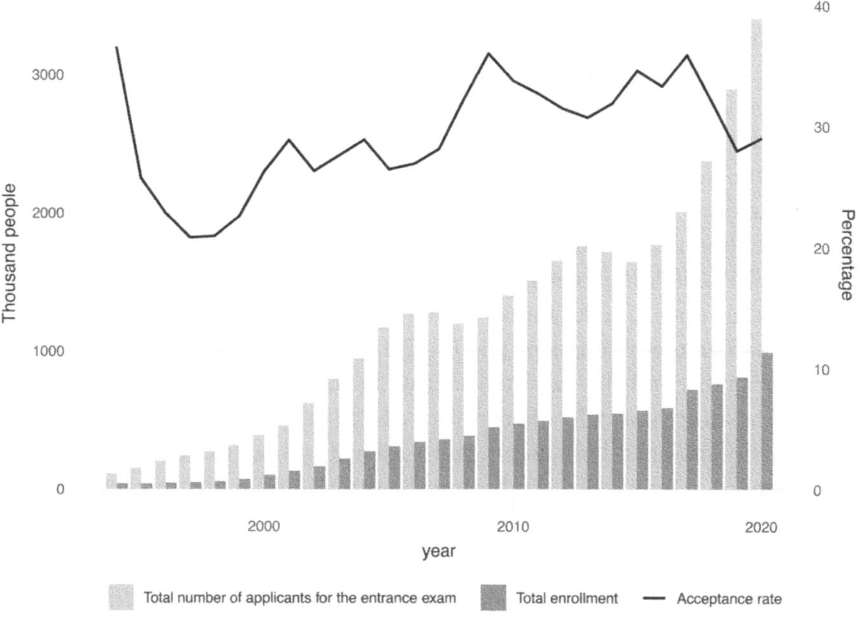

Figure 12. Number of applicants to graduate school and the acceptance rate nationwide, 1994–2020.

Schools. University students consider this a very privileged and prestigious way to obtain opportunities for advanced studies.

Since the mid-1990s, with the expansion of undergraduate admission in China and the depreciated value of the first degree in the job market, the number of applicants for graduate school admission in China has risen dramatically. In 1993, 114,000 applicants registered for the national graduate school admission examinations; in 2020, this number was 341 million. Figure 12 shows the number of graduate school applicants nationwide from 1994 to 2020.[3]

Chinese universities must work relentlessly to screen graduate school candidates, which results in a lengthy, complicated, and confusing process of application, vetting, and admission. Given the number of required examination subjects and the level of difficulty of the exams, especially the universal requirement of a passing grade in a politics course, a tremendous amount of preparation is necessary, which must be carried out on top of a student's normal course load for at least one full year. However, the actual preparation time is usually much longer than that. The difficulty of the examination has resulted in the flourishing of tutoring schools, as attending a costly preparation class in Beijing or one of the provincial capital cities has become a natural choice for most examination candidates. The tuition for good-quality tutoring schools might be as high as 8,800 yuan for a course on a single subject. According to PRC researchers, nationwide, the average tuition is 2,500 yuan per subject (Liang and Liu 2009). It was estimated that in 2003, the revenue generated by preparation for these examinations was around 3 billion yuan; in 2005, the estimated amount was 5 billion yuan (Wang and Chen 2020, 86). In 2009, reporters from the Central People's Radio estimated that the total capital value for the business of tutoring for educational examinations might be as high as 300 billion yuan for that year (Liang and Liu 2009). The costs for expensive tutoring programs and the subsistence costs in the metropolitan cities where such classes are normally offered place a huge financial burden on ordinary university students. Thus, getting into graduate school through the normal channel of examinations can be an exhausting journey that involves huge investments of time and money.

Compared with the high costs associated with the agonizing normal channel, the parallel mechanism of direct admission to graduate school is an extremely desirable option for undergraduate students looking for opportunities to study for higher degrees. Each year, a considerable number of the slots for graduate school admission are allocated via this parallel scheme. In one provincial university, in 2013, the Ministry of Education allocated quotas of admission via the special mechanism equivalent to approximately 3 percent of the total number of that university's entire graduating undergraduate students (Hubei University 2013). The number of quotas allocated for this secondary channel of graduate school admission nationwide, albeit formally untabulated, is vast. Although different universities may have their own procedures for selecting students under this highly desired alternative scheme (*baoyan*, literally "guaranteed admission to graduate school"), most give considerable weight to political performance. The state's most loyal collaborators—student Party members, student cadre, Communist Youth League activists—are given priority and a large share of such quotas.

Career Interests

With expanding higher education in China since the 1990s, the employment market has become extremely competitive for university graduates. In an article entitled "How Could This Year's 6.6 Million University Graduates Find a Job?," *Guangming Daily*, a national newspaper widely read by the Chinese intelligentsia, reported that the total number of undergraduate students who would graduate in 2010 was six times the number in 2000. In 2011, this number rose to 6.6 million (Feng 2011).[4] In 2013, 6.99 million graduating undergraduate students in China entered the job market—a record—but the number of available job openings decreased by 15 percent from the previous year (Feng 2013). This unusually large number of university graduates, together with the shrinking job market for entry-level professionals, has placed enormous pressure on fresh university graduates and their families. In 2001, about 340,000 Chinese university students could not find a job on graduation. The number has been rising steadily since; in 2006, about 1.24 million students had no job offer in hand at the time of their commencement (Zhang 2007, 72). In 2013, by 10 May (two months before the usual graduation season), only 44.4 percent of the graduating classes in traditionally prestigious universities in Shanghai had secured job offers (Zhang 2013). This situation has further deteriorated: according to the National Bureau of Statistics of China, in 2021, China had 9.09 million graduating undergraduate students, and "the difficulty for university graduates to find a job and for the enterprises to find a qualified worker exists simultaneously" (Reuters 2021). A survey conducted by China Youth Daily revealed that 76.12 percent of university graduates in the class of 2021 deemed the job market "very difficult" and 32.59 percent expected to obtain a job offer through a referral from their respective universities (Li 2021). The grave state of the job market for fresh university graduates is obvious.

The transition to a socialist market economy and the growth of China's private sector have significantly weakened university administrations' control over their students' career prospects. Nevertheless, given the fierce competition for opportunities, university political officials still wield considerable influence over the job placement process. After the compulsory job allocation system for university students was abolished in 1997, career advising offices (CAO, *jiuye bangongshi* or *jiuye chu*) were established by the student work bureaucracies in almost all Chinese institutions of higher education. Political counselors at all levels work under instruction from this office to provide career development services for senior students. Accordingly, employers who come to the universities for job postings and recruitment are required to go through this office. In addition, job information is disseminated through this office, which also organizes recruitment activities. In the 2021 survey conducted by *China Youth Daily*, 76.29 percent of the interviewed students identified "insufficient information about employment opportunities" as a main obstacle to finding a satisfac tory job (Li 2021). The university's control of employment information has become an important resource of power and influence.

Typically, CAOs publicize less desirable job postings to the entire student community and reserve information regarding highly sought-after positions for favored students. One student cadre member who served as a part-time assistant in her university's career service recalled,

> The job postings, after they were input in the CAO's database, would be classified into different levels. For the best job openings, the CAO would make a list and send [it] to the Head of the Student Work Department and the Communist Youth League for them to recommend potential candidates, usually at a 3:1 or 5:1 ratio. For the job openings that are considered fairly good, they would be first posted to the mailing list of graduating student Party members and student cadres for response. Only if not enough self-nomination is attained through this process will these job postings be released to the larger student community. And the job openings that were classified as "Level 3"—which denotes . . . the "less desirable" positions—are immediately released to political counselors for onward dissemination to the entire student community. But even when [this] "Level 3" job information reached the hands of the political counselors, they will always first share with students who had good work relations with them and, if not enough response is obtained, publicise [it] to the entire class.[5]

The university also actively uses the political reference system—a certification required in most hiring decisions in the public sector in China—to reward the best students. Political referral takes place in three ways. First, the Party organizations of institutions of higher education can recommend their preferred job candidates to state agencies or SOEs directly. Such employers can also solicit recommendations from the university's political cadres at the outset of their hiring process. Second, for the most sensitive and important state agencies, advanced political clearance from the Communist Party committee of the candidate's home institution is required. Third, for all other students, even when they have secured a job offer, to register for a new residential permit (*hu kou*) and complete the official personnel recruitment procedures regulated by the state, they require a political reference form issued by their university's student work bureaucracy. After the form has been endorsed by the hiring company or agency, the university's Student Work Department must issue a "certificate of dispatching" (endorsed by the Ministry of Education) to the graduating student. Only with this certificate is the hiring formally recognized as legitimate and enforceable by state agencies nationwide. In addition, university departments oversee a variety of special programs that provide fast-track admission to state agencies, SOEs, and the military, all of which are especially desirable for university students from modest family backgrounds. For example, the nationwide "cadre trainee" (*xuandiao sheng*) program provides opportunities for university graduates with outstanding political performance to be appointed directly to entry-level official posts in grassroots state agencies in rural areas or underdeveloped western provinces. The Communist Party's Central Organisation Department instructed that "candidates for the cadre trainee programmes must be students who have a good political character and are committed to working for the state."[6] The ability to select candidates for cadre trainee programs provides the Party committees in these institutions with an important resource for rewarding their most favored students. In 2018, 457 of the 9,603 graduates from Peking University were selected by the University Party Committee to be cadre trainees, serving in twenty-nine different provinces or provincial-level municipalities of China (Jiangsu Provincial Committee of Chinese Communist Youth League 2019).

Material Awards

Universities in China, like their counterparts in the West, offer a wide range of academic scholarships, awards, and prizes (generally termed *jiangxue jin* in Chinese) to the best students, usually in the form of one-off cash payments. The competition for scholarships, academic awards, and prizes in Chinese universities is overseen by the Student Work Department. Competition for scholarships and academic awards is highly politicized, as political performance is heavily weighted in the vetting of awardees.

In Chinese universities, competition for scholarships and prizes is an important component of the state's on-campus incentivization infrastructure. In Chinese universities, the selection of awardees for academic scholarships is overseen by the university-level Student Work Department. In some provincial universities where the Student Work Department is not adequately staffed, this work may be delegated to the Communist Youth League, too. Each year, the Student Work Department determines a comprehensive set of vetting criteria and procedures for scholarship competition and allocates award quotas to each administrative unit. At this level, competition for scholarships is supervised by the political counselor and run by the Student Communist Party Branch. In most institutions, competition for scholarships uses a point system, whereby the criteria issued by the Student Work Department are entered into a numerical formula to calculate a score for each student.

The point systems used for scholarship competitions vary from institution to institution, but nearly all of them combine a student's academic achievements and political performance. Compared with other forms of incentives, direct cash awards in the form of academic scholarships are given to a wider pool of recipients and play a simultaneous role of political inclusion. In competitions for scholarships, academic talent or outstanding performance in one's studies can compensate for political passivity or even indifference. One-off material awards do not involve long-term career development benefits or membership in the ruling elites; thus, they are an ideal way for the regime to reward professional talent and show favor to technically savvy students.

As the state's desire to reward political compliance increased, even need-based financial aid for university students was gradually merged into the overall incentivization infrastructure. Chinese universities have devoted extensive financial resources to help students from poor family backgrounds, endeavoring to shape them into an important supporting base for the regime. According to the MoE, in 2010, 23.06 percent of registered university students in the PRC came from a "poor" family background, and 7.27 percent came from families with "extremely difficult" financial conditions (Guo 2010). The provision of financial assistance for poor students has become one of the top priorities for universities across China. In some universities, financial aid programs ought to be much more generous than academic scholarships. And financial aid packages—in essence, monetary support from the state—are more attractive for university students than academic scholarships or student loans (which require repayment). The full scale of state-sponsored financial aid has not been publicized, but according to publicly available information, at Hunan University alone, for the spring semester of 2010, the university administration issued a total of 8.764 million yuan in financial aid to undergraduate students (Hunan University 2010).

Given the central leadership's high degree of attention to poor university students, these aid measures have at times even become excessive. In one provincial university, an early alert system was established to warn political counselors when the money in any student's dining account remained below 150 yuan for a certain period of time. On receiving such a notification, student affairs officers are dispatched to see whether the student is in any difficulty that the school can help with—a measure deemed unnecessary even by most of the potential beneficiaries. When winter comes, poor students enrolled in the state's financial aid schemes receive new coats from the government free of charge. Some poor students under the state's care tend to be more politically active in official student activities and demonstrate much closer ties to the regime than their better-off peers. As one senior political official in a prestigious national university commented,

> The poorer students would be more cooperative with the university authority or even work for us. As far as I can see, students who are on the university's financial aid programmes tended to be more politically loyal and they attended political education with significantly higher morale. Among the lower-level student cadres, those students account for a remarkable percentage. Students who are very active in officially held collective activities and contributed more to the official university newspaper mostly came from modest family background[s].[7]

Standing Closer to the Organization

The Communist Party also considers the psychological aspect of its incentivization infrastructure. Indeed, the political authorities on campus work earnestly to ensure that student loyalists experience "psychic gratification"—a sense of satisfaction related to the feeling of prominence among one's peers, favorable attachment to power, or the perception of sharing in the power and influence of the state. This psychological aspect of the incentivization infrastructure should not be overlooked.

As spiritual welfare dispensed to political loyalists, psychic gratification is forged through numerous channels on campus. For example, the Student Work bureaucracy and the University Party Committee routinely hold grand ceremonies and rituals glorifying new Party members, reward and prize recipients, and other political role models selected by the regime. On these occasions, new Party members, recipients of awards, and selected role-model students feel prominence among their peers. Moreover, all of these ceremonies involve the construction of political meaning. From the red flags displayed on stage to the solemn processes of oath-taking and award-granting, the spectacular ritualistic elements of these events strengthen the attendees' sense of belonging to a powerful ruling establishment.

Other means of forging psychic gratification are selective access to uni-

Figure 13. An oath-taking ceremony for new student Communist Party members in a university, July 1, 2021 (Xi'an, China).

versity affairs and the hierarchical dissemination of information. The state apparatus on campus intentionally builds a social ladder whereby students are invited to join the governance of the university at various levels. The most trusted student cadre members and Party members are regularly invited to serve on university-level committees, and they thus enjoy a close relationship with university leadership. They are often officially designated student representatives who speak to university management on behalf of their fellow students. In conducting political reviews and evaluations, the university Party apparatus also delegates power to this corps of "backbone students" (*xuesheng gugan*). Through this process, a sense of shared power and authority naturally develops among these student loyalists. Lesser student cadre members serve in faculty-level governance structures.

On Chinese university campuses, political officials often call for students to "stand closer to the 'organisation'" (*xiang zuzhi kaolong*), where "organisation" customarily refers to the Party. The implicit discourse behind this call is that by staying close to the state, loyal students obtain not only political accreditation but extra privileges, advantages, material gains, and psychic gratification, which make their university life easier and improve their future career prospects. The tiered structure of positive incentives—from membership in the ruling Party to material awards in the form of one-off cash allowances—has enabled the state to construct an incentivization infrastructure from which it can dispense rewards and mete out penalties to ensure a high level of political compliance from university students.

Punishing Defiance

Although dispensing incentives has enabled the state to effectively signal its preferred patterns of behavior and to secure cooperation in this regard in everyday campus life, on less frequent occasions, the state also feels the need to exercise coercion and display its power by punishing outright defiance, trouble-making, and inappropriate political behavior to stop such actions from signaling symbolic force to society, snowballing into other sectors of the student community, threatening the tranquility of the campus, and harming the political regime itself.

According to Joel Feinberg, "punishment is the infliction of hard treatment by an authority on a person for his [or her] prior failing in some respect [usually an infraction of a rule or command)]" (Feinberg 1965, 397). Punishment to maintain political order on university campuses serves at least three functions. First, it has a reformist function, as the state hopes to change an individual or a group's behavior away from actions or speech that the state disapproves of. Second, punishment deters other members of the university community from engaging in behavioral or discursive patterns that the state opposes, thus establishing and securing conformity in this critical social space. Punishment is thus a social event and cognitive process that affects observers, who not only "react . . . in a behavioural sense" but also "process social information in order to make sense of the situation and its implications for them and their group" (Trevino 1992, 648). Third, punishment serves an expressive function. By publicly condemning wrongdoers, the state clearly expresses its disapproval of their behavior and thus establishes boundaries of action or speech for its subjects.[8] Like rewards, punishments are an indispensable component of the incentivization infrastructure that the state uses to define, differentiate, regulate, and manage everyday life in society.

In Chinese universities since the 1990s, punishment for political, social, or academic offenses is exclusively overseen by the Communist Party Committees on campus. The foundation of the Communist Party's penalty structure is a formal disciplinary mechanism governed by a set of published codes established by each institution based on guidance issued by the MoE. University authorities across China almost universally classify disciplinary actions into five levels based on the nature and level of the offense.

The lowest level of punishment for minor disciplinary offense is *warning*. The convicted student is given a warning letter, which is to be posted on the campus bulletin board and included in the student's personnel dossier. Some institutions may remove the record from the student's dossier on graduation, subject to a panel review. The second-lowest level of punishment for common disciplinary offenses is *demerit*. The convicted student is suspended from all competitions for scholarships, financial aid, or academic prizes for a minimum of one year. Communist Party membership is usually denied to the convicted student for an extensive period, even beyond graduation. The decision is posted on the campus bulletin board and permanently included in the student's personnel dossier.

A higher level of punishment, *serious demerit*, is administered in response to a major or very serious offense, or to behavior that triggers action from state law enforcement agencies. Usually, the convicted student is suspended from all competitions for scholarships, financial aid, or academic prizes for the duration of his or her university studies. If the offense is of a political nature, Communist Party membership is unlikely to be granted in the student's lifetime. The decision is posted on the campus bulletin board, announced at a public event, and permanently included in the student's personnel dossier.

Probationary review for expulsion is the second-harshest level of formal punishment, which is administered in response to serious antiregime legal codes. The student is put on probationary review under the Student Communist Party Branch and the Student Work Department for a designated period of time. Any unsatisfactory performance or new offense committed during that period leads directly to expulsion. Party membership is denied to the student during his or her natural life. The decision is posted on the campus bulletin board, broadcast on the campus TV network, announced at a public event, and permanently included in the student's personnel dossier. *Expulsion* is the highest level of formal punishment, which is administered for the most serious antiregime actions, repeated moral failures of the most serious nature, convictions for felonies under state legal codes, and confirmed allegations by state law enforcement agencies for antiregime activities outside of campus. The convicted student's university studies are terminated immediately and the student is barred for life from enrolling in any public institution of higher learning in China. Expulsion also entails the loss of cadre membership for the student's lifetime, which means that she or he cannot be recruited by any state agencies to serve as an official, civil servant, or professional. Party membership is denied to the student during his or her natural life. The decision is posted on the campus bulletin board, broadcasted on the campus TV network, announced at a specifically organized public rally, and permanently included in the student's personnel dossier. The student's family and the municipal state of his place of origin are notified.

In China, the disciplinary actions received during university studies will almost certainly affect a student's life and career long beyond graduation. A permanent record of an offense in one's personnel dossier (and ineligibility for Communist Party membership) can block a student from getting a job in the public sector. In addition, the public nature of the penalty serves an expressive purpose, as disciplinary actions indicate the state-designated boundaries of acceptable student action and speech on campus. Members of the student community must refrain from crossing these boundaries to avoid public humiliation.

In Chinese universities since the 1990s, although negative sanctions—whether in the form of formal disciplinary action or informal obstruction of the rhythm of everyday life—are used less frequently than positive incentives, they nevertheless constitute an indispensable segment of the incentivization infrastructure that supports the reestablished state control and political order. Compared to the penalty system's usually undeclared reformist functions, on university campuses, the expressive and deterring roles seem to be more salient. Punishments define the boundaries of the behavioral and discursive space acceptable to the state and establish community-wide knowledge about the state's prohibited modes of action, speech, and elements of everyday life. The state thus not only firmly establishes its own authority, through repetitive shaping of the everyday rhythm of a critical social space, it also effectively internalizes its preferred pattern of public interaction, expression, and disposition into the minds, hearts, and routines of members of the critical social groups who occupy that space.

The Maintenance of Normalcy

Mental-Health Auditing

With the decline of traditional means of mobilization and monitoring on campus, mental-health auditing (*xinli weisheng jiance*) has gradually become a novel instrument for the state to monitor students' mental conditions and to detect irregularities. In 2005, the Ministry of Education, Ministry of Health, and Central Committee of the Communist Youth League issued a joint document entitled "Opinions on the Further Enhancement and Improvement of Mental Health Work among the University Students."[9] This document states that "the purpose of the enhancement and improvement of mental health work among the university students is to thoroughly implement the Communist Party's general policies on education under the new social circumstances" and "[mental-health work] is a crucial component in the overall strengthening and betterment of the ideological and thought work among the university students" (Ministry of Education, the Ministry of Health, and the Central Committee of the Chinese Communist Youth League 2005).

The state requires all universities to create an alert system to report on students who may have potential mental problems or whose deviant thoughts or audacious behavior might cause political instability.[10] Universities are also required to conduct periodic mental screening of students and to maintain a constant mechanism for mental-health auditing that operates throughout a student's university studies. In a provincial university located in central China, all first-year students are required to undergo a lengthy mental-health screening process during their freshman class orientation. The results are carefully analyzed by the university's political officials, and students are interviewed or investigated if any irregularities are identified. All first-year students were classified into one of four categories: "Normal," "Slightly Problematic," "Problematic," or "In Need of Special Attention." The finalized survey results and names of the students identified as potentially problematic or beyond are distributed to counselors and Party secretaries in charge of student affairs in each faculty or department. Based on the information obtained from the screening, follow-up consultations might be arranged for students identified as problematic or needing special attention.

Each *banji*—the basic "grid-like" structure of university students—includes a special student cadre position entitled "commissioner of mental health" (CMH). The official Student Union features a special Mental Health Department to coordinate the work of CMHs at lower levels and collect their reports. In fact, as the joint document issued by the three central agencies states, "it is necessary to create a teacher-on-duty system, quick reporting system of irregular situations, and a fast and effective crisis handling mechanism—all three to be staffed by student cadres, Political Counsellors, Class Directors, all the way up to the Faculty and University level" (Ministry of Education, the Ministry of Health, and the Central

Committee of the Chinese Communist Youth League 2005). As one PRC researcher summarized on-campus mental-health monitoring, institutions of higher education are required to implement four crucial mechanisms: a mental-health auditing and counseling mechanism, a command and intervention mechanism, a monitoring and surveillance mechanism, and a follow-up and support system (Ouyang 2009, 62). Mental-health monitoring and intervention have remained an important device to identify abnormalities, issue early alerts, and intervene in crises whenever necessary.

Compulsory Consultation and Thought Guidance

In March 2011, news media in China widely reported that Peking University had established a "consultation system" (*huishang zhidu*) for "ideologically radical students" (*sixiang pianji xuesheng*). This system required political cadres at the university to monitor the thoughts and behavior of ten categories of students, including students with "radical ideas," "failing academic performance," "financial difficulty," "independent lifestyle," "addiction to the Internet," "conviction of disciplinary offence," and "mental fragility" (Zhang 2011b, 2011c). According to Party officials, the purpose of these compulsory consultations was to "integrate forces from all aspects to solve the special problems with individual students" (Hang Zhang 2011). The scope of the criteria for inclusion in such a consultation is so broad that one student, as the *Beijing Evening News* reported half-jokingly, "immediately recognised that she met the standards for at least three of the ten categories upon just the first sight of the regulations" (Zhang 2011c).

Although it is presented as a normal student aid program and administrative procedure, the political and coercive nature of the compulsory counseling scheme is so obvious that even official news media have questioned its rationale and criticized its methods (Jia 2011). Nevertheless, a program designed by the CYL is still being implemented nationwide, requiring university political cadres to provide adequate guidance to students on "critical points in their thought development" (*sixiang jiedian yindao*). In a 2011 speech, Lu Hao, then first secretary of the Chinese CYL, stated that the "thought guidance" program should operate in such a way as to make the younger generation acknowledge China's rapid development while maintaining a reasonable expectation for the increase of personal wealth, to pursue material wealth along with spiritual enrichment, and to have a "correct" understanding of the problems remaining in China's development model (Communist Youth League Committee of Hunan Institute of Humanities, Science and Technology 2012, 16–18).

Conclusion

An effective incentivization infrastructure is the foundation of a stable political order. Rewards and punishments are essential components of the Chinese state's reconstructed infrastructure of incentivization. A tiered structure of positive incentives, which includes elite membership, preferential advantages, and earmarked opportunities, not only facilitates the formation of a group of young loyalists on campus, it provides a model pattern of speech and action for other students to follow and sufficient enticement for them to do so. Various forms of punishments are imposed for delinquency, defiance, and rebellious action on campus; more importantly, through the public exercise of punitive power, the state clearly defines the limits of its tolerance of "trespassing" speech and behavior.

The state's methods of dispensing positive incentives for preferred patterns of behavior and use of sanctions for deviations create in the student populace habitual adaptation to and internalization of the norms of state-approved behavior and thought. The standards expressed and defined through the workings of this incentivization infrastructure are naturalized into the norms and codes for the campus community, and over time, they become a natural part of the critical social space and indispensable to the social group living in that space. Through these parallel processes of rewarding and punishing, the reinvented Chinese state can carve out a space marked by a constructed congruence between the student populace and the standards established by the state. By signaling its preferred behavior and creating zones of prohibition, the state uses the incentivization infrastructure to generate a culture of congruence that is shaped by the Party's official identity, symbolism, and meanings. This organizational culture then grows into the institutional environment in which young students grow up, receive higher education, develop their own value systems, and forge their own worldviews. The long-term influence of this unique institutional culture should not be overlooked.

SIX

At the Perilous Moment

Critical and Sensitive Periods

Power . . . is tolerable only on condition that it mask a substantial part of itself. Its success is proportional to its ability to hide its own mechanisms.

> —Michel Foucault, *The History of Sexuality*, vol. I,
> *An Introduction*, 1978, 86

They came together . . . in the lives of individuals—not as empty "isms" but as personal experiences, which exposed contradictions underlying systems of power.

> —Robert Darnton, *Censors at Work*, 2015, 89

Political Crisis and Triggering Event

"Students have often been in the vanguard of revolutionary movements" (Altbach 1967, 77). A modernizing and democratizing force in the twentieth century, university students provide—as C. Wright Mills rightly suggested—"a major potential mass base for new revolutionary movements" in an era when radical politics is gradually losing its appeal to other sectors of postindustrialized societies (Lipset 1972, xvi). However, the enormous revolutionary energy and political potential of the student body is not realized until it is waged into concrete large-scale social movements set off by certain "triggering events" in a situation of crisis. As Stephen Skowronek argued, a crisis is "a sporadic, disruptive event that suddenly challenges a state's capacity to maintain control and alters the boundaries defining the legitimate use of coercion" (1982, 10). A triggering event, according to E. Wright Bakke and Mary S. Bakke (1971), is one that "brings into focus, as a cause for action and as relevant to the interests of large numbers of students, one or more . . . experience-verified allegations of institutional shortcomings and/or inconsistences" (493). Peking University defines a "triggering event" in its crisis response plan as one "that has caused or is expected to cause serious damage, threatening the safety of the life and property of the faculty and students of the university, or harming the over-all stability of the university or of society at large" (Peking University 2017, 5). As the most crucial activating factors for student activism, triggering events usually have three distinctive features: symbolism, impact potential-ity, and cohesiveness. Table 4 on describes these three characteristics of a potential triggering event in everyday experiences on university campuses.

The nationwide revolutionary movements that have taken place in China over the last century often began as student movements seizing opportunities provided by dramatic political events on the national or international stage. Whether it be the death of a popular political figure, the anniversary of a previous rebellion swept back into consciousness by the tidal waves of history, or a major international event in which China might be considered to have "lost face" in one way or another, a regime striving to maintain stability and safeguard a quiescent order is at its most vulner-able and exposed on these politically volatile occasions. Having grasped the energetic nature of the university student population from past encounters, it is all the more important for the post-Tiananmen Chinese Party-state to ascertain that it has the capacity, arrangements, and resources available to keep university campuses calm and cool at times of political susceptibility.

The capacity of a political regime to handle politically sensitive moments in the nation's public life reflects and shapes its strength in terms of responding to crises and maintaining its grip on power. Indeed, regimes have been ousted when they failed to safely handle their last moments of crisis. If Nicolae Ceauşescu had survived the demonstrations in the city of Timişoara triggered by the government-sponsored attempt to evict László Tőkés, he would not have been removed from power in December 1989. Ferdinand Marcos had to flee the Philippines when his regime could not handle the crisis after his "snap election" and the national uprising after Cardinal Vidal's call for civil disobedience in 1986. Observers of events in the Arab Spring of 2011 could easily discern that the variation in different regimes' capacity to handle politically sensitive events and the ensuing cri-ses was a major factor in their ultimate fate. Juan J. Linz, commenting on

TABLE 4: Characteristics of a triggering event or situation

Notation	Description of Characteristics
Symbolism	"The event or situation dramatically and vividly symbolises and provides specific verifying evidence of the perceptions of activists concerning particular objectionable characteristics of the university, economic, or political institutions, concerning the way in which the Establishment manages and governs these institutions, and particularly concerning the degree to which their managing and governing run counter to the life interests of the people involved."
Impact Potentiality	"The event or situation shall have a negative impact on the personal aspirations and life expectancies of the majority of students or is intricately associated with some event or circumstance which has such a negative impact."
Cohesiveness	"The event or situation co-joins the interests of several of the groups of students . . . [who are characterized as] separate or lonely, and who are seeking integration and fellowship with their fellow students by developing a following in a cause which has widespread appeal."

Source: Bakke and Bakke 1971, 493–94.

the collapse of the Stalinist regime, wrote that "The decay, the ossification and ritualisation of an ideology that could not serve as a mobilising utopia, in the end meant that the cadres . . . did not feel legitimised to use the intact and large coercive apparatus in a crisis situation" (2000, 30).

In China also, history shows that politically sensitive moments in the nation's public life have been vulnerable times for outbursts of large-scale student unrest. The May Fourth Movement was triggered by China's diplomatic failure in negotiating the Treaty of Versailles at the Paris Peace Conference in 1919. The June Fourth Movement of 1989 was initiated by the death of Hu Yaobang, an ousted political leader who was purged due to his alleged weakness in fighting liberal thoughts and in defending the Party's orthodox ideologies against the threat of a Westernized intelligentsia. In 1999, when thousands of university students went onto the streets of Beijing in the largest student movement since 1989, it was precipitated by the NATO air force's unexpected bombing of the Chinese Embassy in Belgrade on May 8 in that year—an incident considered by many Chinese citizens as an ostentatious insult to Chinese national dignity. Given the political impact of university students as a prominent social group, large-scale student unrest directly threatens the safety of the regime.

Scholars in the PRC acknowledge both the threat to the stability of university campuses in a changing society and the potential impact of a student uproar on the safety of the overall political order. Zhao Yun and

Yao Kunpeng rightfully argued that the "Topical events and controversies in society eventually will influence the security and stability of university campuses" (Zhao and Yao 2013, 71).[1] As Zhang Dexiu, another PRC researcher specializing on the political control of universities, contended,

> If political stability on university campuses cannot be preserved—for example, if the university students forge contentious movements in the format of collective petitions, sit-ins, self-organization among the students, or even street protests—there will likely be a "butterfly effect." The unrest will soon be spread to the whole country and threaten the overall stability of the entire society. (Zhang 2011a, 1)

Since the 1990s, securing the stability of university campuses during politically sensitive moments has thus become the top priority for government agencies and Party cadres across China who are responsible for either the higher-education sector or public security at large. In official discourse, these sensitive moments that attract the most attention from the state are called "Critical and Sensitive Periods" (*min gan qi*, CSPs).

Critical and Sensitive Periods

Although political work has been constant on Chinese campuses since the 1990s, universities are required to impose extra control during the designated CSPs each year. A CSP can be designated by the state for a variety of reasons. Some are statutory and regular (e.g., the week before and after the anniversary of the June Fourth Movement of 1989 and the week before the plenary session of the National People's Congress every spring), others are sporadic but somewhat predictable (usually before major social or political events), and others are sudden or unpredictable (e.g., the SARS epidemic and the Jasmine Revolution). Table 5 lists some of the designated CSPs at a provincial university in a given year.

Many CSPs on university campuses are designated for when political or social tension is expected to be high and the Party-state anticipates a higher likelihood of student unrest. This can follow a criminal case involving a member of the university community. For example, the student protests at Peking University in 1988 and 1999 were both caused by the death of a student in a murder case.[2] In 1999, students from Peking University and Tsinghua University were outraged by the news that a first-year female

TABLE 5: Major critical and sensitive periods at a provincial university

Time In Year	Duration	Reason
January 1	3 days	Large crowd gathering on campus for New Year's Eve concert and celebration
Early March	7–10 days	Plenary meetings of the National People's Congress and the Chinese People's Political Consultative Conference
Mid-late March	7 days	Anniversary of the 1959 Tibetan Rebellion
Early April	3 days	Qingming Festival: A traditional memorial day for the deceased
Early May	3 days	Anniversary of the NATO bombing of the Chinese Embassy in Belgrade in 1998
Early June	7–10 days	Anniversary of the 1989 June Fourth Movement
Early July	7 days	Anniversary of the 2009 Xinjiang Uighur Riots
Early October	3 days	Celebration for the Founding Day of the People's Republic of China

Source: Interview with political cadres in a provincial university in central China in 2011.

Peking University student—Qiu Qingfeng—was found dead in the wilderness after a midnight ride in an unregistered cab. A large protest broke out, involving students from both universities. In the aftermath of such a tragic event that may emotionally engage the university student community, a brief CSP is declared.

On 9 May 2009, Tan Zhuo, a recent graduate of Zhejiang University, was hit and killed by a Mitsubishi Lancer SUV. The driver of the SUV—Hu Bin, the son of a wealthy local family—appeared not to take the death of the victim seriously enough. Furthermore, at a press briefing held immediately after the incident, local police claimed that Hu was driving at a speed of 70 kilometers per hour—which happened to be exactly the maximum speed at which the collision would be defined by law as a simple traffic incident rather than a criminal offense of "reckless driving" or "threatening public security by dangerous means." Outraged by the driver's attitude and the alleged favoritism of the local police toward him, students of Zhejiang University called for a city-wide demonstration to demand justice for their deceased young alumnus. The university and government immediately announced a CSP and requested all of the political cadres to return to campus immediately. Special control measures were implemented as quickly as possible.

A political cadre described this unexpected incident in the following terms:

Last time, we were somewhat successful in handling the haphazard situation after the widely reported traffic incident [the "70 km/h Incident" of Hu Bin, or *qishi ma shijian*]. As one of our alumni was hit and died in such a tragic and cruel way, students on campus were indeed outraged and agitated. Many of them started to prepare for a large-scale demonstration. We certainly did not want the situation to deteriorate and threaten the overall political stability. . . . We declared a Critical and Sensitive Period immediately to all of the teachers and staff who were responsible for security affairs. We worked closely with the police and put in place a series of upgraded control measures. Political officers—from Deputy Party Secretaries to the political counselor in each *banji*—all stood by in their university dorms without leaving campus. Political cadres tried to talk to as many students as possible and persuaded them individually to keep calm. The university updated its instructions to all of the teachers, staff, and security personnel involved in the handling of the matter on an hourly basis. With help from the police, the campus computer network was also effectively controlled and closely monitored. . . . Eventually, although there was a high level of stress and anxiety, no major demonstration took place and we successfully safeguarded proper order on campus.[3]

Some CSPs are declared before and during major national events that symbolize nationhood and pride. The Beijing Olympics held in 2008 was such a national event that was considered to present the face of the Party-state. The periods before and during the Beijing Olympics were certainly designated as a CSP, and tightened control measures were implemented on university campuses nationwide. The plenary sessions of the National People's Congress and the Chinese People's Political Consultative Conference—meetings of the supreme national legislature and political consultative body of China—are held in March in most years and are also considered a time to demonstrate harmony, achievements, and prosperity under the leadership of the CCP—especially given that a large number of journalists from international news media gather in Beijing during that week. Hence the time before and during the *liang hui* ("Dual Sessions") is a fixed CSP across all of China's colleges and universities.

China's major diplomatic issues may also become triggering events for student unrest—particularly when China's national dignity is considered to have been trampled on by "Western powers." For example, Sino-Japanese disputes over the Diaoyu Islands, anniversaries of the Nanjing Massacre, a

Japanese politician's official visit to the Yatsukuni Shrine, and other historical and contemporary occurrences imbued with strong symbolic meaning are a rich reservoir of potential triggering events that can lead to student movements of various scales. Any event that can be linked to these collective memories may therefore trigger the declaration of a CSP. For example, on 9 September 2010, after the Japanese Maritime Police seized a Chinese fishing boat and arrested the captain, university authorities all over China announced a CSP immediately, and the control machinery was set in full motion to prevent any public unrest from being initiated on university campuses. Events that unexpectedly erupt on campus can also trigger the declaration of a CSP.

Overall, CSPs are periods the regime identifies as politically sensitive and as potentially able to expose state vulnerabilities, revolving around a potential triggering event. Due to the perceived sensitivity and vulnerability, tightened security measures are put in place and all-around attention is devoted to the situation on university campuses. The measures implemented during a CSP attempt to limit the mobility of student groups, censor information flow on campus, disperse gathering crowds, and distance students from any outside contentious challengers to the state. The primary purpose of the extra control during CSPs is to prevent potential student activists from seizing the opportunity provided by a triggering event and from assigning it any "symbolic political connotations" from which a movement might be mobilized (Johnston 2011, 112).

State-University Collaboration

During a CSP—whether it be statutory or temporarily declared—the control mechanisms and measures implemented on university campuses become stricter and more rigid, and penalties for violation are harsher. Additional surveillance measures are put in place to find and nip in the bud any sparks of potential protest. The operations of the state on campus during a CSP feature efficient, intimate, on-site, real-time collaboration between the university administration and state law-enforcement agencies, including information sharing and control, behavioral control and deterrence, and preventive punitive measures targeting potentially defiant students.

The close collaboration between state agencies and university authorities during CSPs can first be seen in the rapid and efficient transmission of commands, instructions, and information. Nanjing University, in its

Contingency Plan for Social-Political Crises, clearly requires that during a political crisis, "the University's Leadership Group should report any related information to the Ministry of Education, the Provincial Communist Party Committee, the Provincial Government, and the Provincial and City Police, requesting assistance and support. At the same time, the control of the campus computer network must be heightened and harmful information firmly blocked from being spread."[4] The unusually efficient flow of information and swift action are also meant to ensure that every student becomes aware before dawn that joining street demonstrations on the next day will have very negative consequences for their future career.

One political cadre in charge of student affairs at a national university recalled that in the wake of NATO's bombing of the Chinese Embassy in Belgrade in 1999, the government informed university officials and demanded that the university announce a CSP as quickly as possible. The NATO bombing of a Chinese embassy was considered a major affront to China's international dignity, and the state anticipated that it would arouse enormous anger and outrage among university students. The cadre recalled,

> That was a Saturday and all of our colleagues in charge of student management were at a scenic area outside the city center for a staff retreat. It was about 7 p.m. and we were about to have a group dinner. A phone call from the government to the Head of our Student Work Department informed us that the students were outraged and planned to walk to Shanghai to launch a public protest in front of the U.S. Consulate-General. The government official asked all of us to return to campus immediately as a number of students had already gathered in front of the statue of Chairman Mao, which is located in a central spot on campus. As soon as we returned to campus, we immediately declared a CSP and busily engaged ourselves with work, which involved chatting to different stakeholders, bargaining with student leaders, and monitoring any developments among the outraged student community.[5]

When a CSP is in effect, internal information transmission and chains of command are effectively set in motion.[6] Within the university community, a public Short Message Service (SMS) system that delivers mass text messages to all students and members of the university community is also used to facilitate the sharing of information and coordination of extra control measures. As the cadre recalled,

After the university-level meeting, we immediately issued a notification via our mass SMS system. We, the Communist Party Committees at the faculty level, were responsible for ensuring that the information and instructions were delivered to each and every grassroots political cadre as well as the students in time. With the text message system and mobile phones, we could reach all of the political cadres, counselors, or other staff members in charge within half an hour after the government issued the instructions for the CSP. Also, grassroots cadres in charge of student management were required to physically stay with all of the students for whom they were responsible for half an hour—at most 1 hour—after the CSP was declared. All of the extra control measures had to be put in place within the same time period.[7]

For more serious situations, the Communist Party Committee will hold small meetings with senior political officials, student cadres, and Communist Party members to relay the information and instructions from the state. For example, when the then–French President Nicolas Sarkozy met with the Dalai Lama in 2008—the spiritual leader of Tibet and a political exile from the PRC—students at a university in central China considered it an insult to the ongoing Beijing Olympics torch relay and were outraged. A boycott against Carrefour—the French supermarket chain operating in the town—was proposed, and a public demonstration in front of the store was scheduled. One student cadre recalled her experiences at the eve of the breakout of this anti-France nationalist movement. She said,

It was a certain night before the Beijing Olympics. I was summoned to school at 3 a.m. for a meeting. The Provincial Party Committee must just have completed their meeting [on that matter] at around 9 p.m. in the evening and university leaders met at 1 a.m. At 3 a.m., all of the faculty-level administrators, political officials, and student cadres were already in the meeting hall. The classroom directors[8] were supposed to meet all of the students between 5 and 6 a.m.[9]

To prevent the students from rushing downtown and launching a public protest, the Communist Party Committee in each faculty summoned internal meetings attended by the most loyal students. These student loyalists were tasked with helping the Party-state calm their more independent peers and monitoring and reporting any new developments among the student populace. In the Carrefour incident, political officials of the university relied heavily on the voluntary collaboration of student cadres in pacifying their outraged peers.[10]

The state can plan some CSPs well in advance. Every anniversary of the 1989 student movement, for example, is a time of high alert for government agencies, university officials, and student cadres all over China. For these fixed CSPs, the university authorities, working with government law-enforcement agencies, have fine-tuned action plans ready to implement for any imaginable scenario. However, as previously discussed, there are many other CSPs that appear abruptly but are no less dangerous. According to one official's account,

> Now we have very effective information transmission and sharing mechanisms between us and state authorities during sensitive periods. Important information about a possible student collective action can be disseminated efficiently from the university to the state or from the state to the university. Once signs of a potential public protest are confirmed, the university takes action very promptly. In such a scenario, the provincial Department of Education will usually send an alert to the Student Work Department of our university. Administrators in charge of student affairs will then be summoned to an urgent meeting to discuss the situation and subsequently all of the political counsellors are notified about any decisions made at that meeting about the additional security measures to be implemented.[11]

During declared CSPs, law-enforcement agencies may intervene directly in the management of certain university facilities and the control of students. The university administration also used the campus public SMS platform to assist in disseminating warnings and messages from the local police or other law-enforcement agencies concerning political stability. Some universities respond to the state agencies' requests for assistance with "two-handed preparations" (*liangshou zhunbei*). A student from a university in Sichuan said that during the Diaoyu Islands incident of 2012, the university on the one hand collaborated with state agencies in persuading students not to participate in the public anti-Japan demonstrations; on the other hand, the university instructed the official Student Union to secretly prepare stocks of national flags and patriotic banners with politically correct slogans. If the university could not stop the students from protesting, these banners and slogans would be distributed to the students to create an image of a "patriotic student movement" instead of one that was antiregime.

Indeed, the collaboration between state agencies and university authorities is full of calculations, maneuvers, and struggle on both sides. During these critical periods for the state, the state-university relationship can become more complex. The state is reluctant to intervene directly into the daily operations of institutions of higher learning and thus relies on the voluntary collaboration of academic institutions to help prevent public protests, collective action, or any similarly "chaotic" scenarios from taking place. The universities therefore shoulder the responsibility of maintaining order. This collaborative relationship is testimony not only to the extensive reach of the reinvented state across the social realm, but to its reliance on voluntary cooperation from social institutions, and to the symbiotic relationship between the reinvented state and the institutions of higher learning under its constant control.

"Thought Work Is the Lifeline"

During any declared CSP, the state requires university authorities to put all of their effort into conducting enhanced "thought work" (*sixiang gongzuo*) with students. The enhanced thought work during CSPs is implemented in three ways: strengthened broadcasting of the Party-state's official stance, expanded persuasive talk about the undesirability of undertaking any politically audacious activity, and the dissemination of information on the negative consequences of defiance. These represent the propagation of a standing discourse, an inveigling discourse, and a preclusion discourse, respectively. These three discourses constitute the main lines of the state's narrative directed toward the student community during a CSP, delivered though the student-control apparatus. As Deng Xiaoping once pointed out, "Thought work is the lifeline for the Communist Party's work . . . on all fronts" (Deng 1994, 364). It has remained the principal weapon for the reinvented state to survive political crises.

During any declared CSP, the first thing an observer notices on campus is the increased density of propaganda about the state's official stance toward the issue at hand. This includes extended media coverage throughout the campus of the Party-state's official policy lines, public seminars by invited officials or pro-state scholars to expound on the specific topics in question, and special political study sessions organized by the Communist

Party Committee or the Communist Youth League. University political cadres' visits to student residences become more frequent, and special consultation sessions with "problematic" students become longer and more intensive.[12]

In fact, increasing the targeted social group's exposure to the Party's contingency narrative, including a standing discourse, an inveigling discourse, and a preclusion discourse, is a standard procedure in handling politically sensitive scenarios. During CSPs that are declared by universities nationwide, the state deploys national propagandist outlets to promote this kind of enhanced thought work and deliver the state's message to the country's entire student body. For example, on 9 May 1999, after the NATO bombing of the Chinese Embassy in Belgrade, Hu Jintao—the then-vice-president of China—delivered a televised speech that was broadcast live by every television station in China and appealed directly to students to "voluntarily protect the overall political stability" and "ensure that the protests be lawful and orderly" (Xinhua News Agency 1999).

For another example, during the escalation of the Sino-Japanese disputes over the Diaoyu Islands in 2010—especially after the Japanese government seized a Chinese fishing boat operating in disputed waters on September 7 of that year—large-scale anti-Japan demonstrations and protests flared up in major cities all over China. To maintain political stability on university campuses, the central state dispatched numerous "lecturing corps" (*xuanjiang tuan*) to hold special public seminars in "prestigious universities and universities in cities in which the 'patriotic sentiment' is particularly high." Meanwhile, China Central Television replaced its prime-time programs with a live broadcast of a public seminar on Sino-Japanese relations given by a former minister of foreign affairs. The Party's major official newspapers also published a series of editorials, op-eds, and related material during this period for the use of the political officials and cadres who were in charge of conducting emergency "thought work" and maintaining stability on university campuses (Zhang 2011a, 16–17).

Public seminars are also used as a convenient and efficient means of conducting thought work with large crowds of students during a designated CSP. In October 2010, Yao Jiaxin, a university student from the Xi'an Institute of Music, stabbed a woman to death after accidentally hitting the victim when driving his car to a date with his girlfriend. When the death sentence was handed down by the court in May 2011, there was major concern that students of Yao's home institution might wage a public protest over the use of capital punishment—especially given that a rumor was spreading that more than 400 students of the institute had signed a public petition asking for mitigation—and a CSP was immediately declared by the university concerned. Immediately after the judgment was announced and Yao was executed, the Institute organized for its party secretary and several prominent legal scholars to give a series of public seminars explaining the rationale behind the death sentence to students of Yao's alma mater. Party secretaries of various departments of the Institute were also asked to hold seminars to further explain the case to their students and discuss any questions that might be raised by the student populace (Xi'an Conservatory of Music 2009).

Conducting "political and thought work" with the student community in a timely and efficient manner is a high priority for Party-state officials at all levels who are responsible for maintaining security. In 2009, a large-scale and violent ethnic riot broke out in Urumqi, the capital city of Xinjiang. This incident led to more than 140 causalities and more than 800 injuries (China News Service 2009), and social unrest and violent confrontations continued between the Chinese and Uighur population in the region for at least three months afterward. On 6 July 2009, the day after the riot, one of the first things Nur Bekri, the then-governor of Xinjiang, did was to appear on the campus of Xinjiang University. Bekri held public seminars and attended discussion sessions with students of "all ethnicities" (*geminzu xuesheng*) and made the following request:

> The Communist Party Committee in each and every institution of higher education of Xinjiang should carry out their responsibilities seriously and play an essential leadership role [in stabilizing the situation]. They should organize the staff of their institutions quickly and effectively . . . and safeguard the normal order of work and life for students and teachers alike. . . . It is critically important to strengthen our education and control of students [during this sensitive time] and carry out deep and detailed "political and thought work." (Jiang 2009)

Governor Bekri gave very specific and detailed instructions on the issues and themes that should be discussed and emphasized in postcrisis thought work with the university students of Xinjiang, which would include a clear understanding of the violent and separatist nature of the ethnic riot, an acknowledgment of the complexity of the political situation in Xinjiang, and a firm agreement on the necessity to safeguard the stable sociopolitical conditions of the region. After the Uighur Riot of 2009, the high level of attention to the threat posed by ethnic groups on university campuses extended nationwide: even political cadres belonging to universities far from Xinjiang were busy telling their students that they had received special instructions from the state that anyone who dared to join a public demonstration or protest in the streets (regardless of whether they were protesting against the state or against the Uighur communities) would be detained immediately by the police.

The enhanced thought work during declared CSPs is also reflected in the increased frequency and intensity of university political officials' meetings and conversations with the students for whom they are responsible. The purpose of these meetings is to understand the shifting trends of thought among students, to identify their grievances, and to persuade them not to organize or join any antiregime actions. Compared to official propaganda, this kind of thought work usually appears more personal and considerate, and in some cases carries nuanced but effective connotations of threat and deterrence. For example, one university political cadre described what he had to say during such a visit:

> I told the students that this kind of thing [political protest] is very sensitive. . . . Our principal concern as teachers is the safety of our students. Going into the streets for a protest is a very dangerous activity in itself and all kinds of unanticipated things might happen. I have no way to monitor each and every one of you as you are already adults, and you have your freedoms. I would not stop you by force, but you need to consider it over and over again before taking any steps. . . . At times, I would also tell the students that the government will catch them if they engage in a public protest—and this possibility should not be hidden from the young students.[13]

To deliver a strong yet unprovocative message to students during these precarious moments can be difficult; political officials thus use language in a more strategic manner. When asked how she dealt with the 2010 CSP concerning the Sino-Japanese diplomatic skirmish over the Diaoyu Islands, a university political official said,

> When the political atmosphere was the most intense during the Sino-Japanese territorial disputes, I intentionally "injected" my views to the students, but in a way that they would not notice. For example, I told them it was important to be rational. In a territorial dispute, China is not necessarily the just side and Japan the unjust.

We need to be reasonable. Vandalizing other people's private cars while protesting against Japan does not help your country at all. Also, you need to first hear and analyse the story from both sides—China and Japan—and think twice before you engage in any political action and express anger.[14]

During these politically sensitive periods, even proregime events are discouraged.

It is apparent that even during this kind of individual thought-work session, which is full of personal "back-patting," pressure and deterrence are exercised in a subtle manner, and the state's message is duly delivered through a caring, considerate conversation between the political counselor and the student in question. Thus, the Party-state's efforts to reestablish control and order on university campuses involve the strategic use of threats, which have become an increasingly important form of inveigling discourse in the Party-state's efforts to demobilize students and curb political tensions on campus.

Tightened Monitoring

During a declared CSP, university authorities require the responsible teachers and political cadres to know "the location of each student 24 hours a day." University authorities also require teachers to deploy student loyalists to monitor other students' activities, conduct "stability-preservation" education in the classrooms, and make sure that none of the students can leave campus. To implement this last point, university authorities will at times seek the assistance of armed police to guard the university's gates and lock down the campus.

At some universities, student cadres and political officials also attentively monitor students' status updates on social media platforms and the latest messages shared in group chats on instant-messaging services. Any irregularity or the slightest indication of potential student unrest is reported. Political cadres, especially those who maintain daily contact with the student body, are requested to actively join their students' online chat groups and monitor any ongoing discussions. One student recalled that during the declared CSP in 2012, one of his friends was summoned by the police immediately after he sent a single message related to the call for the Jasmine Revolution in China. As one student from a national university recalled,

When China's dispute with the Philippines on the sovereignty of the Huangyan Shoal was widely reported by the news media, public demonstrations broke out in a number of places. In our university, there were banners and slogans posted by the students, protesting against the Philippines' occupation of the Huangyan Shoal. When this first emerged, officials from the Communist Youth League immediately notified us that we should not be involved in any activities related to political issues, and that they will never approve such activities. Communist Youth League officials also attended many classroom and student group meetings to reiterate these points. They implemented strict measures and asked student cadres to observe the situation in each *banji*. Cadres were told that if any student under their watch indeed planned to organise or attend [a protest], they should report this to the university immediately. If they failed to do so, they would be held personally accountable for any unpleasant consequences.[15]

At another provincial university, political officials on campus mentioned that when the anti-Japan movement broke out in 2010, the university asked all political counselors and other university officers to check the location of each student and ask each student not to go outside—or they would have to shoulder all of the consequences. According to the university's requirements, this warning message had to be delivered very quickly to every member of the student community. The official Student Union also organized the student cadres on campus to check attendance at every class and to account for any absences.

Student meetings are more frequently convened by political counselors or university officials during a declared CSP. The official Student Union or the Communist Youth League will usually organize additional recreational or extracurricular activities during these periods to distract the students from political events, and activities organized by other voluntary student groups and clubs are either cancelled or severely restricted. Student meetings and activities organized by the university authorities during a CSP serve as an effective means to restrain the students' mobility and fill most of their time outside of the classroom.

Students also recalled that during the same CSP, the official Student Union organized many more extracurricular activities than usual, including an unplanned university-wide *bahe* (a Chinese version of tug-of-war) contest that would usually engage all of the students as either participants or cheerleaders and spectators. The university administrators and political officials also reach out to the most critical members of the student popu-lation (*zhongdian xuesheng*). During the 2009 Xinjiang Uighur Riot, for example, political officials in a provincial university in central China were asked to call on each student hailing from the Xinjiang region and make sure that she or he did not harbor any form of grievance or discontent against the state. Student cadres were also asked to pay closer attention to these students' thoughts and behavior during this period.

The campus associational space, comprised primarily of student groups and societies, is an important arena during a declared CSP. During CSPs, university political officials therefore exert considerable pressure on the leaders of each student interest group and club, asking them to take respon-sibility and make sure that members of their group do not participate in any political activity.

Control of Information

Tightened control over campus computer networks is another impor-tant measure taken by Chinese universities during declared CSPs. This includes enhanced monitoring of posts on campus online forums, mes-sages appearing on social media platforms, and information exchanged through instant-messaging services. University administrators perform around-the-clock monitoring of online posts, social media status updates, and content transferred through instant-messaging services. When certain agitating and influential political events take place, state law enforcement agencies become directly involved in monitoring and controlling commu-nications over the university computer network. One senior political cadre from a national university said,

> During politically sensitive periods, the popular online student forums on our university's computer network are closely monitored [by different state agencies], and the university administration is fully aware of this. . . . In addition, the provincial police depart-ment dispatches officers to campus to conduct online monitoring work. . . . I think most students do not about know things like the Jasmine Revolution if we control their exposure to such online information. . . . From the perspective of the university, we are of the opinion that these measures are necessary. Students do not under-stand how complicated these things can be . . . and may make very radical remarks or take politically aggressive actions. If such unfor-

tunate things indeed take place, we as university administrators do not have the power to handle the case and will only assist the police in dealing with it.[16]

Monitoring the campus network is an important way to shape public discourse on campus, but it also serves other, trickier purposes. Through monitoring and screening, spreaders of political rumors, authors of radical commentaries, and originators of agitating messages are carefully identified, traced, warned, and—in a few more-serious instances—investigated. Sometimes, when officials feel that online remarks have become too radical or are stirring up trouble, student cadres and hired "student online commentators" are asked to write follow-up posts to rebut the deviant remarks. This endeavor is referred to in the Party's official discourse as "opinion guiding" (*yulun yindao*).[17]

To more proactively shape the information space on campus during the precarious moments, Chinese universities also deploy the "red" student websites that the Party has financially supported. During CSPs, university administrators might temporarily suspend unofficial campus websites while allowing the officially endorsed student websites to continue operating and thus to enjoy a monopoly over public discussion during the sensitive period. In recent years, with Web 2.0 services such as social media websites with rich content (e.g., TikTok), instant messaging services with multiple functions (e.g., WeChat), and individual content-publishing platforms (e.g., Weibo and the public accounts on WeChat) flourishing in China, students have tended to use these more convenient means to associate and communicate more creatively. Most classes, organizations, and dormitories have created their own Internet groups in various formats. Political counselors and student cadres are therefore asked to closely monitor these internet groups to police student thinking and take control of potential energies in times of heightened political sensitivity, too.

In the era of "big data," the post-Tiananmen Chinese universities are also trying to deploy the voluminous data generated during everyday life on campus to further enhance the state's surveillance capacity in this critical social space. A study published in 2020 by information officers from Nanjing University of Science and Technology reported a new model of using big data from the campus network to monitor everyday experiences on campus. According to the design, six early-alert modules are constructed based on campus big data: one module to identify the whereabouts of any particular student; an alert system for unusual student spending; an online activity alert system that covers visits to "sensitive websites" and searches on "sensitive keywords," based on a list "provided by the state security and public security agencies"; an alert system for congregations of people; a library alert system that "detects if a student borrows sensitive books"; and a system for other forms of early alerts. In addition to providing early alerts, the new big-data system can perform such functions as providing a "user portrait" of the detailed daily activities of any member of the campus community, analyzing online behavior by digging into "the time, location, and user identity of every website visit" and checking the logs against "an embedded list of sensitive websites provided by the police," and providing a social network analysis of any member of the campus community (Cui et al. 2020). This new information infrastructure will surely further strengthen the state's capacity to manage politically sensitive periods on campus and nip any signs of unrest in the bud.

Conclusion

Critical and Sensitive Periods are declared on Chinese university campuses at politically precarious and thus demanding moments for the reinvented state. These are vulnerable moments for the state because the potential for political unrest or the development of a student movement is very high and there is an imminent danger of antiregime activities. To guard the safety of the political order, the state takes extraordinary measures to pacify the tension, monitor critical social spaces, exert tightened control over critical social groups, and deter people who might dare to exercise defiance from taking any real action. To attain these goals, the state feels a need to deploy a series of measures on university campuses, such as persuasion in the form of thought work to reach out to the student community, and heightened measures to limit the students' mobility and prevent the mobilizing energies on campus from materializing. The authorities keep an eye on information flows to regulate the public discourse on campus more closely. Together, these measures become a woven net of persuasion, monitoring, control, and deterrence that the state relies to keep university students calm and cool even in the most critical and sensitive moments of national and international politics.

SEVEN

Conclusion

We have come to the end of a short century, which extended from 1914 to 1989, but we do not know what century we have entered.

—Robert Darnton, *George Washington's False Teeth*, 2003, 11

No such titan ever visited / during my days as aedile. Yet wisps / still buttonhole us in random moats: / Was it this you were expecting, and if not, why not?

—John Ashbery, "Gravy for the Prisoners," 2013

In the Long Shadow of Tiananmen

On that early summer day in 1989, when the sun finally set on the horizon of Beijing, the future of China was anything but certain. In the fifty anxious days and nights prior to that evening, rebellious university students had led a nationwide uprising against the mighty state. The educated youth were joined by millions of Chinese people from all walks of life. The politically charged spring ended in a national tragedy, with the state on edge and in limbo.

In the wake of the military operation, the paramount leader, Deng Xiaoping, held an audience with the generals who had gathered in Beijing. To the surprise of many, an unflappable Deng stopped short of blaming the now-ousted liberal reformists as the culprits in the eclipsing upheaval; instead, after giving an extended account of the reform and opening-up programs he had advocated throughout the preceding decade, Deng emphasized that the basic ideas adopted and upheld by the post-Mao Party elites were anything but wrong. These ideas included not only their developmental strategy, the Four Cardinal Principles,[1] but also, and most crucially, the Party's decision to approach and engage with the capitalist West on an unprecedented scale. Probably intending it for an audience beyond the narrow meeting hall, Deng Xiaoping emphasized his final point succinctly: "If our efforts have fallen short in any respect, it was that we had not done enough to thoroughly implement the policies" (1994 302–8).

In 1992, against the backdrop of a fervent national debate on the future direction of China's market reforms, Deng Xiaoping, aged eighty-eight, paid an unannounced visit to the southern province of Guangdong, the home of China's frontier special economic zones. During that trip, Deng, whose advice was rapidly adopted by the reigning Politburo, reaffirmed his determination to implement further liberal reforms in China and demanded the expansion and acceleration of those reforms. At the 14th National Party Congress held in October of that year, the Party decided to abandon the centrally planned economy and replace it with a "socialist market economy." In 2001, the Chinese government concluded its marathon negotiations with the West and became a full member of the World Trade Organization, precipitating a major realignment of global supply chains in which China would have a major share.

Instead of regime change, the Tiananmen Movement of 1989 resulted in China's full-fledged transition into a socialist market economy, and opening up to global capitalism began to accelerate across the country in the ensuing decades. Reform and opening-up bestowed new blessings on the Chinese economy. In the decade following the Tiananmen Movement, China achieved a record-high economic growth rate. But the sea change that took place in the economic sphere was a double-edged sword—the preservation and expansion of the liberal reformist agenda temporarily stabilized the regime, yet the sweeping forces of marketization and globalized capitalism caused the utopian ideology, revolutionary zeal, and central-planning apparatchiks' old ways of control to lose their practicality.

Since the 1990s, with the implementation of a series of special laws regulating social movements, the communist state finally ditched the large-scale, unbridled, and fanatical mobilization of educated youth as a device of governance.[2] This "new normal" signified the terminal decay of the old socialist edifice of mobilizational control operated by a revolutionary state, serving as a prompt for the succeeding techno-bureaucratic state to forge a new institutional order. The largely unexpected collapse of the Soviet Union and its Eastern European satellite states in the late 1980s and early

1990s increased the urgency of China's state-rebuilding mandate. Trapped in the impasse of a national political crisis, the ruling political party of China wasted no time in starting its self-salvaging project to reinvent the state from the ruins of a clearly bygone era.

A New Social Reality

The new forces unleashed by marketization and globalization created not only a new reality that was almost beyond Party leaders' recognition, but also unfamiliar obstacles to the self-salvaging campaign of a compromised state. The establishment of a market mechanism transformed China's economic regime by abolishing the state's monopoly over scarce resources and social opportunities, thus altering the leverage of state apparatchiks in negotiating and shaping the terrain of people's speech and actions. The market transition also invalidated established norms of control through the national-scale free movement of capital and other factors of production, wiping out barriers erected by the old state apparatus that restricted people's freedom to choose their place of residence, employment, and political affiliation.

China's accelerated entry into the World Trade Organization and the shift to global capitalism created opportunities for people to generate large amounts of wealth in a relatively short time. In the 1990s, millions of young white-collar professionals and university graduates in China redrew the urban landscape on new terms. Global capitalism led to the globalization of Chinese talent. For the first time since the communist victory over China in 1949, the Party-state had to share the country's top professional and technological talent with foreign investors, global corporations, and Wall Street chiefs. Moreover, Western capitalism brought with it a modern civil society. Since the late 1990s, developmental, environmental, and humanitarian nongovernmental organizations have flourished in China, encouraging social awareness and action among younger people. These new sociopolitical fabrics have further compromised the communist state's traditional control infrastructure.

In addition, new cultural forces undermined the outdated state machine on a daily basis. The Party and the state both needed a new set of legitimating narratives that could effectively justify their ruling mandate and reestablish the righteousness of the political order they strove to uphold. Simultaneously, China's engagement with the West enabled global culture to infiltrate Chinese society, which was only accelerated by the universal availability of the internet in the late 1990s. These challenges to the Party-state's cultural hegemony shook its grip on the country's younger generation, especially university students, weakening its long-held decisive edge over rival suppliers of authority in the social realm. To rescue itself from utter systemic failure, the state yearned for overhauled, practical political arrangements to restore control under new circumstances. At the end of the day, as Herbert Marcuse argued, "the very mechanism which ties the individual to his society has changed, and social control is anchored in the new needs which it has produced" (1991, 11).

The People and the Space

Deficient legitimacy, functional paralysis, and competitive disadvantage are the main obstacles that a compromised state needs to overcome to rescue itself from utter collapse. For this complex and multifaceted undertaking of state reconstruction, the central goal for builders of the post-Tiananmen Chinese state is to reestablish an effective, consolidated, and justifiable political order and control over the critical social groups and critical social spaces of the country. Critical social groups are the weakest link in the edifice of state control. Members of these groups suffer the most from prior crises, given that they bear the largest share of overall losses and make the most significant sacrifices relative to other groups. Internally, members of these groups usually maintain close professional or fraternal networks. Members of a critical social group usually have an intentionally or unintentionally alternative vision and diagnosis of sociopolitical reality and different aspirations and plans for the future of the country than those touted by the ruling authority. From time to time in history, such critical social groups have been imbued with strong antisystem potentiality, remarkable mobilizational energies, and a proven capability to provide alternative or even revolutionary imageries for the future.

Accordingly, critical social groups remain the focal point for the post-crisis state's endeavors to reinvent both organizational and symbolic order. Members of critical social groups inhabit and live their everyday experiences in critical social spaces. Within this socially produced spatiality, mobilizational networks, political symbolism, or a shared identity may be nurtured, and activities deemed harmful by the ruling political order may take place. These spheres usually have physical boundaries (such as university campuses, public squares, dissident bookstores, underground churches, and the jungle camps of guerrilla fighters), but their more important dimensions are the symbolism, networks, solidarity, and identities that are generated, maintained, revived, and disseminated within them. The effectuation of an institutionalized political order relies on the extensive and effective projection of state power to the furthest reaches of these social spatialities, bringing their various constitutive elements under state rulers' firm control.

For the Chinese state, places such as university campuses and the Grand Bazaar in Urumqi[3] are critical social spaces. To exert control over these spaces, the state attempts to establish effective systems of signification, regulation, incentivization, and surveillance. These functional-institutional infrastructures converge into a form of domination that both constitutes and supports the political order that the state seeks to reinvent, reeffectuate, and sustain. The state takes advantage of but does not exhaust the creativity embedded in the activities that take place in these critical social spaces. In a sense, critical social spaces function symbiotically with the state: although these spaces depend on the state's endorsement and tolerance for their survival, the state benefits from the legitimizing, innovative, economic, cultural, and organizational backing that they provide. For a compromised state that seeks to avoid permanent breakdown, critical social spaces are pivotal sites for the state's remedial undertakings.

The Infrastructures for Statism

From this recounting of the experiences of state reinvention in China since the 1990s, it can be discerned that the state reconstruction project entails rebuilding key infrastructures of government: a significative infrastructure that creates and projects the state's legitimating narratives, a regulatory infrastructure that controls public life, and an incentivization infrastructure that shapes individual behavior by dispensing rewards for loyalty, meting out penalties for defiance, and deterring potential opponents. Additionally, the regime constructs an institutional infrastructure that organizes the social realm into a "grid-like" structure that is made and operated in the image of the state itself, completing its hideous enterprise of effectuating and maintaining control.

The term "institutional infrastructure" denotes an interconnected web of institutional arrangements that effectively shapes and structures people's everyday experiences at both the individual and community levels. It is the organizational foundation of the state's rebuilding project, enabling the state "to impose [its] own image of a just order" on elites and nonelites alike (Scott 1985, 39). The institutional infrastructure facilitates the state's reach into each small human or social unit, streamlining the reproduction of a consistent pattern of control and operation over identical groups of subjects and demarcated social spaces. It also increases the legibility of each demarcated spatial unit and its inhabitants, facilitating the state's surveillance at the everyday level. The identical institutional structure of each unit makes the everyday operation of the entire system a natural reproduction of the overall institutional culture. Ultimately, "the unknown, the unpredictable, the indeterminable are avatars of the enemy" (Lefort 1986, 288). The state builders stand firm in their determination to conquer the wilderness of society.

Using the significative infrastructure, the state seeks to manufacture, consolidate, and project a state catechism, or what I call "the baseline political rhetoric," onto critical social groups and in critical social spaces. This metanarrative legitimizes, rationalizes, and naturalizes the order and control that the state seeks to impose. This baseline political rhetoric serves as the official legitimating narrative, justifying the state's power and rendering the people's compliance both natural and purposeful. This state-enforced catechism usually includes a metaphysical theory explaining the state's right to rule, a founding myth justifying the righteousness of the state through a tailor-made historiography, and a visionary anecdote reconstructing social realities and shaping the collective imagination of the day to the state's liking. For ordinary citizens, the state's baseline political rhetoric provides a bond, a teleological confirmation of meaning, a solemn assignment of purpose, and a red thread connecting daily events and occurrences to a defined order, connecting individuals and supplying a wider identity focused on the state.

A country's lively public life is another important field in which the state can undertake its project of reinvention, where the state strives to rebuild an effective regulatory infrastructure to shape the systems of connection, information flow, and institutional culture within its social spatiality, and thereby combats rival suppliers of authority, spirituality, and organizational influence. A community-based public space that exists in parallel with the state provides an alternative arena for public debate and deliberation. Public opinion is formed in such a space; organizational life, communal bonds, discursive power, underground culture, and hidden political activism are also cultivated there—all outside of state supervision, permitting aspirational social forces to rally and eventually grow into opposition movements.

By maintaining its unflinching hold on these spheres, the state maintains a decisive edge in a contested field where multiple sources of order attempt to sway the direction of communal life and collective opinion.

The foundation for the reinvented political order is the state's competency to reward compliance, punish defiance, and closely monitor everyday occurrences in critical social spaces—in Marcusian terms, a capacity to impose "imperatives, rules and structures" on individuals' thought and behavior, thus "colonising" their everyday life (Marcuse 1991, xiv). This process involves reconstructing an incentivization infrastructure, in which the state maintains an updated set of reward instruments, punishment devices, and surveillance mechanisms that coax, measure, and preserve political compliance. By deploying the tools available in this incentivization infrastructure, the revived state can define boundaries and communicate to the social realm its preferences about acceptable types of speech and action. When linked to rewards and penalties, monitoring and surveillance contribute to the effectiveness of this incentivization. Together, the various components of this system serve as both an institutional architecture and a state-imposed cognitive frame, which, as Rousseau wrote, "can compel without violence and persuade without convincing" (1987, 164).

The State in the Everyday

Bernard-Henri Lévy argued that

> power does not appropriate the world; it continually engenders it in all its dimensions. It does not expropriate men and their homes; it places them under house arrest, deepens and fortifies the niches where they literally take root. Far from malignantly tearing the thread of their social fabric, power is what weaves the cloth of every reality. (1979, 40)

The state is manifested in the everyday lifeworld of its citizens, where state forces join (or are joined by) grassroots movements, elite visions mingle with the common imagination, and official discourses combat subaltern narratives. The everyday lifeworld hosts the essential sites in which the state tries to maintain its legitimation footing, to compete for domination over public life, and to manufacture conformism and acquiescence by deploying sets of devices that generate and dispense incentives for compliance.

The political everyday is the space in which an state's claim to power is effectuated. "Everyday-ness" is filled with seemingly unimportant and banal experiences; nevertheless, it is through these quotidian, mundane encounters that a social group wins or loses its fundamental right "to formulate its own frames of reference and its own model of conduct" (Certeau 1997, 14). Michel de Certeau's sentiment is echoed in Robert Darnton's comment on the remarkable convergence of liberalism and imperialism in the colonial power of the British Raj in India: "They came together . . . in the lives of individuals—not as empty 'isms' but as personal experiences, which exposed contradictions underlying systems of power" (2015, 89).

A state's compromisation also takes place in the political everyday lifeworld of its citizens. Normally, declining states first lose their authority to shape and regulate the spatial and temporal structures—however minuscule and nuanced—that form and establish the patterns of citizens' daily lives.[4] The symptomatic predictors of a compromised state first manifest themselves in the everyday lives of the people, including the progressive weakening of the state's coercive menace, the blurring of institutional boundaries, the disorientation of existing hierarchies, the muddling of structural layers, and the waning of the state's signaling mechanisms to targeted audiences. Eventually, a state's compromisation takes place on three interlinked fronts embedded in the everyday experiences lived by ordinary people.

On the *discursive* front, the state's inability to project its legitimation narrative and justify its rule results in the illegitimacy of its baseline political rhetoric, along with a deficient ability to maintain "the symbolic miasma that blocks revolutionary thoughts" (Scott 1985, 39). On the *associational and communal* front, the state's weakened competency leads to the loss of its competitive edge over rival suppliers of authority and organizational influence in public life. The associational space thus becomes an "automated" social spatiality, gradually operating on alien ideals, principles, and human capital free from state control. Through the everyday channels provided by an overly excited civil society, rival powers with competing ideological claims creep into the state edifice, further complicating the domestic political landscape and state order.

On the *individual* front, the state's traditional devices used to incentivize people to comply with official preferences and behave become progressively less effective over a relatively short time. In this situation, the state is unable to encourage compliance, reward loyalty, punish defiance, or foresee rebellious behavior in everyday experiences. Given this strong demonstrative effect, citizens are likely to find themselves in a social milieu of accumulating doubts, disobedience, noncooperation, and disrespect toward state authorities. This noncompliance clears the way for a major political crisis.

Finally, as a result of the state's diminished capacity, it has neither the will nor the strength to detect in advance danger from a contentious anti-regime movement, and thus it is prevented from either suppressing such a movement when it arises or ending the crisis in a peaceful manner and at a strategic moment that is advantageous to the state. For state rulers, this doomsday scenario can be escaped only by rebuilding a new political order that is compatible with contemporary demands, in which the state does not rule as "an externality through mere surveillance" but instead weaves its logic into "the fabric of society, into norms, rules, institutions, and relations of power" in everyday life (Bayat 2013, 26).

The Pursuit of Order

State rulers share a cult of order. They go all out to transform themselves from "territorial sovereign[s]" into "architect[s] of the disciplined space" (Foucault 2004, 29). The key infrastructures—institutional, significative, regulatory, and incentivization—uphold the state's order-building project, which, as Slavoj Žižek put it, "has to be re-invented in each new historical situation" (2009, 6). Institutional infrastructure assists the state in classifying, sorting, and organizing individual subjects into artificially divided components, with which the state both rearranges the spatial-temporal structure of people's everyday experiences into small, interconnected units and reestablishes control over the production of their primary identity and interpersonal networking through those encounters.

Structurally, the state creates a concentric circle in the targeted social realm, with the core group loyal to the state at the center and each extending circle covering one subcategory of people categorized according to their expected level of political trustworthiness, providing practical knowledge that the state can use to cultivate order. This infrastructure further reinstalls a separate governing structure in each grid—the basic unit—that resembles the institutional arrangements of the state. Although members of critical social groups simply experience their everyday lifeworld within this grid-like structure, they (probably unbeknownst to them) are engaged in repetitive experiences that mirror national political processes, rendering these processes habitual and natural. These miniature institutional structures eventually morph into "political organisations that are grassroots extensions of the party-state itself" (Walder 1984, 85).

A *significative infrastructure* refreshes, restrengthens, and reconsolidates the state's basis of legitimation. The state's signification project is multivocal, involving a variety of channels, arenas, and forms. Often disguised as scientific, educational, or administrative formalities, it is designed to reach every aspect of people's lived experiences in a subtler, more nuanced, and more invasive manner. With it, the state creates an immersive, experiential, and pragmatic system of projection for its official treatise. Effectively signifying its legitimating narratives, the state makes society accept the official order as both justifiable and purposeful. The discursive landscape continuously forged by the state in the political everyday lifeworld becomes so pervasive that the targeted audiences, despite experiencing occasional fatigue, nevertheless consider it familiar, natural, and instinctive. They possess neither the freedom nor the practical ability to escape.

The state deploys a revamped *regulatory infrastructure* to regain its decisive edge as it competes with alternative centers of authority in public life, particularly in the associational space directly involved in the communal experiences lived by the people. With the help of such an infrastructure, the state produces and maintains a monopoly over shared spaces, channels for information dissemination, symbolic systems, timetables, and other important resources and means that are necessary for the functioning of public life. In addition, the state rebuilds a stern yet operational set of mechanisms to monitor, filter, approve, and sanction occurrences in the country's public life under a watchful eye. With a revived regulatory infrastructure, the state regains a strong grip over this organizational process, enabling it to minimize potential social demands and, *faute de mieux*, to shape the contours of these demands in advance.[5]

The *incentivization infrastructure* provides the state with new and effective sets of tools to generate the required motivation or negative sanctions that shape individuals' behavior in the political everyday lifeworld. The state can use these varied forms of inducement to redraw the boundaries of permissible behavior and specify the limits of the state's tolerance of transgressions, making concrete what Erikson terms the "symbolic boundaries" of a community (Wilson, Greenblatt, and Wilson 1977, 10). The state's refreshed incentivization infrastructure must be compatible with the range of available resources under changing circumstances and include a layered system of dispensing. The infrastructure is also incomplete without a mechanism that provides proactive, real-time, around-the-clock, ubiquitous surveillance of critical social spaces. Such a surveillance mechanism gives the state ways to monitor compliance, measure loyalty, and detect resistance.

The state's renewed capacity to effectuate and sustain order hinges on the existence of this type of compelling incentivization infrastructure.

State Order on the University Campus

"One of the classic themes in the social sciences" is the "sources of political order" (Bates et al. 1998, 3). The modern university is a vital source for the political order upheld by the nation-state. Ever since the Westphalian nation-state came to dominate the global political landscape, the university has evolved gradually from a medieval institution of masters and students into a cultural project that holds the "single and dominant image" and "fragmented practices" of the nation-state together (Migdal 2011). In the modern era, the baseline political rhetoric of the state and that of its antitheses are both often manufactured, fine-tuned, and projected in the university, protected by its institutional mandate for the free pursuit of knowledge.

Prominent national universities serve the modern state as a training ground for future elites by facilitating the education and socialization of future national political, economic, and cultural leaders and by building solidarity among them. In the era of the knowledge-based economy, the university is a hub for producing professional elites who will later control the country's innovative capacity, investment arrangements, and technological breakthroughs. The university thus occupies a central position in the nation-state's developmental agenda and the consolidation of its material foundation.

The university is also a politically charged space that reflects the uncertainties and anxieties of modern sociopolitical life. There is an inherent tension within the university between nurturing the loyalty of future political elites and encouraging innovation for national development purposes. Culturally, the university is a project with a mission statement guided by multiple stakeholders. Socially, the university is the locus in which existing social relationships meet and new networks are forged, and as such, it is natural that the campus experience may also involve high social tensions. The university is a microcosm of the complex social landscape at large. Perhaps that is why György Péteri, when discussing the communist idea of the university, warns against "essentialising" the university, preferring to view it as something "socially embedded" that changes according to time and place (Connelly and Grüttner 2005, 12).

Universities are also politically critical because of their students. Free of realpolitik interests, students usually uphold a normative standard for the nation-state and adhere to pure principles. Students' rebellious nature reflects their age, as they populate university campuses from adolescence to early adulthood. University students mature physically, mentally, and sociopolitically during their educational experience. This transition is naturally reflected in their strong desire to escape from the censure of both parental authority and state power. As a "preparatory abeyance structure,"[6] the university hosts the rebellious momentum derived from both the natural transformation and the ideological purity of its students, making it one of the most precarious sites for the invention, effectuation, stabilization, and maintenance of a political order.

"Universities, like other institutions, were both a support for and a danger to the Communist political regime" (Péteri 2005, 164). Post-Tiananmen, Chinese universities provide an unusually detailed glimpse into the operations undertaken by a crisis-ridden communist state to rebuild political order and reestablish political control over the social realm. Chinese universities are closely coupled with the modern Chinese state, providing the impetus and manpower for an array of political revolutions, from the May Fourth Movement of 1919 to the June Fourth Movement of 1989. Military suppression crippled the capacity of the run-down Maoist state machine, and for the surviving communist regime, the erosion of the foundations of the communist state in terms of its significative, regulatory, and incentivization competence on university campuses necessitated the systematic overhaul and reconstruction of the state's bedrock infrastructures of control.

Over approximately three decades, the Chinese state built a tightly knit web of institutional control on university campuses that was directly connected to the larger state apparatus. This web was a grid-like structure with an internal operating system resembling the state, weaving together all of the actors, but primarily the students, in the political everyday lifeworld on university campuses. This web featured a concentric structure, by order of allegiance, that supported the exercise of state power and a workforce with a dual teacher-cadre capacity to infiltrate students' everyday lives, networks, and experiences. In this way, the state reestablished in post-Tiananmen Chinese universities a complete infrastructure of control with a renewed set of legitimating narratives, a revived capacity to signify the state's narrative, a restrengthened capacity to regulate public life, and a refreshed tool kit to reward loyalty, punish defiance, and deter potential opposition.

Coupled with a sophisticated, extensive web of surveillance, the state regained the upper hand in shaping the everyday behavior of Chinese students at both the individual and the group levels. This revived state apparatus also gave the regime the means to detect, respond to, and curb crisis situations. The early-alert capability and installation of an entire bureaucracy intended as a preemptive response to political crises became part of the new normal that both secured the stability of the regime and facilitated the robust control of the state over the university and university students on an everyday basis.

Certainly, the university is a multiagent and multiactor social field in which faculty members, administrators, and students are all elemental stakeholders in the everyday lifeworld on campus. In this book, I focus on the state-directed control systems foisted on students; however, it is important to note that to reinvent a political order on university campuses and manufacture an acquiescent academia also involves systems of signification, regulation, and incentivization for nonstudent stakeholders. In addition, this study used the sociopolitical field of the university as a microcosm for the larger apparatus of control that the communist state has sought to establish over Chinese society at large in the post-1989 era. Similar control devices and systems being established outside of university walls—such as a similar "grid-like" structure for grassroots neighborhood organizations, a strict regulatory infrastructure that commands the media space, and an incentivization and surveillance system deployed in sectors such as state-owned enterprises—illuminate that the university's experiences reflect some of the shared features of the new state power that has been reinvented across China.

This holistic system of state intervention in the political everyday lifeworld has created a milieu of conformism, acquiescence, and loyalty to the state. This milieu is crucial for the Chinese state's overall rebuilding project. In other words, the manner in which the state reinvents its strong hold over the power to shape people's quotidian experiences is at the center of inquiries into state rule and the reasons for its endurance. Echoing calls to recognize the importance of the political everyday lifeworld under autocracies and its essential relevance to state formation, this book seeks to shift scholarly attention from a perspective dominated by a focused glimpse into the high politics of the state to down-to-earth, mundane, concrete, lived experiences under the rule of the state.

In the Final Analysis

The forms of states are not ephemeral occurrences in the political history of *Homo sapiens*; their emergence is usually some kind of response to fundamental change in terms of economic forces, cultural norms, and social structure. The reinvented state in China is constructed from the ruins of the bygone state apparatus and in accordance with the new circumstances of the post-Tiananmen era. It is a mixture of an escape from Maoist chaos, a cursory return to technocratic rule, a soul-search for the Party's lost ideological cause, and a remaking of the forward-facing new capacity that has just arrived with unprecedented leaps in information technology and the arrival of big data and new methods of communication. This book provides a detailed glimpse into this reinvented state: what it looks like, how it works, and most importantly, how the Chinese communist regime effectively uses it to reassert control over the society in the post-Tiananmen era.

"Events . . . are constituted as well as constitutive," argued William H. Sewell Jr. (1990, 23). The people's massive withdrawal of their compliance during the Tiananmen Movement of 1989 was not only a watershed moment for Chinese politics of the 1980s, but also a history-shaping transformative event for the Chinese state. As Grzegorz Ekiert noted, "major political crises and ways in which particular regimes responded to the crisis were more important in shaping political processes in these countries than the formal characteristics of their political and economic systems or their politically dependent status" (1996, 307). The military suppression of a student-led national uprising against the political establishment discredited the old legitimating narratives of the state and highlighted a somber political reality. The iron fist used to crush contentious social forces alienated members of critical social groups whose compliance and support would be vital for the long-term survival of the regime.

Different regimes undertake different actions to achieve political stability, thus effectuating and sustaining the political order. The reinvented Chinese state in the post-Tiananmen era represented a clear rupture from the Maoist paradigm of governance. The Maoist state, seeking to realize its utopian goal of a class-leveled society, discharged its hegemonic project through an ideological congruence forged by large-scale societal mobilization. In contrast, the post-Tiananmen Chinese state seeks primarily to "destabilize" society and strives to engineer social stability through a normalized, quotidian, and pervasive web of control, along with visible and invisible operations that signify the state's baseline political narrative, regulate public life, and dispense incentives for conformism, securing the regime's claim to power.

"Authority is the agent of order," argued Edward Shils (1982, 96). Acknowledging the pluralist social landscape with multiple competing centers of authority under an all-out market transition, the post-Tiananmen Chinese state implements its hegemonic project and reinvents a state order through institutionalized, bureaucratized, and standardized means and methods, supplemented only by occasional mass mobilization at uncontroversial moments. When the Party-state identifies the maintenance of long-term stability and order (*changzhi jiuan*) as its overall goal, its demands on society are no longer allegiance and devotion but primarily quiescence and obedience. In the university, one of the most critical social spaces for implementing the state's hegemonic order, the overhauled state operates on different fronts only to prevent the displacement of university students in terms of their integration and compliance with the new political order. In particular, the state strives to remove the precarious social space and draconian meaning previously assigned to the student population and to create new community spaces, norms, culture, and timetables that ensure that China's new generations of educated youth remain calm, despite the confusing domestic and international environment.

"The state is to politics what the hidden hand is (à la Adam Smith) to economics" (Rosenau 1989, 14). If the Maoist Chinese state was ideological, paternalistic, and agitative, engaging society through its advocacy of a revolutionary and futuristic consensus on a class-leveled society, the revamped post-Tiananmen state is pedagogical, disciplinary, and patronizing, shaping society with powerful devices of signification, regulation, and incentivization. Whereas the Maoist state asked for authentic piety, the new state demands dutiful observance that involves "self-discipline and subjective coercion" (Turner 2008, 89). The new state creates and enforces a set of bureaucratic rules that standardize and rectify social interaction, public spaces, and the individual behavioral landscape; it appears to be more routine in terms of its operation. Through the norms of exchange of loyalty and benefits, the state's preferred pattern of speech and actions is internalized in the minds and hearts of the governed. This conformity is manifested through their everyday encounters with the state and their collective lifeworlds, where people are socialized into compliance. Eventually, as the legal maxim states, *etsi coactus, tamen voluit* (I may have been compelled, but in the final analysis I committed my will). In doing so, the new state has overhauled its own appearance, structure, and functioning to become more resilient and relevant under the new political and social reality. A reinvented state has thus emerged, finally, from the ruins of a compromised state.

Notes

1. Asef Bayat (2021) noted that "'youth affordance'—that is, strategic agility, endurance, and 'structural irresponsibility' (relative freedom from dependence on and responsibility for others)—offered [students a] comparative advantage to act more daringly on the stage of street politics" (103). Francis Fukuyama (2014) also found that the rising political demand pressed by a university-educated new middle class in the Middle East is an important variable to explain the Arab Spring. He wrote, "Tunisia and Egypt had experienced lower rates of growth than Turkey or Brazil; nonetheless, both produced large numbers of university graduates whose hopes for work and career were stymied by the cronyism of those countries' political regimes" (6).

2. For the United States, see Rim 2020; Zaveri 2020; Paul 2020; Pierson 2020. For Hungary, see Vass 2020; *Hungary Today* 2020; Kalan 2020; Dunai 2020; Reuters staff 2020. For Iraq, see Abdul-Zahra 2019; Alsaafin 2020; *Al Jazeera* 2019. For Indonesia, see Karmini 2020; Budiman and Costa 2020; Costa and Widianto 2020; Doherty 2020.

3. On the tradition of Chinese student activism, see, among others, Wasserstrom 1991; Calhoun 1994; Perry 1994; Wasserstrom and Liu 1995; Wright 2001; Zhao 2001; Andreas 2009; Huang 2010; Perry and Yan 2020.

4. This resonates with the question Teresa Wright asked in 2010: "Although university students in the 1980s participated in numerous political protests, since 1989 they have been remarkably quiescent. Indeed, rather than challenging the CCP, post-1989 college students have displayed a remarkable interest in joining it. What accounts for this shift?" (Wright 2010, 65). For a discussion, see the next chapter.

5. For a discussion, see chapter 6.

6. In 2020, China had 2,738 institutions of higher education, among which

827 offered postgraduate programs. In the same year, 41.83 million students were studying in tertiary institutions in China, and Chinese universities that offered first degree programs had an average of 15,749 students. The gross enrollment ratio of China's higher education sector in 2020 was 54.4 percent, a 2.8 percent increase on the previous year. See Ministry of Education, 2021a.

7. For state building see, for example, Evans, Rueschemeyer, and Skocpol 1985; Tilly 1992; Ertman 1997; Ziblatt 2006; Zhao 2015; Acemoglu and Robinson 2019. For an overview of the development of state theory, see Wang 2021.

8. This resembles Michael David-Fox's (2005) description of the Russian students: "From the point of view of official party ideologues and moralists, youth was at once a specially plastic group to be fashioned and protected, a source of deviation, and a potential force to be unleashed and mobilised" (35).

9. In many non-Western cultures, modern universities represent a foreign force with no indigenous cultural roots (Zhao 2001, 96); in such a scenario, the university also stands in tension with the national culture.

10. By focusing on the political professionalization of student cadres in the Communist Youth League on campus, Doyon (2023) depicts how the forging of "behavioural homogeneity" and an intermingled clientism network facilitates the formation of loyalty and commitment to the state of these future political officials. This book, instead, studies how the post-Tiananmen Chinese state reinvents itself on university campuses and reestablishes its control over the university student populace from the perspective of state rebuilding.

11. This holds despite the occasional adoption of the older instrument of campaign mobilization by the state, albeit at a much smaller scale, when it deems the strategy necessary to realize governance goals. Again, see Perry 2011.

12. See, for example, Sayer 1994; Bayat 2013, 2021; Blaydes 2018; Ong 2022.

CHAPTER 1

1. Sebastián Mazzuca (2021) discussed the concept of state weakness, which denotes the weakness in the development of a state's capacity to produce satisfactory quantity, quality, and efficiency of governmental goods and services. State weakness is the consequence of historical pathways of state formation—a narrowly defined process involving territorial consolidation and coercion monopolization. When a state is compromised—the concept I discuss in this book—the focus is on legitimation and control. It is conceptually different from Mazzuca's definition of state weakness, which stresses the state's reduced capacity in providing public goods and services.

2. See, for example, Sayer 1994; Bayat 2013, 2021; Blaydes 2018; Ong 2022.

3. For example, studies have demonstrated how in the Soviet Union, social formations such as the Russian nature protection movement, the professional organization of Soviet composers, and the "Soviet Technical Intelligentsia" craved "breathing space," where a community of professionals operated on alternative norms, narratives, and ideologies under soviet-socialist political control (Bailes 1971; Weiner 1999; Tomoff 2006; David-Fox 2005).

4. This refers to a political order that was supported by a "rich subculture of instrumental-personal ties independent of the party's control." See Walder 1984, 7, 24.

5. Yet in Vietnam, the biggest obstacle in the way of the state's efforts to invent a socialist politico-economic order was people's everyday resistance. See Kerkvliet 2005. In other cases, societies may willingly provide the cognitive bedrock for effectuating and maintaining an institutionalized political order in the quotidian details of the political everyday. In the 1930s and 1940s, German society's collective sense of belonging to a genuine "volksgemein-schaft" (a national community) and the shared cognitive and value structures of monolithic antisemitism are believed to have played an essential role in securing the people's willing compliance with fanatic state projects as hideous as the Holocaust. See Goldhagen 1997; Fritzsche 1998.

6. For the transformation from a mass campaign to managed campaigns in the post-Mao era, see Perry 2011.

7. For the rise of modern universities, see Reuben 1996; for the origin of liberal education, see Newman 1996; for the origins of the research university, see Clark 2006; for the transformation of the university under globalization, see Readings 1996; for the commodification of higher education, see Apple 2012; for a comparative overview of higher education and the state, see Goodman, Kariya, and Taylor 2013.

8. For example, the university has been said to embrace a "liberal education" agenda (Newman 1996), but has also been blamed for "the closing of the American mind" (Bloom 1987). There has been extensive debate over whether the modern university is built on "the Kantian concept of reason," the "Humboldtian idea of culture," or the "techno-bureaucratic notion of excellence." See Readings 1996.

9. As being argued, "the university was a ready infrastructure to serve the growing needs of a relatively independent public sphere" (Péteri 2005, 159).

10. For state-mobilized social movements, see Ekiert, Perry, and Yan 2020; also see Zhao 2004; Wang 2012b; Gries 2004, 2014.

11. See Calhoun 1994; Zhao 2001; Wasserstrom and Liu 1989; Hinton 1972.

12. Susan Shirk argues that "the vague and subjective standards, peer judges, and mutual destructiveness that char- acterise virtuocracies make it possible for people to succeed through opportunism, fakery, or sycophancy. Political competition on such virtuocratic grounds generates social mistrust and conflicts" (1982, 184).

13. For an overview of the transformation of China's youth culture in the post-Mao era, see Clark 2012.

14. The article defines the term "involuted" as follows: "The Chinese term for involution, *neijuan*, which is made up of the characters for 'inside' and 'rolling,' suggests a process that curls inward, ensnaring its participants within what the anthropologist Xiang Biao has described as an 'endless cycle of self-flagellation.'" See Liu 2021.

CHAPTER 2

1. For the Chinese Communist Party's reorganization of higher education in China from 1949 to 1961, see Hsu 1964.

2. After 1989, the Communist Party Committees in most PRC universities created a new "Student Work Department (SWD)" on a par with the traditional

Organizational, Propaganda and United Front Departments. Today, SWDs are a major component of the Communist Party apparatus (instead of university administration) on university campuses. An interesting account of the creation of SWD in Tsinghua University can be found in the memoir of Fang Huijian (the then–University Party Secretary). See Fang 2003, 373–74.

3. See later in this chapter.

4. See Xu 2007, 239; also see Interview 201106017–01.

5. In the past two decades, "grid management" (*wangge hua guanli*) has become increasingly popular in China, especially in communal policing. For grid management outside of the university space, see Schwarck 2018; Jiang 2021; Zenz and Leibold 2020; Hu, Tu, and Wu 2018; Chen and Kang 2016; Leibold 2020; Tang 2020.

6. A "year cohort" is not normally considered a formal organizational unit of the student populace, though.

7. Interview FFAA-with MoE official.

8. The majority of Chinese youth under the age of twenty-eight have to join the CYL at some point in middle school.

9. Interview 20110606–01.

10. Interview 20110606–02.

11. Interview 20110607–01.

12. Interviews 20110607–06, 20110607–01, 20110315–01, 20110419–01.

13. Interview 20110225–01.

14. A few universities used the less politicized title of "classroom director" (*Ban zhuren*) for this post prior to Ministry of Education Instruction No. 24 (2006). See Gong, Zhang, and Zhang 2003, 497.

15. It is also considered an effective institutional channel for the Communist Party to identify, train, and promote loyal political talent for the regime's future officialdom. In fact, a number of senior Communist Party leaders, including Hu Jintao, the supreme leader of China between 2002 and 2012, served as political counselors for some time after graduating from college. See Wen Wei Po 2011.

16. Interview 201103617–01.

17. Interview 20110308–01.

18. Interview 20110315–01; also see 20110318–01.

19. These powers include (1) publicizing and implementing the Communist Party's political lines, guidance, and policies, (2) managing all Party organizations on campus, (3) making decisions on all important issues involved in the university's teaching, research, and administration, (4) overseeing the university's political and ideological work, in addition to work on moral education, (5) selecting, appointing, training, and promoting all university cadres (i.e., faculty or staff members who serve on administrative posts), (6) supervising the Communist Youth League, the Women's Federation, and the Student Union, and (7) implementing the Party's United Front Policy and overseeing all activities organized by officially endorsed minor democratic political parties on campus. See the Central Committee of the CCP 1996; for a revised version of the regulations, see the Central Committee of the CCP 2021.

20. Interview 20110608–07.

21. Interview 20110608–05.

22. Interview 20110315–01.
23. Interview 20130618–01.
24. Interview 20130614–04.

CHAPTER 3

1. It has to be noted that the state used a politico-ideological curriculum as a major weapon to reform the old educational systems prevalent in China's colleges and universities in the 1950s after the Party's military takeover of those institutions. Yet after the initial period of state-building in the early 1950s, the Maoist regime's perception of the utility value of a formal curriculum for ideological education in universities was at best dismissive.

2. For a review of China's education reform after 1976, see Epstein 1991.

3. For example, for peasant workers who recently emigrated from the countryside to urban centers, the aims of ideological training activities set by the state are modest, involving "helping them become aware of the Communist Party-state's care [for them] and understand the unavoidable problems . . . in the process of industrialisation and urbanisation" (Chinese Communist Youth League, CCYL 2010). Document No. 17 advised that attention should be paid to providing them with "humanitarian care and psychological easement" and "assisting with real life difficulties and issues" (Chinese Communist Youth League, CCYL 2010).

4. Qiu's previous posts include chief justice of a northwestern province and the Communist Party secretary of the Bureau of State Security of Beijing.

5. In addition, the Xinguang Civilian's Development Association (also known as the New Light People's Development Association) at Renmin University of China (Zhou 2018; Yang 2018; Xinguang Civilian's Development Society 2018a, b), Qimin Society at the University of Science and Technology Beijing (Wen 2018; Zhan 2018; Zhang 2018), the Marxism Studies Society at Nanjing University (Wang 2018; Hu 2018a, b; Zhu 2018a, b), and the Xinxin Youth Society at Beijing Language and Culture University (Hai 2018; Xinxin Youth Society 2018a, b, c, d) were either forced to dissolve or denied registration by their respective university administrations.

CHAPTER 4

1. This book deals primarily with the post-1989 period. For the activism and political implication of student groups in earlier periods, see Wasserstrom 1991; Walder 2009.

2. See Communist Party Group of the MoE and the Central Committee of the CYL 2020.

3. Interview 20110415–01.

4. Interview 20110608–06.

5. See the Central Committee of the CCP and the State Council 2004.

6. For studies of China's online censorship regime in general, see King, Pan, and Roberts 2013, 2014, 2017; Lorentzen 2014; Roberts 2018.

7. For a more detailed account of this process, see Han 2018.

8. To accomplish this mission, the Ministry directed that Communist Party

and CYL organizations on university campuses should identify topics that "indicate the future direction or emerging tendency of public discussion, or that may have a wider social impact."

9. See Ministry of Education and the Central Committee of the Chinese Communist Youth League 2016.

10. Rumor has it that online commentators receive fifty cents from the state for each message they post online, but this might not be true. My interviews show that most of these student online commentators receive a monthly stipend from their respective university's Communist Youth League, rather than working on a per-piece salary. For very interesting studies on the Chinese "five-cents army," see Han 2015a, b, 2018.

11. Interview 20110608–04.

12. These included Peking University's "Red Flag Online," Nankai University's "Awakening Web," Nanjing University's "Young Communists School," Central China Science and Technology University's "Party School Online," and Southwestern University of Communications's "Frontline." See Cao 2012, 152.

13. For an overview of the Communist Party's policy toward religion, see Laliberte 2011; Cao 2020.

14. This perception is perhaps caused by the heavy use of theological terms and jargon.

15. See Ministry of Education and Central Committee of the Chinese Communist Youth League 2004.

16. For China's decision in 2009 to expand its higher education sector, see Bai 2006.

17. A similar situation could be found in Eastern European countries after World War II. The specialization and expansion of higher education institutions in those countries, following the Soviet model, have resulted in higher levels of conformity, anxiety, and pressure on university campuses. See Neave 2011.

CHAPTER 5

1. See Organization Department of the Central Committee of the Communist Party of China 2021; Ministry of Education 2021b.

2. See Interview 20110608–02.

3. For data sources, see Department of Planning and Construction of the National Education Commission 1994, 34–35; Department of Planning and Construction, National Education Commission 1995, 34–35; Department of Planning and Construction, National Education Commission 1996, 34–35; Han 1997, 36–37; Ji 1998, 38–39; Ji 1999, 38–39; Mou 2000, 40–41; Mou 2001, 40–41; Mou 2002, 44–45; Mou 2003, 24–25; Han 2004, 26–27; Han 2005, 26–27; Han 2006, 24–25; Han 2007, 26–27; Han 2008, 26–27; Han 2009, 24–25; Xie 2010a, 26–27; Xie 2011, 24–25; Xie 2012a, 26–27; Xie 2013, 24–25; Xie 2014, 26–27; Xie 2015, 26–27; Liu 2016, 26–27; Liu and Li 2017, 29; Liu and Li 2018, 29; Liu and Li 2019, 29; Chinese Education Online 2014; Chinese Education Online 2021; Ministry of Education 2021a. The surge in the number of graduate school applications has multiple causes. First, harsh competition on the Chinese job market has made an advanced degree a considerable advantage for university graduates seeking employ-

ment. With the increasingly fierce competition for jobs in the state apparatus and SOEs, an advanced degree has become a virtual necessity. The Chinese state has also taken the granting of higher degrees seriously, as this is one of the primary channels of upward social mobility.

4. Bai (2006) provides a rich analysis of the so-called "graduate unemployment problem" associated with China's rapid expansion of higher education enrollment in the 1990s.

5. Interview 20130905–01.

6. See Central Organization Department 2000. For an example of the qualification requirements of such a program, see Organization Department of the CPC Henan Provincial Committee et al. 2021.

7. Interview 20110603–01.

8. Regarding the expressive function of punishment, see Feinberg 1965.

9. See the Ministry of Education, the Ministry of Health, and the Central Committee of the Chinese Communist Youth League 2005.

10. See the Ministry of Education, the Ministry of Health, and the Central Committee of the Chinese Communist Youth League 2005.

CHAPTER 6

1. Zhao and Yao (2013) listed four categories of events and topics that may have such an influence in China: political and ideological trends, livelihood issues, campus safety issues, and problems arising from the reform and rapid development of higher education. See Zhao and Yao (2013), 71

2. In 1988, the student protest was provoked by the death of a postgraduate student, Chai Qingfeng, who was beaten by young gangsters in a Beijing restaurant close to campus.

3. Interview 20110617–01.

4. See Nanjing University 2014, 6.

5. Interview 20110617–01.

6. After the CSP was announced in the wake of the NATO bombing, according to political cadres I interviewed, the Public Security Department of the provincial government summoned a meeting attended by all of the faculty-level Communist Party secretaries. At the meeting, the official from the provincial government emphasized the importance of maintaining political stability on campus and issued detailed instructions on how to prevent students from joining the planned public demonstrations. The Communist Party Committee of each faculty then held a meeting with all of the political counselors under their supervision and the information from the government was relayed to them promptly. See Interview 20110617–01.

7. Interview 20110617–01.

8. In Chinese, *ban zhuren*, a title similar to political counselor.

9. Interview 20110617–01.

10. As one student cadre recalled, "When I was a freshman, I experienced the Carrefour incident. It was at 6 a.m. one morning that our political counsellor called all of the student cadres and invited us to an immediate breakfast meeting. At the meeting, the political counsellor asked us to persuade students in each class not to

participate in any public protest or demonstration in front of the French supermarket Carrefour." See Interview 20110606–06.

11. Interview 20110607–05. It is interesting, however, that some students regard the university's prompt response to politically sensitive events as an "overreaction." One student told of not even knowing what the Jasmine Revolution was until being summoned to a meeting at which political officials warned students about the negative sanctions if any of them joined protest actions. In some cases, the preventive measures taken by the university somewhat facilitated the spread of an originally obscure message about a possible oppositional movement (see Interview 20110608–03).

12. A political counselor described her university's arrangements during the declared CSP before the Communist Party's 18th National Congress in 2012 as follows: "During that time, we were ordered to organize more political study sessions for the students than we usually did. . . . At these sessions, we led the students in a group study of the relevant Communist Party documents. . . . At the routine meetings for all political counsellors, the Deputy Party Secretary of the CCP Committee instructed us to organize more reading sessions during the CSP and conduct enhanced patriotic education. As part of the preparation for the 18th Party Congress CSP, the university organized many additional public seminars to explain to students the Party's official political lines during that period, and all students were required to attend. We even promised the students that we would award extracurricular credits to everyone who attended those mandatory political seminars." See Interview 20130617–04.

13. Interview 20130617–05.

14. Interview 20130618–01.

15. Interview 20130619–02.

16. Interview 20110617–01.

17. See Interview 20110617–01. Also see Xu 2007, 229.

CHAPTER 7

1. These include the principles of upholding the socialist path, upholding the people's democratic dictatorship, upholding the Chinese Communist Party's leadership, and upholding Maoist thought and Marxism-Leninism.

2. The Maoist paradigm of state-directed mass mobilization first lost its constitutional legality in 1982. In 1982, the so called "Four Bigs"—the Party's familiar instruments for youth mobilization—were criminalized in the new constitution promulgated by a stability-seeking Party leadership The "Four Bigs" (*sida*) refer to speaking out freely (*da ming*), airing views fully (*da fang*), holding large-scale debates (*da bianlun*), and writing "Big Character Posters" (*da zibao*). See chapter 2.

3. The Grand Bazaar in Urumqi is where Uighur merchants sell food items. In 2009, the ethnic riots in Xinjiang first broke out there.

4. Just imagine on a cold morning, the fictional manager of a fruit and vegetable shop à la Václav Havel stops placing in his window, among the onions and carrots, the slogan "Workers of the World, Unite!" See Havel 2018 [1978], 14.

5. As Francis Fukuyama argued, "society organised into cohesive groups . . . is much more likely to demand and receive accountability than one consisting of disorganised individuals" (2004, 30).

6. See chapter 4 of this book.

Bibliography

Abdul-Zahra, Qassim (2019). "Students Join Iraq Protests as Clashes Kill 3 Demonstrators." URL: https://apnews.com/article/ap-top-news-baghdad-middle-east -religion-iraq-9e643b7c5da045c7aab777fdb883f820 (visited on 6/21/2022).

Acemoglu, Daron, and James A. Robinson (2019). *The Narrow Corridor: States, Societies and the Fate of Liberty*. New York: Penguin Press.

Al Jazeera (2019). "Iraqi Students Join Thousands in Ongoing Anti-Gov't Protests." URL: https://www.aljazeera.com/news/2019/10/28/iraqi-students-join-thousa nds-in-ongoing-anti-govt-protests (visited on 6/21/2022).

Alsaafin, Linah (2020). "Students Are the 'Backbone' of Iraq Anti-government Protests." URL: https://www.aljazeera.com/news/2020/2/10/students-are-the-bac kbone-of-iraq-anti-government-protests (visited on 6/21/2022).

Altbach, Philip G. (1967). "Students and Politics." In *Student Politics*. New York: Basic Books.

Altbach, Philip G. (2009). *Rise of the Red Engineers: The Cultural Revolution and the Origins of China's New Class*. Stanford, CA: Stanford University Press.

Andreas, Joel (2006). "Institutionalized Rebellion: Governing Tsinghua University During the Late Years of the Chinese Cultural Revolution." *China Journal* 55: 1–28.

Ang, Yuen Yuen (2020). *China's Gilded Age: The Paradox of Economic Boom and Vast Corruption*. Cambridge, UK: Cambridge University Press.

Apple, Michael W. (2012). *Education and Power*. New York: Routledge.

Arendt, Hannah (1969). "On Violence." In *Crises of the Republic*, 103–98. Orlando, FL: Harcourt.

Bachrach, P., and M. S. Baratzm (1970). *Power and Poverty: Theory and Practice*. New York: Oxford University Press.

Bai, Limin (2006). "Graduate Unemployment: Dilemmas and Challenges in China's Move to Mass Higher Education." *China Quarterly* 185: 128–44.

Bailes, Kendall E. (1971). *Technology and Society under Lenin and Stalin: Origins of the*

Soviet Technical Intelligentsia 1917–1941. Princeton, NJ: Princeton University Press.

Bakke, Wight E., and Mary S. Bakke (1971). *Campus Challenge*. Hamden, CT: Archon Books.

Balogh, Brian (2009). *A Government Out of Sight: The Mystery of National Authority in Nineteenth-Century America*. Cambridge, UK: Cambridge University Press.

Bates, Robert H., ed. (1998). *Analytical Narratives*. Princeton, NJ: Princeton University Press.

Bates, Robert H. (2008). *When Things Fell Apart: State Failure in Late-Century Africa*. Cambridge, UK: Cambridge University Press. 213

Bayat, Asef (2013). *Life as Politics: How Ordinary People Change the Middle East*. Second Edition. Stanford, CA: Stanford University Press

Bayat, Asef (2021). *Revolutionary Life: The Everyday of the Arab Spring*. Cambridge, MA: Harvard University Press.

Beasley-Murray, Jon (2010). *Posthegemony: Political Theory and Latin American*. Minneapolis: University of Minnesota Press.

Bellin, Eva (2005). "Coercive Institutions and Coercive Leaders." In *Authoritarianism in the Middle East: Regimes and Resistance*, 21–42. Boulder, CO: Lynne Rienner Publishers.

Berger, Peter L., and Thomas Luckmann (1966). *The Social Construction of Reality: A Treatise in the Sociology of Knowledge*. New York: Anchor Books.

Bernard-Henri Lévy (1979). *Barbarism with a Human Face*. New York: Harper and Row.

Blaydes, Lisa (2018). *State of Repression: Iraq under Saddam Hussein*. Princeton, NJ: Princeton University Press.

Bloom, Allan (1987). *The Closing of the American Mind: How Higher Education Has Failed Democracy and Impoverished the Souls of Today's Students*. New York: Simon and Schuster Paperbacks.

Borton, James (2004). "A Blogger's Tale: Stainless Steel Mouse." URL: http://www.atimes.com/atimes/China/FG22Ad04.html (visited on 10/11/2021).

Bourdieu, Pierre (1996). *The State Nobility: Elite Schools in the Field of Power*. Cambridge, UK: Polity Press.

Bourdieu, Pierre (1999). "Rethinking the State: Genesis and Structure of the Bureaucratic Field." In *State/Culture: State-Formation After the Cultural Turn*, ed. George Steinmetz, 53–75. Ithaca, NY: Cornell University Press.

Bourdieu, Pierre (2020). *On the State: Lectures at the Collège de France 1989–1992*, eds. Patrick Champagne et al. Cambridge, UK: Polity Press.

Bregnbæk, Susanne (2019). *Fragile Elite: The Dilemmas of China's Top University Students*. Stanford, CA: Stanford University Press.

British Broadcasting Channel (2018a). "深圳佳士工人维权: 左翼青年与政治诉求" [Shenzhen Jasic workers' rights defense: Left-wing youth and political aspirations]. URL: https://www.bbc.com/zhongwen/simp/chinese-news-45296032 (visited on 9/21/2021).

British Broadcasting Channel (2018b). "深圳佳士工人维权发酵: 多名声援团成员失联" [Shenzhen Jasic workers' rights protection fermented: Many support group members lost contact]. URL: https://www.bbc.com/zhongwen/simp/chinese-news-45296032 (visited on 9/21/2021).

Brownlee, Jason (2007). *Authoritarianism in an Age of Democratization*. Cambridge, UK: Cambridge University Press.

Budiman, Yuddy Cahaya, and Agustinus Beo Da Costa (2020). "Indonesia Islamic Groups, Students Join Movement to Scrap Jobs Law." URL: https://www.reut ers.com/article/us-indonesia-economy-protests-idUSKBN26Y18Q (visited on 6/21/2022).

Burns, John P., and Xiaoqi Wang (2010). "Civil Service Reform in China: Impacts on Civil Servants' Behavior." *China Quarterly* 201 (March): 58–78.

Calhoun, Craig (1994). *Neither Gods nor Emperors: Students and the Struggle for Democracy in China*. Berkeley: University of California Press.

Cao, Nanlai (2020). *Constructing China's Jerusalem: Christians, Power, and Place in Contemporary Wenzhou*. Stanford, CA: Stanford University Press.

Cao, Yinzhong (2012). "大学生网民群体研究" [A study on the university student netizen population]. PhD thesis. University of Electronic Science and Technology of China.

Cary, Eve (2013). *Reforming China's State-Owned Enterprises*. URL: https://thedi plomat.com/2013/06/reforming-chinas-state-owned-enterprises/ (visited on 10/11/2021).

Central Committee of the CCP (1996). "中国共产党普通高等学校基层组织工作条例" [The Chinese Communist Party's regulations on basic level work in ordinary institutions of higher education]. URL: http://cpc.people.com.cn/GB/641 62/71380/71387/71589/5527096.html (visited on 9/21/2021).

Central Committee of the CCP (2021). "中国共产党普通高等学校基层组织工作条例" [Regulations on the operations of the grassroots organizations of the Chinese Communist Party in ordinary institutions of higher education]. URL: http://www.gov.cn/zhengce/2021-04/22/content_5601428.htm (visited on 9/28/2021).

Central Committee of the CCP and the State Council (2004). "关于进一步加强和改进大学 生思想政治教育的意见" [A few opinions on the further enhancement and improvement of thought and political education among the university students]. Document No. 16 (2004).

Central Committee of the CCP and the State Council of the People's Republic of China (2004). "中共中央国务院关于进一步加强和改进大学生思想政治教育的意见" [Instructions from the Communist Party Central Committee and the State Council on the further strengthening and improvement of thought and political work among university students]. URL: http://www.wfxy.neu.edu.cn /2016/0311/c471a19992/pagem.htm (visited on 9/24/2021).

Central Committee of the Chinese Communist Youth League and the Ministry of Education (2005). "关于加强和改进大学生社团工作的意见" [Opinions on strengthening and improving the work of college student associations]. URL: http://www.gqt.org.cn/documents/zqlf/200703/t20070321_14553.htm (visited on 9/24/2021).

Central Organization Department (2000). "关于进一步做好选调应届优秀大学毕业生到基层培 养锻炼工作的通知 (组通字 [2000] 3 号" [Notice on further doing a good job in selecting outstanding university graduates to train and exercise at the basic level (*zu tong zi* [2000] no. 3)]. URL: https://career.tsinghua.edu .cn/info/1040/2392.htm (visited on 10/26/2021).

Certeau, Michael de (1984). *The Practice of Everyday Life*. Berkeley: University of California Press.

Certeau, Michel de (1997). *Culture in the Plural*, ed. Luce Giard. Minneapolis: University of Minnesota Press.

Chai, Wei (2016). "高扬信仰的风帆-党的十八大以来高校思想政治工作综述" [Raising the sail of faith: Summary on the university thought work since the Party's 18th National Congress]. URL: http://www.moe.gov.cn/jyb_xwfb/s51 47/201612/t20161207_291086.html (visited on 10/20/2021).

Chen, Feng, and Yi Kang (2016). "Disorganized Popular Contention and Local Institutional Building in China: A Case Study in Guangdong." *Journal of Contemporary China* 25, no. 100: 596–612.

Chen, Junwang, Xi Cheng, and Ping Li (Nov. 2005). "实名制让高校 BBS 变脸" [Real name system makes university BBS change face]. 楚天都市报 [*Chutian Metropolitan*].

Chen, Peng (2015). "高校辅导员怎样离学生更近一点?" [How could university counselors get closer to the students?] URL: https://epaper.gmw.cn/gmrb /html/2015-07/13/nw.D110000gmrb_20150713_1-06.htm?div=-1 (visited on 10/20/2021).

China Daily (2021). "Young People Make Their Commitment to National Rejuvenation." URL: http://en.people.cn/n3/2021/0702/c90000-9867735.html (visited on 1/09/2022).

China Internet Network Information Center, CNNIC (2013). "中国互联网发展状况统计报告" [A statistical report on the condition of the development of China's internet]. URL: http: //www.cnnic.cn/hlwfzyj/hlwxzbg/hlwtjbg/2013 01/P020130122600399530412.pdf (visited on 9/21/2021).

China News Service (2009). "七·五暴力事件目击记: 乌鲁木齐，尸体躺在路上" [Witnesses of July 5th violence: Urumqi, body lying on the road]. URL: http://www.chinanews.com/gn/news/2009/07-06/1763270.shtml (visited on 10/11/2021).

Chinese Communist Youth League, CCYL (2010). "中青发 [2010], no.17. 号关于在全团开展分类引 导青年工作的通知" [Notice on the work of classification and guidance of youth work in the whole League]. URL: http://www.gqt.org.cn /documents/zqf/201011/t20101126_432589.htm (visited on 9/21/2021).

Chinese Education Online (2014). "数字看考研: 历年考研报名人数与录取人数统计" [Look at the Postgraduate Entrance Examination by numbers: Statistics on the number of applicants and the number of admissions for the postgraduate entrance examination over the years]. URL: https://kaoyan.eol.cn/nnews/2014 01/t20140123_1067583.shtml (visited on 10/24/2021).

Chinese Education Online (2021). "历年考研报名人数与录取统计" [Statistics on the number of applicants and the number of admissions for the Postgraduate Entrance Examination over the years]. URL: https://www.eol.cn/e_ky/zt/com mon/bmrs/ (visited on 10/24/2021).

Ci, Jiwei (1994). *Dialetic of the Chinese Revolution: From Utopianism to Hedonism*. Stanford, CA: Stanford University Press.

Clark, Paul (2012). *Youth Culture in China: From Red Guards to Netizens*. Cambridge, UK: Cambridge University Press.

Clark, William (2006). *Academic Charisma and the Origins of the Research University.* Chicago: University of Chicago Press.

Clemens, Elisabeth S. (2017). "Reconciling Equal Treatment with Respect for Individuality: Associations in the Symbiotic State." In *The Many Hands of the State: Theorizing Political Authority and Social Control,* eds. Kimberly J. Morgan and Ann Shola Orloff. New York: Cambridge University Press.

Colletta, Nat J., Markus Kostner, and Ingo Wiederhofer (2004). "Disarmament, Demobilization and Reintegration: Lessons and Liabilities in Reconstruction." In *When States Fail: Causes and Consequences,* ed. Robert I. Rotberg, 170–81. Princeton, NJ: Princeton University Press.

Communist Party Group of the MoE and the Central Committee of the CYL (Jan. 2020). "中共教 育部党组共青团中央关于印发高校学生社团建设管理办法的通知" [Notice on the governance of different kinds of student groups on university campuses].

Communist Youth League Committee of Hunan Institute of Humanities, Science and Technology (2012). "湖南人文科技学院大学生思想引导手册" [Handbook of ideological guidance for college students of Hunan Institute of Humanities, Science and Technology]. URL: http://www.hnrku.net.cn/txkz/upfiles/201203 /20120323111753646.doc (visited on 9/13/2013). 216

Connelly, John (2000). *Captive University: The Sovietization of East German, Czech, and Polish Higher Education 1945–1956.* Chapel Hill: University of North Carolina Press.

Connelly, John, and Michael Grüttner (2005). *Universities Under Dictatorship.* University Park: Pennsylvania State University Press.

Corrigan, Philip, and Derek Sayer (1985). *The Great Arch: English State Formation as Cultural Revolution.* Oxford, UK: Basil Blackwell.

Costa, Agustinus Beo Da, and Stanley Widianto (2020). "Indonesia Police Fire Warning Shots at Papua Student Protest." URL: https://www.reuters.com/arti cle/us-indonesia-papua-idUSKBN26J1T0pr (visited on 6/21/2022).

Cui, Cong, et al. (2020). "基于大数据的高校安全与维稳系统设计与实践" [Design and practice of university security and stability maintenance system based on big data]. *Chinese Journal of ICT in Education* 5: 61–65.

Darnton, Robert (2015). *Censors at Work: How States Shaped Literature.* New York: W. W. Norton.

David-Fox, Michael (2005). "Russian Universities Across the 1917 Divide." *Universities Under Dictatorship,* eds. John Connelly and Michael Grüttner. University Park: Pennsylvania State University Press.

Deng, Xiaoping (1994). "邓小平文选" [Selected works of Deng Xiaoping], 2nd ed., vol. 2. Beijing: Renmin Chuban She.

Department of Ideological and Political Work, MOE (2008). "加强和改进大学生思想政治教育 重要文献选编 1978–2008" [Enhancing and improving the selection of important documents on college students' ideological and political education 1978–2008]. Beijing: China Renmin University Press.

Department of Planning and Construction of the National Education Commission (1994). "中国教 育统计年鉴 1994" [Educational statistics yearbook of China 1994]. Beijing: People's Education Press.

Department of Planning and Construction, National Education Commission (1995). "中国教育统 计年鉴 1995" [Educational statistics yearbook of China 1995]. Beijing: People's Education Press.

Department of Planning and Construction, National Education Commission (1996). "中国教育统计年鉴 1996" [Educational statistics yearbook of China 1996]. Beijing: People's Education Press.

Department of Science and Information of Ministry of Education (2021). "电子科技大学突发公 共事件应急预案 (2020 年 8 月修订)" [Emergency plan for public emergencies of the University of Electronic Science and Technology of China (revised in August 2020)]. URL: https://xxgkw.uestc.edu.cn/info/1093/3818.htm (visited on 10/29/2021).

Department of Student Societies and Clubs of the CYL Committee of Tsinghua University (2006). "清华大学学生社团协会工作手册" [Work Manual of Student Societies and Clubs at Tsinghua University]. URL: https://bbs.pku.edu.cn/attach/a4/21/a4213fa137bf8151/%E6%B8%85%E5%8D%8E%E5%A4%A7%E5%AD%A6%E5%AD%A6%E7%94%9F%E7%A4%BE%E5%9B%A2%E5%8D%8F%E4%BC%9A%E5%B7%A5%E4%BD%9C%E6%89%8B%E5%86%8C.pdf (visited on 9/24/2021).

Doherty, Ben (2020). "Protests Flare in Papua as Students Demand Independence Referendum." URL: https://www.theguardian.com/world/2020/sep/29/protests-flare-in-papua-as-students-demand-independence-referendum (visited on 6/21/2022). 217

Donahue, Francis (1971). "Students in Latin-American Politics." *Student Activism: Town and Gown in Historical Perspective*, 253–69. New York: Scribner's.

Doyon, Jérôme (2023). *Rejuvenating Communism: Youth Organizations and Elite Renewal in Post-Mao China*. Ann Arbor: University of Michigan Press.

Duara, Prasenjit (1988). *Culture, Power, and the State: Rural North China 1900–1942*. Stanford, CA: Stanford University Press.

Dunai, Marton (2020). "Hungary Arts University Protesters Defy Order to End Blockade." URL: https://www.reuters.com/article/hungary-politics-education-theatre-idINKBN2712OI (visited on 6/21/2022).

Economist (2016). "Youthful Nationalists: The East Is Pink." URL: https://www.economist.com/china/2016/08/13/the-east-is-pink (visited on 12/29/2021).

Economy, Elizabeth C. (2022). *The World According to China*. Cambridge, UK: Polity Press.

Editorial Group (July 2009). "思想道德修养与法律基础" [Moral education and the basics of law]. fourth. Beijing: Higher Education Press.

Editorial Group (June 2010a). "中国近现代史纲要" [Outlines of China's modern and contemporary history]. fourth. Beijing: Higher Education Press.

Editorial Group (June 2010b). "毛泽东思想和中国特色社会主义理论体系概论" [Introduction to Mao Zedong thoughts and the systematic theories of socialism with Chinese characteristics]. third. Beijing: Higher Education Press.

Editorial Group (June 2010c). "马克思主义基本原理概论" [Introduction to the basics of Marxism]. fourth. Beijing: Higher Education Press.

Education and Publicity Group of Peking University 2020 Freshman Military Training Corps (2020). "北京大学 2020 级本科生军训开训仪式举行" [The opening ceremony of the military training of Peking University's 2020 undergraduates was held]. URL: https://news.pku.edu.cn/xwzh/564367317499479aa 83d6d361058b794.htm (visited on 9/21/2021).

Eisenstadt, S. N. (2017). *The Political Systems of Empires*. New York: Routledge.

Ekiert, Grzegorz (1996). *The State Against Society: Political Crises and Their Aftermath in East Central Europe*. Princeton, NJ: Princeton University Press.

Ekiert, Grzegorz, Elizabeth J. Perry, and Xiaojun Yan (2020). *Ruling by Other Means: State-Mobilized Movements*. Cambridge, UK: Cambridge University Press.

Epstein, Irving (1991). *Chinese Education: Problems, Policies, and Prospects*. London, UK: Garland Publishing.

Ertman, Thomas (1997). *Birth of the Leviathan: Building States and Regimes in Medieval and Early Modern Europe*. New York: Cambridge University Press.

Evans, Peter B., Dietrich Rueschemeyer, and Theda Skocpol, eds. (1985). *Bringing the State Back In*. Cambridge, UK: Cambridge University Press.

Evans, Sara M., and Harry C. Boyte (2003). "Free Spaces: The Sources of Democratic Change in America." *Civil Society Reader*, eds. Virginia A. Hodgkinson and Michael W. Foley, 255–69. Hanover, MA: University Press of New England.

Fang, Huijian (2003). "清华大学工作五十年" [Fifty years of work at Tsinghua University]. Beijing: Tsinghua University Press.

Fang, Li, and Yuanhui Liu (2013). "浙江省举行专场招聘会" [Opinions on the enhancement and improvement of the thought and political work on junior faculty members in institutions of higher education No. Jiaodang (2013)] 12. URL: https://zjnews.zjol.com.cn/system/2013/06/28/019431462.shtml (visited on 10/11/2021).

Fazal, Tania M. (2007). *State Death: The Politics and Geography of Conquest, Occupation, and Annexation*. Princeton, NJ: Princeton University Press.

Feinberg, Joel (July 1965). "The Expressive Function of Punishment." *The Monist* 49, no. 3: 397–423.

Feng, Bilian (2013). "垄断才是大学生就业最大障碍" [Monopoly is the biggest obstacle for the job placement of university graduates]. URL: http://edu.people .com.cn/n/2013/0521/c1053-21559057.html (visited on 10/11/2021).

Feng, Gang (2009). "高校思想政治教育创新发展研究" [Research on the innovation and development of ideological and political education in colleges and universities]. Beijing: China Renmin University Press.

Feng, Lei (2011). "今年 660 万大学生将如何就业?" [How would this year's 6.6 million university graduates find a job?] URL: https://epaper.gmw.cn/gmrb/html /2011-02/23/nw.D110000gmrb_20110223_2-05.htm (visited on 10/11/2021).

Feng, Zhiyue, Yibin Qian, and Congping Pan (2012). "社会转型期高校 BBS 话题特征及功能，地位探讨" [Analysis on campus BBS topic feature, function and status on social transformation in China]. *Guanggao Daguan* [Theoretical Edition] 12: 66–70.

Foucault, Michel (2004). *Security, Territory, Population*, ed. Michel Senellart. New York: Palgrave Macmillan.

Fritzsche, Peter (1998). *Germans into Nazis*. Cambridge, MA: Harvard University Press.

Fukuyama, Francis (2004). *State-Building: Governance and World Order in the 21st Century*. Ithaca, NY: Cornell University Press.

Fukuyama, Francis (2014). *Political Order and Political Decay: From the Industrial Revolution to the Globalization of Democracy*. New York: Farrar, Straus and Giroux.

Gallagher, Mary E. (2005). *Contagious Capitalism: Globalization and the Politics of Labor in China*. Princeton, NJ: Princeton University Press.

Gandhi, Jennifer (2008). *Political Institutions under Dictatorship*. New York: Cambridge University Press.

Gao, Chanjuan, et al. (2013). "谈敏感时期规范教工政治参与与舆论引导—从我校教工思政'一岗双责'创新管理机制说起" [Talking about standardizing the political participation of faculty and the guidance of public opinion in the sensitive period]. *Innovation Education* 8: 158.

Gaventa, John (1980). *Power and Powerlessness: Quiescence and Rebellion in an Appalachian Valley*. Urbana: University of Illinois Press.

Geddes, Barbara, Joseph Wright, and Rica Frantz (2018). *How Dictatorships Work*. Cambridge, UK: Cambridge University Press. 219

Geertz, Clifford (1980). *Negara: The Theatre State in Nineteenth-Century Bali*. Princeton, NJ: Princeton University Press.

Genevaz, Juliette (2019). "Defense Education in Chinese Universities: Drilling Elite Youth." *Journal of Contemporary China* 28, no. 117: 453–67.

Germani, Gino (1978). *Authoritarianism, Fascism and National Populism*. New York: Routledge.

Giddens, Anthony (1987). *The Nation-State and Violence*. Berkeley: University of California Press.

Gill, Graeme (2011). *Symbols and Legitimacy in Soviet Politics*. 6. Cambridge, UK: Cambridge University Press.

Ginsburg, Tom, and Tamil Moustafa (2008). *Rule by Law: The Politics of Courts in Authoritarian Regimes*. New York: Cambridge University Press.

Goldhagen, Daniel Jonah (1997). *Hitler's Willing Executioners: Ordinary Germans and the Holocaust*. New York: Vintage Books.

Gong, Haiquan, Jinfeng Zhang, and Yaocan Zhang (2003). "20 世纪的中国高等教育" [China's higher education in the 20th century]. Beijing: Higher Education Press.

Goodman, Roger, Takehiko Kariya, and John Taylor (2013). *Higher Education and the State: Changing Relationships in Europe and East Asia*. Oxford, UK: Symposium Books.

Gramsci, Antonio (1971). *Selections from Prison Notebooks*. New York: International Publishers.

Greitens, Sheena Chestnut (2016). *Dictators and Their Secret Police: Coercive Institutions and State Violence*. Cambridge, UK: Cambridge University Press.

Gries, Peter Hays (2004). *China's New Nationalism*. Berkeley: University of California Press.

Grzymala-Busse, Anna (2007). *Rebuilding Leviathan: Party Competition and State Exploitation in Post-Communist Democracies*. Cambridge, UK: Cambridge University Press.

Guan, Chenghua (2004). "北京大学校园文化" [The campus culture of Peking University]. Beijing: Peking University Press.

Gueorguiev, Dimitar D. (2021). *Retrofitting Leninism: Participation Without Democracy in China*. Oxford, UK: Oxford University Press.

Guha, Ranajit (1997). *Dominance without Hegemony: History and Power in Colonial India*. Cambridge, MA: Harvard University Press.

Guo, Gang (May 2005). "Party Recruitment of College Students in China." *Journal of Contemporary China* 14, no. 43: 371–93.

Guo, Shaofeng (2010). "贫困生占大学生总数 23/100 教育部开通资助热线" [Poor students account for 23 percent of the total number of college students, the Ministry of Education opens a funding hotline]. URL: http://news.xinhuanet .com/school/2010-08/16/c_12448358.htm (visited on 5/10/2012).

Guriev, Sergei, and Daniel Treisman (2022). *Spin Dictators: The Changing Face of Tyranny in the 21st Century*. Princeton, NJ: Princeton University Press.

Guthrie, Douglas J. (1995). "Political Theatre and Student Organizations in the 1989 Chinese Movement: A Multivariate Analysis of Tiananmen." *Sociological Forum* 10, no. 3: 419–54. 220

Habermas, Jürgen (1991). *The Structural Transformation of the Public Sphere*. Cambridge, MA: MIT Press.

Hai, Yan (2018). "北语左翼学生社团被疑因参与工运遭校方注销" [A leftist student society at Beijing Languages and Culture University was forced to dissolve, suspected for its participation in labor movement.] URL: https://www .voachinese.com/a/Leftiest-Student-Bodies-Cancelled-At-A-Beijing-Universi ty-20190108/4733385.html (visited on 9/24/2021).

Han, Jin (1997). "中国教育统计年鉴 1997" [Educational statistics yearbook of China 1997]. Beijing: People's Education Press.

Han, Jin (2004). "中国教育统计年鉴 2004" [Educational statistics yearbook of China 2004]. Beijing: People's Education Press.

Han, Jin (2005). "中国教育统计年鉴 2005" [Educational statistics yearbook of China 2005]. Beijing: People's Education Press.

Han, Jin (2006). "中国教育统计年鉴 2006" [Educational statistics yearbook of China 2006]. Beijing: People's Education Press.

Han, Jin (2007). "中国教育统计年鉴 2007" [Educational statistics yearbook of China 2007]. Beijing: People's Education Press.

Han, Jin (2008). "中国教育统计年鉴 2008" [Educational statistics yearbook of China 2008]. Beijing: People's Education Press.

Han, Jin (2009). "中国教育统计年鉴 2009" [Educational statistics yearbook of China 2009]. Beijing: People's Education Press.

Han, Rongbin (2015a). "Defending the Authoritarian Regime Online: The 'Voluntary Fifty-Cent Army.'" *China Quarterly* 224: 1006–25.

Han, Rongbin (2015b). "Manufacturing Consent in Cyberspace: China's 'Fifty-Cent Army.'" *Journal of Current Chinese Affairs* 44, no. 2: 105–34.

Han, Rongbin (2018). *Contesting Cyberspace in China: Online Expression and Authoritarian Resilience*. New York: Columbia University Press.

Hang Zhang (2011). "北大将会商" 思想偏激" 等十类" 重点学生" [Ten types of "key students" including "extreme thinking" students to be consulted in Peking University]. URL: http://edu.people.com.cn/GB/14234143.html (visited on 8/31/2013).

Haskins, Charles Homer (1923). *The Rise of Universities*. Ithaca, NY: Cornell University Press.

Havránek, Jan (2005). "Czech Universities under Communism." *Universities Under*

Dictatorship, eds. John Connelly and Michael Grüttner. University Park, PA: Pennsylvania State University Press.

Hayhoe, Ruth, and Ningsha Zhong (1997). "University Autonomy and Civil Society." *Civil Society in China*, eds. Timothy Brook and B. Michael Frolic, 99–121. Armonk, NY: M. E. Sharpe.

He, Liquan (2017). "人大工友夜校坚持 6 年后停办: 为生计已无工友来上课" [RUC night school for coworkers insists on closing after 6 years: No coworkers come to class for their livelihood]. URL: http://news.cctv.com/2017/04/27/AR TIpRad5ryTBDRIpyJ6Ylug170427.shtml (visited on 9/21/2021).

Hechter, Michael (2013). *Alien Rule*. New York: Cambridge University Press.

Henderson, Gail E., and Myron S. Cohen (1984). *The Chinese Hospital: A Socialist Work Unit*. New Haven, CT: Yale University Press. 221

Herbst, Jeffery (2000). *States and Power in Africa: Comparative Lessons in Authority and Control*. Princeton, NJ: Princeton University Press.

Hernández, Javier C. (2019). *Professors, Beware. In China, Student Spies Might Be Watching*. URL: https://www.nytimes.com/2019/11/01/world/asia/china-stude nt-informers.html (visited on 3/08/2022).

Hinton, William (1972). *Hundred Day War: The Cultural Revolution at Tsinghua University*. Monthly Review Press.

Howard, Christopher (1997). *The Hidden Welfare State: Tax Expenditures and Social Policy in the United States*. Princeton, NJ: Princeton University Press.

Hsu, Immanuel C. Y. (1964). "The Reorganisation of Higher Education in Communist China 1949–61." *China Quarterly* 19: 128–60.

Hu, Hongfei (2018a). "南京大学本科生胡弘菲向全社会的求助信" [The help letter from Nanjing University undergraduate Hu Hongfei to the whole society]. URL: https://jiashigrsyt1.github.io/hhfqzx/ (visited on 9/24/2021).

Hu, Hongfei (2018b). "就南京大学最近出现的校园暴力联名抗议书" [A joint protest letter regarding the recent campus violence in Nanjing University]. URL: https://jiashigrsyt1.github.io/kyndblsj/ (visited on 9/24/2021).

Hu, Jieren, Yue Tu, and Tong Wu (2018). "Selective Intervention in Dispute Resolution: Local Government and Community Governance in China." *Journal of Contemporary China* 27, no. 111: 423–39.

Hua, Hua (Nov. 2010). "大学生信仰基督教的原因与路径分析" (Analysis on the reason and pathway of the conversion of university students to Christianity)." *China Youth Study* 11: 75–80.

Huang, Jianli (2010). "难展的双翼: 中国国民党面对学生运动的困境与决策:1927–1949 年" [The politics of depoliticization in Republican China: Guomindang policy towards student political activism, 1927–1949]. Beijing: The Commercial Press.

Hubei University (2013). "我校为优秀本科生" '开天窗'16 名毕业生保送名校名所读研攻博" [Our university "opens the sky window" for outstanding undergraduates and 16 graduates are recommended to prestigious universities for postgraduate studies]. URL: http://www.hubu.edu.cn/Html/2013-6/hdyw5018 .shtml (visited on 8/31/2013).

Hunan Institute of Technology (2013). "湖南工学院学生教学信息员工作管理规定" [Regulations on the work management of student teaching information officers in Hunan Institute of Technology]. URL: https://www.hnit.edu.cn/jpc /info/1018/2772.htm (visited on 10/29/2021).

Hunan University (2010). "湖南大学学生在线" [Disciplinary codes for students of University of Science and Technology of China]. URL: http://students.hnu.cn /show.php?id=1266 (visited on 10/11/2021).

Hungary Today (2020). "Theater Uni Leadership Demands 'Student Republic' to Be Terminated with 'Immediate Effect.'" URL: https://hungarytoday.hu/hungary -theater-university-leadership-student-republic/ (visited on 6/21/2022).

Huntington, Samuel P. (1968). *Political Order in Changing Societies*. New Haven, CT: Yale University Press.

Huntington, Samuel P. (1991). *The Third Wave: Democratization in the Late Twentieth Century*. Norman: University of Oklahoma Press. 222

Jasic Workers Support Group (2019). "佳士工人声援团新年献词" [New Year's message from Jasic Workers Support Group]. URL: https://jiashigrsyt1.github .io/sytxnxc/ (visited on 9/21/2021).

Jason, Zachary (2018). *Student Activism 2.0*. URL: https://www.gse.harvard.edu/ne ws/ed/18/08/student-activism-20 (visited on 9/24/2021).

Jesse, Ralph (2005). "Between Control Band Collaboration: The University in East Germany." *Universities Under Dictatorship*, eds. John Connelly and Michael Grüttner. University Park: Pennsylvania State University Press.

Ji, Baocheng (1998). "中国教育统计年鉴 1998" [Educational statistics yearbook of China 1998]. Beijing: People's Education Press.

Ji, Baocheng (1999). "中国教育统计年鉴 1999" [Educational statistics yearbook of China 1999]. Beijing: People's Education Press.

Jia, Yanxiu, and Congbiao Zhou (June 2012). "地方高校大学生宗教信仰问题调查分析" [Investigation and analysis on religious belief of provincial university students]. 学校党 建与思想教育 [*School Party Building and Thought Education*] 425: 68–70.

Jia, Zhiyong (2011). "会商" 思想偏激" 学生源于大学的" 偏激" [Discuss the "extreme thinking" students from the "extreme" of the university]. URL: http://opinion.china.com.cn/opinion_36_13536.html (visited on 10/25/2021).

Jiang, Fu'er (2009). "以强有力措施确保高校安全稳定" [Ensuring the safety and stability of colleges and universities with strong measures]. URL: http://pa per.jyb.cn/zgjyb../page/1/2009-07/09/01/2009070901_pdf.pdf (visited on 10/11/2021).

Jiang, Jue (2021). *A Question of Human Rights or Human Left? The "People's War against COVID-19" under the "Gridded Management" System in China*.

Jiangsu Provincial Committee of Chinese Communist Youth League (2019). "2018 届中国名 校毕业生有所增加, 选调生成就业重要去向" [The number of graduates from prestigious universities in China in 2018 has increased, and the selected graduates is an important destination for employment.] URL: https:// www.thepaper.cn/newsDetail_forward_2809851 (visited on 10/26/2021).

Johnson, Chalmers (1970). "Comparing Communist Nations." *Changes in Communist Systems*, ed. Chalmers Johnson, 1–32. Stanford, CA: Stanford University Press.

Johnston, Hank (2011). *States and Social Movements*. Cambridge, UK: Polity Press.

Joseph, Gilbert M., and Daniel Nugent (1994). "Popular Culture and State Formation in Revolutionary Mexico." *Everyday Forms of State Formation: Revolution and the Negotiation of Rule in Modern Mexico*. Durham, NC: Duke University Press.

Kalan, Dariusz (2020). *Orban's Macbeth*. URL: https://foreignpolicy.com/2020/10/13/orban-hungary-theater-vidnyanszky-populism/ (visited on 6/21/2022).

Karmini, Niniek (2020). "Protests Against New Labor Law Turn Violent across Indonesia." URL: https://apnews.com/article/asia-pacific-indonesia-riots-environment-virus-outbreak-d5c64867ff54c884c9bd6339e15d0930 (visited on 6/21/2022).

Kasza, Gregory J. (1995). *The Conscription Society: Administered Mass Organizations*. New Haven, CT: Yale University Press.

Kerkvliet, Benedict J. Tria (2005). *The Power of Everyday Politics: How Vietnamese Peasants Transformed National Policy*. Ithaca, NY: Cornell University Press.

Kertzer, David (1988). *Ritual, Politics and Power*. New Haven, CT: Yale University Press.

Khoury, Dina Rizk (2013). *Iraq in Wartime: Soldiering, Martyrdom, and Remembrance*. Cambridge, UK: Cambridge University Press. 223

King, Gary, Jennifer Pan, and Margaret E. Roberts (2013). "How Censorship in China Allows Government Criticism but Silences Collective Expression." *American Political Science Review* 107, no. 2: 326–43.

King, Gary, Jennifer Pan, and Margaret E. Roberts (2014). "Reverse-Engineering Censorship in China: Randomized Experimentation and Participant Observation." *Science* 345.6199: 891.

King, Gary, Jennifer Pan, and Margaret E. Roberts (2017). "How the Chinese Government Fabricates Social Media Posts for Strategic Distraction, Not Engaged Argument." *American Political Science Review* 111, no. 3: 484–501.

Koss, Daniel (2018). *Where the Party Rules: The Rank and File of China's Communist State*. New York: Cambridge University Press.

Kuran, Timur (1995). *Private Truths, Public Lies: The Social Consequences of Preference Falsification*. Cambridge, MA: Harvard University Press.

Laliberte, Andre (2011). "Contemporary Issues in State-Religion Relations." *Chinese Religious Life*, eds. David A. Palmer, Gleen Shive, and Philip L. Wickeri, 191–208. Oxford, UK: Oxford University Press.

Lanza, Fabio (2010). *Behind the Gate: Inventing Students in Beijing*. New York: Columbia University Press.

Lefebvre, Henri, and Catherine Régulier (2013). "The Rhythmanalytical Project." *Rhythmanalysis: Space, Time and Everyday Life*, ed. Henri Lefebvre, 81–106. Dublin, Ireland: Bloomsbury Academic.

Lefort, Claude (1986). *The Political Forms of Modern Society: Bureaucracy, Democracy, Totalitarianism*, ed. David Thompson. Cambridge, MA: MIT Press.

Leibold, James (2020). "Surveillance in China's Xinjiang Region: Ethnic Sorting, Coercion, and Inducement." *Journal of Contemporary China* 29, no. 121: 46–60.

Levi, Margaret (1997). *Consent, Dissent, and Patriotism*. Cambridge, UK: Cambridge University Press.

Levitsky, Steven, and Lucan Way (2022). *Revolution and Dictatorship: The Violent Origins of Durable Authoritarianism*. Princeton, NJ: Princeton University Press.

Li, Ding (2017). "共青团组织推动高校学生社团发展与治理的历程研究." 青年研究 5: 1–16.

Li, Huaxi (2021). "近八成受访大学生认为现在就业形势严峻就业难" [Nearly 80 percent of college students interviewed believe that the current employment situation is severe and difficult to find]. URL: http://news.youth.cn/jsxw/2021 06/t20210603_12993373.htm (visited on 10/26/2021).

Li, Jiansheng, and Lei Ye (May 2008). "当代大学生对邪教的认识" [The knowledge of contemporary university students on evil cult]. 科学与无神论 [*Science and Atheism*] 5: 25–30.

Li, Tieying (1992). "高等教育必须坚持社会主义方向" [Higher education must stick to the direction of socialism]. 十一届三中全会以来重要教育文献选编 [*Collection of Important Documents on Education since the 3rd Plenum of the 11th Central Committee*], ed. Department of Policies and State Commission of Education Regulations, 388–95. Beijing: Jiaoyu Kexue Chubanshe.

Liang, Xingwang, and Yulei Liu (2009). "考研升温带动相关产业链市场背后潜伏危机" [The increased enthusiasm in the graduate school admission examination breeds a whole chains of business with crisis behind the market.] URL: 224 http://china.cnr.cn/yaowen/200910/t20091018_505515347.shtml (visited on 10/11/2021).

Liao, Zhicheng, and Xiaofen Xie (Mar. 2012). "现状与反思: 当代大学生宗教信仰问题研究" [Current condition and reflection: A study on the religious belief problem of university students]. 福建论坛人文社会科学版 [*Fujian Forum: Humanities and Social Science Edition*] 3: 150–53.

Linz, Juan (2000). *Totalitarian and Authoritarian Regimes*. Boulder, CO: Lynne Rienner Publishers.

Lipset, Seymour M. (1972). *Rebellion in the University*. London: Routledge and Kegan Paul.

Liu, Changya (2016). "中国教育统计年鉴 2016" [Educational statistics yearbook of China 2016]. Beijing: People's Education Press.

Liu, Changya, and Jiancong Li (2017). "中国教育统计年鉴 2017" [Educational statistics yearbook of China 2017]. Beijing: People's Education Press.

Liu, Changya, and Jiancong Li (2018). "中国教育统计年鉴 2018" [Educational statistics yearbook of China 2018]. Beijing: People's Education Press.

Liu, Changya, and Jiancong Li (2019). "中国教育统计年鉴 2019" [Educational statistics yearbook of China 2019]. Beijing: People's Education Press.

Liu, Xiaoling, and Dan Liang (Dec. 2007). "大学生宗教信仰问题的调查与对策研究" [An investigation and study on the religious belief problem of university students and the policy response to it). 求索 [*Exploration*] 12: 115–17.

Liu, Yi-Ling (2021). *China's Involuted Generation*. URL: https: //www.newyork er.com/culture/cultural-comment/chinas-involuted-generation (visited on 3/09/2022).

Liu, Yunsheng, Chunxi Hao, and Xinsheng He (2009). 裂变与整合 [*Split and Integration*]. Beijing: Guangming Daily Publishing House.

Lorentzen, Peter (2014). "China's Strategic Censorship." *American Journal of Political Science* 58, no. 2: 402–14.

Lovell, David W. (1984). *From Marx to Lenin: An Evaluation of Marx's Responsibility for Soviet Authoritarianism*. London, UK: Cambridge University Press.

Loveman, Mara (May 2005). "The Modern State and the Primitive Accumulation of Symbolic Power." *American Journal of Sociology* 110, no. 6: 1651–83.

Loveman, Mara, and National Colors (2014). *Racial Classification and the State in Latin America*. Oxford, UK: Oxford University Press.

Lukes, Steven (2005). *Power: A Radical View*. Second Edition. Palgrave Macmillan.

Luo, Xiao, et al. (Jan. 2010). "基督教渗透高校现状及对大学生的影响" [The current conditions on the permeation of Christianity on university campuses and its impact on the student populace]. [*Lanzhou Xuekan*] 196: 70–73.

Lust-Okar, Ellen (2005). *Structuring Content in the Arab World*. New York: Cambridge University Press.

Lv, Chunhui (Mar. 2012). "中国高校学生社团的发展变迁及思考" [Reflections on the development and transformation of student groups in Chinese institutions of higher education]. 长春工业大学学报 [*Academic Gazetteer of the Changchun University of Industry, Special Edition on Higher Education*] 33, no. 1: 88–91. 225

Lyons, Terrence (2004). "Transforming the Institutions of War: Postconflict Elections and the Reconstruction of Failed States." *When States Fail: Causes and Consequences*, ed. Robert I. Rotberg. Princeton, NJ: Princeton University Press: 269–301.

Machiavelli, Niccolò (1998 [1513]). *The Prince*. Second Edition. Chicago: University of Chicago Press.

Magaloni, Beatriz (2006). *Voting for Autocracy: Hegemonic Party Survival and Its Demise in Mexico*. Cambridge, UK: Cambridge University Press.

Mamdani, Mahmood (1996). *Citizen and Subject: Contemporary Africa and the Legacy of Late Colonialism*. Princeton, NJ: Princeton University Press.

Marcuse, Herbert (1991). *One-Dimensional Man: Studies in the Ideology of Advanced Industrial Society*. London: Routledge.

Marquand, Robert (2003). *The "Mouse" that Caused an Uproar in China*. URL: http://www.csmonitor.com/2003/1106/p01s04-woap.html (visited on 10/11/2021).

Mattingly, Daniel C. (2020). *The Art of Political Control in China*. New York: Cambridge University Press.

Mayrl, Damon, and Sarah Quinn (2017). "Beyond the Hidden American State: Classification Struggles and the Politics of Recognition." *The Many Hands of the State: Theorizing Political Authority and Social Control*, eds. Kimberly J. Morgan and Ann Shola Orloff. New York: Cambridge University Press.

Mazzuca, Sebastián (2021). *Latecomer State Formation: Political Geography and Capacity Failure in Latin America*. New Haven, CT: Yale University Press.

McDougall, James I. (Dec. 2020). "Whither the Global in Chinese Higher Education? The Production of Space in China's 'New Era' Universities." *China Quarterly* 244: 1013–30.

Meierhenrich, Jens (2004). "Forming State after Failure." *When States Fail: Causes and Consequences*, ed. Robert I. Rotberg, 153–69. Princeton, NJ: Princeton University Press.

Mendieta, Eduardo, and Jonathan Vanantwerpen (2011). "Introduction: The Power of Religion in the Public Sphere." *The Power of Religion in the Public Sphere*, eds. Eduardo Mendieta and Jonathan Vanantwerpen, 1–14. New York: Columbia University Press.

Meng, Anne (2020). *Constraining Dictatorship: from Personalized Rule to Institutionalized Regimes*. Cambridge, UK: Cambridge University Press.

Mettler, Suzanne (2011). *The Submerged State: How Invisible Government Policies Undermine American Democracy*. Chicago: University of Chicago Press.

Migdal, Joel S. (2011). *State in Society: Studying How States and Societies Transform and Constitute One Another*, 16–17. Cambridge, UK: Cambridge University Press.

Milburn, Thomas W., and Daniel J. Christie (1989). "Rewarding in International Politics." *Political Psychology* 10, no. 4: 625–45.

Mills, C. Wright (Sept. 1960). "Letter to the New Left." *New Left Review* 1, no. 5: 18–23.

Mills, C. Wright (2016). "教育部关于加强学生军事训练管理工作的通知 (教体艺 [2017]3 号)" [Notice of the Ministry of Education on strengthening the management of military training for students]. URL: http: //www.moe.gov.cn /srcsite/A17/moe_1061/s3289/201705/t20170524_305608.html(visitedon9/28/2021).

Mills, C. Wright (2021a). "2020 全国教育事业发展统计公报" [Statistical communiqué on National Education Development in 2020]. URL: http://www .moe.gov.cn/jyb_sjzl/sjzl_fztjgb/202108/t20210827_555004.html (visited on 10/24/2021).

Mills, C. Wright (2021b). "2020 年全国教育事业发展统计公报" [2020 National Statistical Bulletin on Education Development]. URL: http://www.gov.cn/xinw en/2021-08/28/content_5633911.htm (visited on 4/07/2022).

Ministry of Education (2006). "普通高等学校辅导员队伍建设规定" [Regulation on the construction of corps of political counselor in ordinary institution of higher education]. URL: http://www.gov.cn/flfg/2006-07/31/content_350701 .htm (visited on 9/21/2021). 226

Ministry of Education (2013). "关于做好 2013–13 年国有企业招收高校毕业生有关事项的 通知" [Circular on various issues concerning the recruitment of university graduates into state-owned enterprises in the year of 2013–14]. URL: http://www.moe.gov.cn/publicfiles/business/htmlfiles/moe/moe_1779/201305 /152595.html (visited on 10/11/2021).

Ministry of Education and Central Committee of the Chinese Communist Youth League (Dec. 2004). "关于进一步加强高等学校校园文化建设的意见" [Opinions on the Further Strengthening of the Construction of Campus Culture in Institutions of Higher Education]."

Ministry of Education and the Central Committee of the Chinese Communist Youth League (2016). "教育部共青团中央关于进一步加强高等学校校园网络管理工作的意见" [Opinions on the further strengthening of the management of computer networks on university campuses]. URL: https://net.hnuahe.edu .cn/info/1061/1245.htm (visited on 9/24/2021).

Ministry of Education, the Ministry of Health, and the Central Committee of the Chinese Communist Youth League (2005). "教育部卫生部共青团中央关于进一步加强和改进大学 生心理健康教育的意见 (教社政 [2005]1 号)" [Opinions of the Ministry of Education and the Ministry of Health and the Central Committee of the Chinese Communist Youth League on further strengthening and improving mental health education for college students]. URL: http://www .moe.gov.cn/srcsite/A12/s7060/201001/t20100113_179047.html (visited on 10/11/2021).

Mitchell, Timothy (1991). "The Limits of the State: Beyond Statist Approaches and Their Critics." *American Political Science Review* 85, no. 1: 77–96.

Mitter, Rana (2004). *A Bitter Revolution: China's Struggle with the Modern World.* Oxford, UK: Oxford University Press.

Mizruchi, Ephraim H. (1983). *Regulating Society: Marginality and Social Control in Historical Perspective.* New York: Free Press.

Moore, Barrington, Jr. (1978). *Injustice: The Social Bases of Obedience and Revolt*. White Plains, NY: M. E. Sharpe.

Mou, Yangchun (2000). "中国教育统计年鉴 2000" [Educational statistics yearbook of China 2000]. Beijing: People's Education Press.

Mou, Yangchun (2001). "中国教育统计年鉴 2001" [Educational statistics yearbook of China 2001]. Beijing: People's Education Press.

Mou, Yangchun (2002). "中国教育统计年鉴 2002" [Educational statistics yearbook of China 2002]. Beijing: People's Education Press.

Mou, Yangchun (2003). "中国教育统计年鉴 2003" [Educational statistics yearbook of China 2003]. Beijing: People's Education Press.

Nanjing Tech University (2013). "学生信息员工作管理规定" [Regulations on the management of student informant work]. URL: http://bwc.njut.edu.cn/Content.aspx?id=105&code=XYGZ (visited on 7/26/2013).

Nanjing University (2014). "南京大学突发事件总体应急预案" [Overall emergency plan for emergencies in Nanjing University]. URL: https://xxgk.nju.edu.cn/06/49/c215a1609/page.htm (visited on 10/29/2021).

Neave, Guy (2011). "Patterns." In *A History of the University in Europe*, 35–46. London, UK: Cambridge University Press.

New York Times (2019). "中国压制左派青年，北大学生举行抗议活动" [Student defiant as Chinese university cracks down on youth communists]. URL: https://cn.nytimes.com/china/20190102/chinese-university-crackdown-students/ (visited on 9/21/2021).

Newman, John Henry (1996). *The Idea of a University*. New Haven, CT: Yale University Press.

Nisbet, Robert (1975). *Twilight of Authority*. Carmel, IN: Liberty Fund.

Ocean University of China (2014). "勿忘国耻我是中国人" [Do not forget national humility as I am Chinese]. URL: http://wzb.ouc.edu.cn/2014/0826/c5456a25734/page.htm (visited on 9/21/2021).

Ong, Lynette H. (2022). *Outsourcing Repression: Everyday State Power in Contemporary China*. New York: Oxford University Press.

Organization Department of the Central Committee of the Communist Party of China (2021). 中"国共产党党内统计公报" [Intra-party statistical bulletin of the Communist Party of China]. URL: http://politics.people.com.cn/n1/2021/0701/c1001-32145418.html (visited on 4/07/2022).

Organization Department of the CPC Henan Provincial Committee et al. (2021). "关于 2021 年选调优秀大学毕业生到基层工作的通知" [Notice on selecting outstanding university graduates to work at the grassroots level in 2021]. URL: http://xds.haedu.gov.cn/NewsView.aspx?id=1059 (visited on 10/11/2021).

Ouyang, Pengfei (Aug. 2009). "新形势下大学生心理健康教育有效途径探析" [Exploring effective methods of mental health education among university students under new conditions] 江西理工大学学报 *Academic Chronicles of Jiangxi Polytechnic University* 30, no. 4: 60–62.

Pan, Jennifer (2020). *Welfare for Autocrats: How Social Assistance in China Cares for Its Rulers*. New York: Oxford University Press.

Paul, Kari (2020). *"Ban This Technology": Students Protest US Universities' Use of Facial Recognition*. URL: https://www.theguardian.com/us-news/2020/mar/02/facial-recognition-us-colleges-ucla-ban (visited on 6/21/2022).

Peking University (2017). "北京大学突发事件应急处置预案" [Emergency response plan of Peking University]. URL: https://xxgk.pku.edu.cn/docs/201705311150110007163.pdf (visited on 10/29/2021).

Peking University (2019). "北京大学学生社团管理办法" [Regulations on the management of student organizations of Peking University]. URL: https://www.sg.pku.edu.cn/xsfz/gzzd1/1324711.htm (visited on 10/08/2021).

Peking University Center for Extracurricular Activities (Mar. 2015). "北京大学学生社团管理制 度汇编" [Collections of rules on the management of student organizations at Peking University.

Pepinsky, Thomas B. (2009). *Economic Crises and the Breakdown of Authoritarian Regimes*. Cambridge, UK: Cambridge University Press.

Perry, Elizabeth J. (1994). "Casting a Chinese 'Democracy' Movement: The Roles of Students, Workers, and Entrepreneurs." *Popular Protest and Political Culture in Modern China*, eds. Jeffrey N. Wasserstrom and Elizabeth J. Perry, 74–92. Boulder, CO: Westview Press. 228

Perry, Elizabeth J. (2011). "From Mass Campaign to Managed Campaigns: Constructing a New Socialist Countryside." In *Mao's Invisible Hand: The Political Foundations of Adaptive Governance in China*, eds. Sebastian Heilmann and Elizabeth J. Perry, 30–61. Cambridge, MA: Harvard University Press.

Perry, Elizabeth J. (2012). *Auyuan: Mining China's Revolutionary Tradition*. Berkeley: University of California Press.

Perry, Elizabeth J. (2020). "Educated Acquiescence: How Academia Sustains Authoritarianism in China." *Theory and Society* 49: 1–22.

Perry, Elizabeth J., and Xiaojun Yan (2020). "Suppressing Students in the People's Republic of China: Proletarian State-Mobilized Movements in 1968 and 1989." In *Ruling by Other Means: State-Mobilized Movements*, eds. Elizabeth J. Perry, Grzegorz Ekiert, and Xiaojun Yan, 57–85. Cambridge, UK: Cambridge University Press.

Péteri, György (2005). "The Communist Idea of the University." *Universities Under Dictatorship*, eds. John Connelly and Michael Grüttner. University Park: Pennsylvania State University Press.

Pierson, David (2020). "George Floyd's Death Inspires an Unlikely Movement in Indonesia: Papuan Lives Matter." URL: https://www.latimes.com/world-nation/story/2020-07-02/papuan-lives-matter (visited on 6/21/2022).

Podeh, Elie (2011). *The Politics of National Celebrations in the Arab Middle East*. Cambridge, UK: Cambridge University Press.

Poggi, Gianfranco (1990). *The State: Its Nature, Development and Prospects*. Stanford, CA: Stanford University Press.

Posner, Daniel N. (2004). "When States Fail: Causes and Consequences." In *Civil Society and the Reconstruction of Failed States*, ed. Robert I. Rotberg. Princeton, NJ: Princeton University Press.

Qiu, Shuiping (27/08/2021). "把党史作为立德树人的最好教科书" [Regarding party history as the best textbook for setting up morals and nurturing men] [*Xuexi Shibao*] 1.

Readings, Bill (1996). *The University in Ruins*. Cambridge, MA: Harvard University Press.

Reuben, Julie A. (1996). *The Making of the Modern University: Intellectual Transformation and the Marginalization of Morality*. Chicago: University of Chicago Press.

Reuters (2021). "中国统计局称就业仍然有压力大学生就业难与企业招工难并存" [The National Bureau of Statistics of China says employment is still under pressure]. URL: https: //www.reuters.com/article/china-graduates-job-0616 -wedn-idCNKCS2DS0MC (visited on 10/26/2021).

Reuters staff (2020). *Thousands of Students March with Torches in Hungary for Academic Freedom*. URL: https://www.reuters.com/article/uk-hungary-protests-stu dents-idUKKBN2782DK (visited on 6/21/2022).

Rhoads, Robert A. (1998). *Freedom's Web: Student Activism in an Age of Cultural Diversity*. Baltimore: Johns Hopkins University Press.

Rim, Christopher (2020). *How Student Activism Shaped the Black Lives Matter Movement*. URL: https://www.forbes.com/sites/christopherrim/2020/06/04/how-st udent-activism-shaped-the-black-lives-matter-movement/?sh=2bd890564414 (visited on 6/21/2022). 229

Rithmire, Meg E. (2015). *Land Bargains and Chinese Capitalism: The Politics of Property Rights Under Reform*. Cambridge, UK: Cambridge University Press.

Roberts, Margaret E. (2018). *Censored: Distraction and Diversion Inside China's Great Firewall*. Princeton, NJ: Princeton University Press.

Rose-Ackerman, Susan (2004). "Establishing the Rule of Law." In *When States Fail: Causes and Consequences*, 182–221. Princeton, NJ: Princeton University Press.

Rosen, Stanley (1993). "The Effect of Post-4 June Re-Education Campaigns on Chinese Students." *China Quarterly* 134: 310–34.

Rosenau, James N. (1989). "The State in an Era of Cascading Politics: Wavering Concept, Widening Competence, Withering Colossus, or Weathering Change?" *The Elusive State: International and Comparative Perspective*, ed. James A. Caporaso, 17–48. Newbury Park, CA: Sage Publications.

Rotberg, Robert I. (2002). "Failed States in a World of Terror." *Foreign Affairs* 81, no. 4: 127–40.

Rotberg, Robert I. (2004). "The Failure and Collapse of Nation-States." *When States Fail: Causes and Consequences*, ed. Robert I. Rotberg. Princeton, NJ: Princeton University Press.

Rousseau, Jean-Jacques (1987). *The Basic Political Writings*. Indianapolis, IN: Hackett Publishing Company.

Sayer, Derek (1994). "Everyday Forms of State Formation: Some Dissident Remarks on 'Hegemony.'" In *Everyday Forms of State Formation: Revolution and the Negotiation of Rule in Modern Mexico*, eds. Gilbert M. Joseph and Daniel Nugent. Durham, NC: Duke University Press.

Schattschneider, E. E. (1960). *The Semi-Sovereign People: A Realist's View of Democracy in America*. New York: Holt, Rhinehart and Winston.

Schedler, Andreas (2013). *The Politics of Uncertainty: Sustaining and Subverting Electoral Authoritarianism*. Oxford, UK: Oxford University Press.

Schwarck, Edward (2018). "Intelligence and Informatization: The Rise of the Ministry of Public Security in Intelligence Work in China." *China Journal* 80: 1–23.

Schwarcz, Vera (1986). *The Chinese Enlightenment: Intellectuals and the Legacy of the May Fourth Movement of 1919*. Berkeley: University of California Press.

Scott, James C. (1985). *Weapons of the Weak: Everyday Forms of Peasant Resistance*. New Haven, CT: Yale University Press.

Selden, Mark (1971). *The Yenan Way in Revolutionary China*. Cambridge, MA: Harvard University Press.

Sewell, William H., Jr. (1990). "Three Temporalities: Toward a Sociology of the Event." In *The Historic Turn in the Human Sciences*, 1–30. Ann Arbor: University of Michigan Press.

Sewell, William H., Jr. (2001). "Space in Contentious Politics." *Silence and Voice in the Study of Contentious Politics*, eds. Ronald R. Aminzade et al. London: Cambridge University Press.

Shandong University of Technology News (2011). "机械学院抓好学生党员队伍建设" [The faculty of engineering doing a good job in strengthening the construction of corps of student party members]. URL: http://www.ihwrm.com/index/daodu/info/ent_id/1721/release_id/26206.html (visited on 10/11/2021).

Shi, Chunming (2018). "向走过场的学生军训说' 不'" [Say "no" to student military training going through the motions]. URL: 230 http://www.mod.gov.cn/jmsd/2018-08/27/content_4823388.htm (visited on 9/21/2021).

Shils, Edward (1982). *The Constitution of Society*. Chicago: University of Chicago Press.

Shirk, Susan (1982). *Competitive Comrades: Career Incentives and Student Strategies in China*. Berkeley: University of California Press.

Sichuan Agricultural University, SICAU (2017). "经济学院把入党启蒙教育搬到军训场" [School of Economics moved the Party's enlightenment education to the military training field]. URL: https://bwc.sicau.edu.cn/info/1004/1012.htm (visited on 9/21/2021).

Skowronek, Stephen (1982). *Building a New American State: The Expansion of National Administrative Capacities 1877–1920*. London: Cambridge University Press.

Slater, Dan (2010). *Ordering Power: Contentious Politics and Authoritarian Leviathans in Southeast Asia*. Cambridge, UK: Cambridge University Press.

Snodgrass, Donald R. (2004). "Restoring Economic Functioning in Failed States." *When States Fail: Causes and Consequences*, ed. Robert I. Rotberg. Princeton, NJ: Princeton University Press: 256–68.

Soifer, Hillel, and Matthias vom Hau (2008). "Unpacking the Strength of the State: The Utility of State Infrastructural Power." *Studies in Comparative International Development* 43: 219–30.

Standing Committee of the National People's Congress (2020). "中华人民共和国国防教育法" [National Defense Education Law of the People's Republic of China]. Standing Committee of the National People's Congress.

Stasavage, David (2020). *The Decline and Rise of Democracy: A Global History from Antiquity to Today*. Princeton, NJ: Princeton University Press.

State Council and the Central Military Commission (2001). "国务院办公厅中央军委办公厅转发教育部总参谋部总政治部关于在普通高等学校和高级中学开展学生军事训练工作意见 的通知 (国办发 [2001] 48 号." [Notice of the General Office of the State Council and the General Office of the Central Military Commission on forwarding the opinions of the General Political Department of the General Staff of the Ministry of Education on the conduct of military training for students in ordinary colleges and high schools]. General Office, the State Council and the General Office, the Central Military Commission.

State Council and the Central Military Commission (2017). "国务院办公厅中央军委办公厅关于深化学生军事训练改革的意见 (国办发 [2017]76 号." [Opinions of the General Office of the State Council and the General Office of the Central Military Commission on deepening the reform of military training for students]. The General Office of the State Council and the General Office of the Central Military Commission.

Statistics Bureau of Tianjin (2009). "天津: 新时期影响大学生就业主要因素分析" [Tianjin: Analysis on the main factors that might have influenced the job placement of university students in the new era]. URL: http://www.stats.gov.cn/ztjc/ztfx/dfxx/200906/t20090601_34800.html (visited on 10/11/2021). 232

Steinmetz, George (1999). "Introduction: Culture and State." *State/Culture: State-Formation After the Cultural Turn,* ed. George Steinmetz, 1–49. Ithaca, NY: Cornell University Press.

Strand, David (1989). *Rickshaw Beijing: City People and Politics in the 1920s.* Berkeley: University of California Press.

Student Confederation of Beijing (2002). "首都高校学生会, 研究生会及学生社团开展跨校活 动的暂行办法" [Trial methods of the management of cross-institutional student activities organized by student unions, graduate student unions and student societies and groups in institutions of higher education in the capital city]" "北京市学生联合会工作手册, 2002 年." 231

Su, Yifang (Sept. 2009). "不可忽视大学校园里的非法宗教活动" [The illegal religious activities on university campuses must not be overlooked]." 安庆师范学院学报 [*Academic Gazetteer of the Anqing Teachers' College, Social Science Edition*] 28, no. 9: 16–20.

Svolik, Milan W. (2012). *The Politics of Authoritarian Rule.* New York: Cambridge University Press.

Tang, Beibei (2020). "Grid Governance in China's Urban Middle-class Neighbourhoods." *China Quarterly* 241: 43–61.

Tian, Guirong (2005). "学生社团: 大学生成长的重要课堂" [Student groups: An important classroom for university students to grow up in]. URL: https://r.cnki.net/kcms/detail/detail.aspx?filename=CJYB200506100005&dbcode=CFND&dbname=cfnd2005&v= (visited on 9/24/2021).

Tilly, Charles (1992). *Coercion, Capital and European States.* Cambridge, MA: Blackwell.

Tomoff, Kiril (2006). *Creative Union: The Professional Organization of Soviet Composers 1939–1953.* Ithaca, NY: Cornell University Press.

Trevino, Linda Klebe (1992). "The Social Effects of Punishment in Organizations: A Justice Perspective." *Academy of Management Review* 17, no. 4: 647–76.

Tripp, Charles (2013). *The Power and the People: Paths of Resistance in the Middle East.* Cambridge, UK: Cambridge University Press.

Tsai, Lily L. (2021). *When People Want Punishment: Retributive Justice and the Puzzle of Authoritarian Popularity.* Cambridge, UK: Cambridge University Press.

Tsinghua University (2020). "清华大学突发事件总体应急预案" [Tsinghua University's overall emergency plan for emergencies]. URL: https://www.tsinghua.edu.cn/publish/newthu/openness/qt/tfggsjyjya.htm (visited on 10/29/2021).

Tsinghua University (2021). "清华大学学生社团建设管理办法" [Regulations on the management and development of student organizations of Peking University]. URL: https://www.tsinghua.edu.cn/info/1288/1301.htm (visited on 10/08/2021).

Turner, Bryan S. (2008). *The Body and Society*. Los Angeles: Sage Publications.

Vass, Ábrahám (2020). "Theater University Students Protest with Barricades after Leadership Resigns Due to Gov't Restructuring." URL: https://hungarytoday.hu/theater-university-student-protest-barricade-leadership-resign-restructuring/ (visited on 6/21/2022).

Vellela, Tony (1988). *New Voices: Student Political Activism in the '80s and '90s*. Boston: South End Press.

Villa, Dana R. (1992). "Postmodernism and the Public Sphere." *American Political Science Review* 86, no. 3: 712–21.

Walder, Andrew G. (1984). *Communist Neo-Traditionalism: Work and Authority in Chinese Industry*. Berkeley: University of California Press.

Walder, Andrew G. (1995). "The Quite Revolution from Within: Economic Reform as a Source of Political Decline." *The Waning of the Communist State: Economic Origins of Political Decline in China and Hungary*, ed. Andrew G. Walder, 1–24. Berkeley: University of California Press.

Walder, Andrew G. (2009). *Fractured Rebellion*. Cambridge, MA: Harvard University Press.

Waldner, David, and Ellen Lust (2018). "Unwelcome Change: Coming to Terms with Democratic Backsliding." *Annual Review of Political Science* 21: 93–113.

Wallace, Jeremy L. (2014). *Cities and Stability: Urbanization, Redistribution, and Regime Survival in China*. New York: Oxford University Press.

Wallace, Jeremy L. (2023). *Seeking Truth and Hiding Facts: Information, Ideology, and Authoritarianism in China*. Oxford, UK: Oxford University Press.

Wang, Xiaoqi (2012a). *China's Civil Service Reform*. New York: Routledge. 233

Wang, Yuhua (Oct. 2021). "State-in-Society 2.0: Toward Fourth-generation Theories of the State." *Comparative Politics* 54, no. 1: 175–98.

Wang, Yun (2018). "南大学生学马列被禁遭暴力清场" [Nanjing University students were banned from studying Marxism and cleared by force]. URL: https://www.rfa.org/mandarin/yataibaodao/kejiaowen/wy-11022018105559.html (visited on 9/24/2021).

Wang, Zheng (2012b). *Never Forget National Humiliation: Historical Memory in Chinese Politics and Foreign Relations*. New York: Columbia University Press.

Wang, Zifeng, and Li Chen (Apr. 2020). "浅谈我国考研培训市场存在的问题与对策" [A brief analysis on the problems and solutions of the market of preparation for the national admission examination for graduate school in China]. 商品与质量 [*The Merchandise and Quality*] 4: 86–87.

Wasserstrom, Jeffrey N. (1990). "Student Protests and the Chinese Tradition, 1919–1989." *The Chinese People's Movement: Perspectives on Spring 1989*, ed. Tony Saich, 3–24. Armonk, NY: M. E. Sharpe.:

Wasserstrom, Jeffrey N. (1991). *Student Protest in Twentieth-Century China*. Stanford, CA: Stanford University Press.

Wasserstrom, Jeffrey N., and Xinyong Liu (1989). "Student Protest and Student Life: Shanghai, 1919–49." *Social History* 14, no. 1: 1–29.

Wasserstrom, Jeffrey N. (1995). "Student Associations and Mass Movements." *Urban Spaces in Contemporary China: The Potential for Autonomy and Community in Post-Mao China*, eds. Deborah S. Davis et al., 362–93. Cambridge, UK: Cambridge University Press.

Weber, Max (1946). "Politics as a Vocation." *From Max Weber: Essays in Sociology*, eds. H. H. Gerth and C. Wright Mills. New York: Oxford University Press.

Wedeen, Lisa (1999). *Ambiguities of Domination: Politics, Rhetoric, and Symbols in Contemporary Syria*. Chicago: University of Chicago Press.

Wegner, Eva (2007). "Islamist Inclusion and Regime Persistence: The Moroccan Win-Win Situation." *Debating Arab Authoritarianism: Dynamics and Durability in Nondemocratic Regimes*, ed. Oliver Schlumberger, 75–94. Stanford, CA: Stanford University Press.

Weiner, Douglas R. (1999). *A Little Corner of Freedom: Russian Nature Protection from Stalin to Gorbachev*. Berkeley: University of California Press.

Weiss, Jessica Chen (2014). *Powerful Patriots: Nationalist Protest in China's Foreign Relations*. Oxford, UK: Oxford University Press.

Wen, Wei Po (2011). "吴邦国: 学生政治辅导员" [Wu Bangguo: Student political counselor]. URL: http://paper.wenweipo.com/2011/04/22/CH1104220011 .htm (visited on 9/24/2021).

Wen, Yuqing (2018). "曾声援深圳佳士工运北科大学生组织被取缔" [A USTB student organization who echoed for Jasic labor movement was deregistered]. URL: https://www.rfa.org/cantonese/news/student-10122018093126.html (visited on 9/24/2021).

Whyte, Martin King (1974). *Small Groups and Political Rituals in China*. Berkeley: University of California Press.

Wickeri, Philip L. (2011). "Introduction." *Chinese Religious Life*, eds. David A. Palmer, Gleen Shive, and Philip L. Wickeri, 5. Oxford, UK: Oxford University Press.

Widner, Jennifer A. (2004). "Building Effective Trust in the Aftermath of Severe Conflict." *When States Fail: Causes and Consequences*, ed. Robert I. Rotberg, 222–36. Princeton, NJ: Princeton University Press. 234

Wilentz, Sean (1985). "Introduction: Teufelsdrockh's Dilemma: On Symbolism, Politics, and History." In *Rites of Power: Symbolism, Ritual and Politics Since the Middle Ages*, 1–9. Philadelphia: University of Pennsylvania Press.

Wilson, Amy Auerbacher, Sidney Leonard Greenblatt, and Richard Whittingham Wilson (1977). *Deviance and Social Control in Chinese Society*. New York: Praeger Publishers.

"版" [The working manual of the Student Confederation of Beijing. 2002 ed.], ed. eStudent Confederation of Beijing, 27–29. Beijing: Student Confederation of Beijing.

Wright, Teresa (2001). *The Perils of Protest: State Repression and Student Activism in China and Taiwan*. Honolulu: University of Hawaii Press.

Wright, Teresa (2010). *Accepting Authoritarianism: State-Society Relations in China's Reform Era*. Stanford, CA: Stanford University Press.

Wu, Wei, and Lu Sha (2015). "北大学生联名发文指该校克扣工人工资北大称正自查" [Peking University students jointly issued a document accusing the school of deducting workers' wages while Peking University claimed to be checking]. URL: http://news.sciencenet.cn/htmlnews/2015/12/334203.shtm (visited on 9/21/2021).

Xi'an Conservatory of Music (2009). "西安音乐学院: 拥护法院对药家鑫判处死刑" [Xi'an Conservatory of Music: Supporting the court's decision to sentence

Yao Jiaxin to death]. URL: http://www.stats.gov.cn/ztjc/ztfx/dfxx/200906/t200 90601_34800.html (visited on 10/11/2021).

Xiao, Chunfei (2008). "教育部: 未来我国高校将有十万名专职辅导员" [Ministry of Education: Chinese universities will have ten thousand full-time counselors in the future]. URL: http://www.moe.gov.cn/jyb_xwfb/xw_fbh/moe_2069/moe _2070/moe_2126/moe_1968/tnull_33106.html (visited on 10/20/2021).

Xie, Guihua, and Yangyang Zhang (2016). "向党靠拢, 被党接纳: 大学生入党问题研究" [Seeking out the Party: A study of the CCP membership recruitment among Chinese college students]. 社会 [*Society*] 36: 32–63.

Xie, Huanzhong (2010a). "中国教育统计年鉴 2010" [Educational statistics yearbook of China 2010]. Beijing: People's Education Press.

Xie, Huanzhong (2011). "中国教育统计年鉴 2011" [Educational statistics yearbook of China 2011]. Beijing: People's Education Press.

Xie, Huanzhong (2012a). "中国教育统计年鉴 2012" [Educational statistics yearbook of China 2012]. Beijing: People's Education Press.

Xie, Huanzhong (2013). "中国教育统计年鉴 2013" [Educational statistics yearbook of China 2013]. Beijing: People's Education Press.

Xie, Huanzhong (2014). "中国教育统计年鉴 2014" [Educational statistics yearbook of China 2014]. Beijing: People's Education Press.

Xie, Huanzhong (2015). "中国教育统计年鉴 2015" [Educational statistics yearbook of China 2015]. Beijing: People's Education Press.

Xie, Ming (2010b). "当代大学生基督教传播现状调查" [An investigation of the current condition of the spreading of Christianity among contemporary university students]. 民族 教育研究 [*Study on Ethic Minority Education*] 21, no. 101: 70–74.

Xie, Xiang (Nov. 2012b). "社团活动已成 90 后生活方式" [Associational life has become a way of life]. 中国青年报 [*China Youth Daily*]: 11.

Xinguang Civilian's Development Society (2018a). 新光平民发展协会就整改一事的联名抗议 书 [A joint protest letter from the Shin Kong Civilian Development Association on the 235 rectification]. URL: https://jiashigrsyt1.github.io /rdxglmx/ (visited on 9/24/2021).

Xinguang Civilian's Development Society (2018b). "监控, 孤立, 污蔑 . . . 我想把人大新光的遭 遇讲给你听" [Surveillance, isolation, slander . . . I want to tell you what happened to Xinguang Civilian's Development Society at Renmin University of China]. URL: https://jiashigrsyt1.github.io/xgzy/ (visited on 9/24/2021).

Xinhua News Agency (2012). "China focus: China pledges further reforms for state-dominated sectors." URL: http://en.people.cn/90785/7990705.html (visited on 10/11/2021).

Xinhua News Agency (2018). "深圳佳士公司工人' 维权' 事件的背后" [Behind the "rights defense" incident of the workers of Shenzhen Jasic Company]. URL: http://www.xinhuanet.com/local/2018-08/24/c_1123326003.htm (visited on 9/21/2021).

Xinhua News Agency (2021). "坚守为党育人为国育才-党的十八大以来高校思想政治工作综述" [Cultivating talents for the Party and the state: Summary on the university thought work since the Party's 18th National Congress]. URL: http:// www.gov.cn/xinwen/2021-06/25/content_5620851.htm (visited on 10/20/2021).

Xinhua News Agency (May 1999). "1999 年 5 月 9 日胡锦涛就我驻南使馆遭袭击发表讲话" [Hu Jintao delivered a TV speech on the NATO attack on the Chinese Embassy in Yugoslavia]. [*People's Daily*]: 1.

Xinxin Youth Society (2018a). "封杀令: 远离这群学生" [Banning order: Stay away from this group of students]. URL: https://jiashigrsyt1.github.io/byfs/ (visited n 09/24/2021).

Xinxin Youth Society (2018b). "新新青年: 从来没有哪个社团的注销通知有如此多的学生干部转发" [Xinxin Youth｜No club's cancellation notice has been forwarded by so many student cadres]. URL: https://jiashigrsyt1.github.io/byxxqn/ (visited on 9/24/2021).

Xinxin Youth Society (2018c). "正告北京语言大学团委与社团理事会: 你们打击进步社团的司马昭之心已人尽 皆知!" [Notice to the Youth League Committee and the Council of Associations of Beijing Language and Culture University: Your heart of Sima Zhao of the regiment in the fight against the Progressive Society is already well known!] URL: https://jiashigrsyt1.github.io/beiyu/ (visited on 9/24/2021).

Xinxin Youth Society (2018d). "紧急! 新新青年社团被校团委强制注销! 北语娘子军再遭黑手!" [Urgent! The Xinxin Youth Society was forcibly cancelled by the Youth League Committee of the school! Beiyu Women's Army again under attack!] URL: https://jiashigrsyt1.github.io/xxqn/ (visited on 9/24/2021).

Xu, Feng (2013). "新中国大学生思想政治教育研究. 北京，中国: 人民出版社."

Xu, Tao (2007). "新时期高校学生工作研究" [Study on Student Work in Higher Education Institutions in the New Era]. Chengdu: Southwest Jiaotong University Press.

Yang, Guobin (2009). *The Power of the Internet in China: Citizen Activism Online*. New York: Columbia University Press.

Yang, Shengru (2018). "中国人大新光协会遭整改校内现抗议涂鸦" [Xinguang Society at RUC was rectified and graffiti appears as protest]. URL: https://www.cna.com.tw/news/acn/201901050117.aspx (visited on 9/24/2021). 236

Yang, Xiaohui (2006). "大学生宗教信仰问题及德育对策研究" [A study on the religious belief problem of university students and the response of moral education]. 思想教育研究 [*Studies of Thought Education*] 138: 19–21.

Yuan, Chunlin (2009). "高校本专科生专职辅导员成年轻化趋势" [University full-time counselors tend to be younger]. URL: http://zqb.cyol.com/content/2009-05/19/content_2671536.htm (visited on 10/20/2021).

Zaveri, Mihir (2020). *"I Need People to Hear My Voice": Teens Protest Racism*. URL: https://www.nytimes.com/2020/06/23/us/teens-protest-black-lives-matter.html (visited on 6/21/2022).

Zenz, Adrian, and James Leibold (2020). "Securitizing Xinjiang: Police Recruitment, Informal Policing and Ethnic Minority Co-optation." *China Quarterly* 242: 324–48.

Zhan, Zhenzhen (2018). "齐民学社关注团: 正义的人们不会惧怕黑暗!" [Qimin Society Concern Group: Righteous people will not be afraid of the dark!] URL: https://jiashigrsyt1.github.io/qmxsgzt/ (visited on 9/24/2021).

Zhang, Cheng'an (2012). "当代大学生宗教信仰的实证调查" [An empirical study on religious belief of contemporary university students] 新远见 [*New Thinking*] 11: 68–74.

Zhang, Dewang (2018). "张德旺: 在北科，我生活在 1984" [Zhang Dewang: I live like in 1984 at USTB campus]. URL: https://jiashigrsyt1.github.io/bkzdw (visited on 9/24/2021).

Zhang, Dexiu (2011a). "国际涉华事件对高校维稳工作的影响与对策" [Study on the influence and countermeasures of international events related to China on college stability]. MA thesis, Nanchang University.

Zhang, Hang (2011b). "北京大学将对' 思想偏激' 等十类学生进行会商" [Peking University to conduct joint consultation to ten categories of students including those with radical thoughts]. URL: http://news.163.com/11/0325/03/6VV9LS VK00014AED.html (visited on 9/21/2021).

Zhang, Hang (2011c). "北大将对思想偏激学生进行学业会商引争议" [Peking University's consulting with radical students raises controversy]. URL: http:// news.sina.com.cn/c/2011-03-24/175822175153.shtml (visited on 10/11/2021).

Zhang, Jianjun (2007). "基于劳动力市场分割理论透视大学生就业市场" [Looking into the job market for university graduates from the perspective of the division of labour market theory]. 思想理论教育 [*Ideological and Theoretical Education*] 3: 72–76.

Zhang, Peng (2013). "史上最难就业年" 实属夸张 [It is an exaggeration to say this year is the hardest year in history in terms of job placement for university graduates]. URL: http://www1.shedunews.com/zixun/shanghai/liangwei/2013/05 /14/517920.html (visited on 10/11/2021).

Zhang, Zhitu (2011d). "高校特殊群体学生维稳工作探析." [*China Youth Education*] 1: 93–96.

Zhang, Zongxin, et al. (Sept. 2011). "山东省大学生宗教信仰状况调查分析" [An investigation and analysis of the condition of religious belief in university student populace of Shandong Province]. 山东理工大学学报 [*Academic Gazetteer of Shandong Polytech University, Social Science Edition*] 27, no. 5: 84–90.

Zhao, Dingxin (2001). *The Power of Tian'anmen*. Chicago: University of Chicago Press.

Zhao, Dingxin (2015). *The Confucian-Legalist State: A New Theory of Chinese History*. Oxford, UK: Oxford University Press. 237

Zhao, Suisheng (2004). *A Nation-State by Construction: Dynamics of Modern Chinese Nationalism*. Stanford, CA: Stanford University Press.

Zhao, Yun, and Kunpeng Yao (2013). "高校网络舆情动态监控与危机管理" [Dynamic monitoring and crisis management of network public opinions in colleges and universities]. [*Education Exploration*] 12: 70–71.

Zhou, Kai (2021). "首届全国高校辅导员工作创新论坛开幕，全国高校将有十万专职辅导员" [The first innovation forum of national university counselors inaugurated, there will be ten thousand full-time counselors nationwide]. URL: http://zqb.cyol.com/content/2008-02/27/content_2079371.htm (visited on 10/20/2021).

Zhou, Qiang (Feb. 2013). "大学生宗教信仰状况分析及对策研究" [Investigative analysis on the religious belief condition of university students and study on possible policy response]. "学校党建与思想教育" [*School Party Building and Thought Education*] 447: 61–63.

Zhou, Viola (2018). *Why a Marxist Movement Is Emerging in China—and Being Crushed*. URL: https://www.inkstonenews.com/politics/china-cracks-down-ma rxist-student-movement/article/2173582 (visited on 9/24/2021).

Zhu, Guifang (2006). "贫困大学生宗教信仰状况探析." [教育评论] 447: 61–63.

Zhu, Hong, and Zhongjian Zheng (2012). "天津高校毕业生国企招聘会" [SOE recruitment fair held for university graduates in Tianjin]. URL: http://socie ty.people.com.cn/n/2012/1223/c1008-19987319.html (visited on 10/11/2021).

Zhu, Shunqing (2018a). "初雪在即, 看南大如何对马会' 秋后算账'" [See how Nanjing University would do to the Marxist Studies Society as "the revenge after autumn" when it is near the time of the first snow]. URL: https://jiashigrsyt1.gi thub.io/ndmh/ (visited on 9/24/2021).

Zhu, Shunqing (2018b). "朱舜卿: 关于停止在校内使用强权暴力打压学生的呼吁书" [Zhu Shunqing: The appeal to stop cracking down on students on campus with power and force]. URL: https://jiashigrsyt1.github.io/zsqhys/ (visited on 9/24/2021).

Zhuang, Pinghui (2017). *The Rise of the Little Pink: China's Young Angry Digital Warriors*. URL: https://www.scmp.com/news/china/society/article/2095458/rise-lit tle-pink-chinas-young-angry-digital-warriors (visited on 12/29/2021).

Ziblatt, Daniel (2006). *Structuring the State: The Formation of Italy and Germany and the Puzzle of Federalism*. Princeton, NJ: Princeton University Press.

Žižek, Slavoj (2009). *First as Tragedy, Then as Farce*. London: Verso.

Zuo, Peng (2009). "大学校园中的基督教聚会点" [The Christian meeting-points on university campuses]." 北京科技大学学报, 社会科学版 [*Academic Gazeteer of University of Science and Technology of Beijing, Social Science Edition*] 29, no. 1: 6–9. 238

Index

Printed and bound by CPI Group (UK) Ltd, Croydon, CR0 4YY

07/07/2026

14916220-0001